EDUCATIONAL PRIORITIES AND DALIT SOCIETY

Educational Priorities and Dalit Society

V. Muralidharan

KANISHKA PUBLISHERS, DISTRIBUTORS
NEW DELHI 110002

KANISHKA PUBLISHERS, DISTRIBUTORS
4697/5-21A, Ansari Road, Daryaganj
New Delhi -110 002
Phones : 2327 0497, 2328 8285
Fax : 011-2328 8285
E-mail : kanishka_publishing@yahoo.co.in

Educational Priorities and Dalit Society
First Published-1997
Second Edition-2012

ISBN: 978-81-7391-182-7

PRINTED IN INDIA

Published by Madan Sachdeva for Kanishka Publishers, Distributors, 4697/5-21A, Ansari Road, Daryaganj, New Delhi-110 002, Typeset by Sunshine Graphics, Delhi, and Printed at Rajdhani Printers, Delhi.

Preface

The sociological entity known as 'dalit' has added a new dimension to the dynamics of social, economic and political development of the country. The dalit society extends beyond the merely Scheduled Caste and Scheduled Tribe and the recent Other Backward Classes (OBC) categorisations. Dalit society encompasses the deprived, the underprivileged, the poor and the oppressed masses, irrespective of caste, religion or creed. In this context it is necessary to mention that the current issue is the inclusion of deprived and SC/ST Christians in the dalit category. Several decades ago the founding father of the Indian Constitution, Dr. B.R. Ambedkar, gave thrust and direction to the policy and planning objectives in the country by reserving seats in educational institutions and in government jobs for SC and ST aspirants. Dr. Ambedkar knew only too well, and all later political and economic *pundits* have agreed, that the long-term solution to the problems of the deprived population, categorised as 'dalit', was to ensure the growth of education among them, through increased educational opportunities and numerous forms of subsidies to facilitate the economic means to achieve the objectives.

The educational of dalit society, including SC/ST population, has been accorded specific importance through priorities spelt out in the Eighth Plan document as well as the National Policy of Education (NPE). Steps have been outlined to ensure that at both the pre-matric stage and the post-matric stages, problems such as the high dropout rate, stagnation, non-enrolment of girl students, and uneven growth among specified communities, are effectively tackled. At the pre-matric stage, programmes covering scholarships, boarding grants, hostel facilities, free supply of books, stationery, uniforms and mid-day meals are slated for extensive expansion. The post-matric scholarship scheme is sought to be rationalised to (i) provide guidance with reference to employment opportunities and offering appropriate incentives for courses which have a Larger market demand; (ii) improve the performance, if necessary, by prescribing minimum standards, and (iii) identify the causes for disparities among various dalit groups in availing benefits under the scheme and indicate appropriate remedial action. The present publication seeks to focus the major aspects of the educational priorities that are envisaged for the social and economic development of the dalit society in India. It is hoped that the collection, comprising materials from both published and unpublished sources, will provide valuable insights into the problems of dalit society and indicate policy imperatives with regard to educational development.

V. MURALIDHARAN

Contents

1

Introduction: Development Debate and Dalit Society

The colossus of contradictions has existed in India for centuries — the Untouchables. They were named *Atishudras,* Broken men, *Antyaja, Antyevas in, Avarn,* Scheduled Castes, non-Hindus, Down-trodden, Protestant Hindus, *Harijans* — and now Dalits.

What is Dalit? According to Dr. Gangadhar Pantawane, Dalit is not a caste. Dalit is a symbol of change and revolution. The Dalit believes in humanism. He rejects the existence of God, rebirth, should, a sacred books that teach discrimination, fate and heaven, because these have made him a slave. He represents the exploited men in his country. A very determined Hindu social system was developed to destroy him as a human being. Human dignity was insulted and he fell prey to unavoidable circumstances. His lifeless body had to face the agony of pain, but the burden of alienation has been the source of rebirth for thousands of people.

Dalitness is essentially a means towards achieving a sense of cultural identity. The inferiority complex based on 'to be Dalit' has now disappeared. Now Dalitness is a source of confrontation. This change has its essence in the desire for justice for all mankind. In this sense, Dalitness is a matter of appreciating the potential of one's total being. Thus individual, culture social burden and Dalitness cannot be isolated.

According to the manifesto of Dalit Panthers, members of Scheduled Castes and Tribes, Neo-Buddhists, the working people, the landless and poor peasants, women and all those who are being exploited politically, economically and in the name of religion are Dalits.

Though the words "poor", "oppressed" and "exploited" would undoubtedly have a broad class connotation, the term 'Dalit' as it ordinarily understood, today, is considered applicable more or less exclusively to the ex-untouchables, *viz.*, the Scheduled Castes. In fact, it is a term that the untouchables have given 'themselves' as against the terms such as Harijans (children of God), Avarna (coloured), Antyaja (low-born) Humshudra (Scheduled Castes), etc. which were given by 'others'.

Dalit Ideology

To examine Dalit ideology is a difficult task because few systematic documents of their ideology exist. The late Dr. Ambedkar is perhaps the only systematic exponent of Dalit ideology. Years, later, the writings of the Dalit Panthers another source of Dalit ideology.

Dalit movements emerged and spread by the turn of the 19th century. The critical difference between the erstwhile movements — Bhakti, Neo-Vedantic and proselytization movements — and the new Dalit movements was that the latter were initiated by the Dalit themselves.

The oppressive as well as the elastic character of the caste system and the failure of even proselytization movements — to emancipate the lower castes, seems to have prompted many Dalit groups to improve their status through sanskritization. Although as a cultural process aimed at bringing about changes in the states of life of Dalits, it had important structural ramifications in that protest orientation and counter-mobilization were necessary attributes of sanskritizations movements, as Dalits often did it in a spirit of recalcitrance and the upper castes invariably opposed such attempts.

The central tendency in Hindu society was that the jatis in Hindus were the value givers norm setters and institutional builders and others followed them. For once the Dalits provided the lead through the formation of their caste associations, which became the base for self-respect and challenging upper caste authority. We may identify two sub-types of these Dalit movements based on two factors, the resource base of the jaits population size, presence of at least a small section which was economically independent and the consequences of the movement. First, those who had favourable resource base and succeed in crossing the pollution line and ceased to be uptouchables.

The Ezhaves of Kerala and the Naders of Tamil Nadu are the classic cases of this type. Second, those who had a relatively weaker source base (as compared with the first group) and did not succeed in crossing the pollution line, inspite of a vigorous protest movement among them. This type is exemplified by the Pahars. Faced with such a predicament the latter group preferred to opt out of the Hindu fold, as Ambedkar and his followers did by embaracing Buddhism. But even then they may not be entirely successful in shaking of the shackles of untouchability to escape the label of 'scheduled caste's. Given such a situation they may attempt to build — parallel cultural systems and refuse to get absorbed in the mainstream of Hinduism through conversion. This is evident by the emergence of the Dalit Panther movement in Maharashtra.

It is clear from our analysis that unlike the earlier movements initiated by outsiders, the movements in which the Dalits participated consciously and voluntarily brought about a sea-change in their socio-cultural identity and self-change in their socio-cultural identity and self-definition. While some of them like the Ezhaves of Kerala and the Nadars of Tamil Nadu succeeded in emancipating themselves from the inhuman practice of untouchability, others like Mahars of Maharashtra, the Chamars of U.P., though not similarly successful, gained a new sense of self-respect of human dignity. However, generally speaking the potential of these movements too was limited as they did not make a frontal attack on the very framework or caste system.

In fact, the Dalits invariably involved their caste status to wrest benefits from official agencies. This being so all Dalit movements old and new were at best reformist in their ideological orientations and they operated as interest groups to better their socio-economic conditions within the overall framework of the society. Therefore, these movements by themselves could not brought about any substantial social change and development of the Dalits, as a whole, their status as 'untouchables' persists, although untouchables is officially abolished and described by social reform movements of all hues. This histus between their official status as equal citizens before law, and their being treated as untouchables by the clean castes, can at least be partly located in Dalit powerlessness the inadequate development of their political clout.

The prevailing conditions of the Dalits could not have bestowed on them any political bargaining power, their substantial numbers notwithstanding. Freedom as such, had no meaning for them given the conditions of their existence.

At all India level the political articulation of Dalit interests and identity was first initiated by the great lawyer and constitutional expert Dr. B.R. Ambedkar, a Maharashtrian Mahar. The first visible manifestation of this was found in his demand for separate electorates for the scheduled castes. The chief instrument employed by the state in India as to bestow political power on the Dalits in the guarantee of 'reserved' representation to them in the parliament, state legislatures and local self-government bodies, roughly in proportion to their population. More importantly, it has came to be accepted as convention by all political parties (irrespective of their ideological orientation) which succeeded in capturing power, to give representation in the ministries formed by them, to Dalits.

This co-option of the Dalits into the establishment was not without its consequences viewed in terms of their mobilization. To begin with the competing political aspirants from among the Dalits get divided on party lines. They face the serious dilemma of competing loyalty between their ideological party affiliations on the one hand and the welfare of their constituency — the Dalits on the other. Second, those Dalit leaders within the ruling party competed with one another to secure position of power and help. This in turn leads to the emergence of factions and fissions among the Dalits within the same party. The net result of all these has been the political cestration of the Dalits, rendering them a highly fractionated social collectively incapably of serious bargaining with the powers that — that be. The unanticipated consequence of the police of protective discrimination seems to be the vivisection of Dalits.

The Dalit political mobilization of the national scene can be traced to the late 1920s when the British Government initiated as serious of Round Table Conferences to provide political representation to the scheduled castes. In the second conference in 1931, Dr. Ambedkar was invited as the representative of the depressed classes but he soon realized that precious little could be achieved through the official channels. Ambedkar firmly believed that unless the caste system was destroyed the social evil of untouchability could not be removed and he realized that to achieve this objective the Dalits should have political power.

Keeping this end in view in 1942, the All India Scheduled Caste Federation (AISCF), was established at an All-India Depressed Class Conference in Nagpur. In 1957 the (AISCF) was dissolved and the Republican Party of India (RPI) was formed. Although an exclusive political party of the Dalits, the RPI endorsed the fundamental tenets of the Indian Constitution and it pursued these objectives through the medium of parliamentary democracy. The specific aims of party are fighting for equality of all Indian citizens with a provision to give the Dalits some special considerations to bring about a balance Indian society and for the removal of exploitation of man by man and class by class.

After the death of Dr. Ambedkar the RPI gradually weakened and a large number of its followers joined the Congress party. In 1970 with the formal split of the RPI, two factions emerged, one openly favouring the Congress policy and getting co-opted into it, while the other maintained its distinct identity, although without much political clout. The visible indications of the party's existence at the national level are the periodic charts of demands if submitted to the Government, and the very often ineffective and the very infrequent collective actions it launches, focusing on the problems of the Dalits. However, though its persistent demands the RPI was successfully persuing. The Government to pass the protection of Civil Rights Act, 1976 which prescribes more stringent punishment for those who practise untouchability replacing the Untouchability Offences Act, 1955. The RPI failed to make an impact at the national level for the reasons: — for not having an ideology of an action programme radically different, from that of other parties. The RPI leaders often co-opted into the ruling parties at the State and Central levels, thereby eroding the potentially of the party for any serious or sustained mobilization of the Dalits.

Faced with such predicaments the Dalit-youths gradually have become restive. The visible expression of their mental unrest was first manifested in finding a 'voice' for themselves the Dalit Literacy movement gradually emerged.

The development of Dalit literacy movement from 60s onwards established deep relationship between Dalit writers and Dalit Panther Movement of 70s. This literary movement among Dalits has played a significant role in bringing behind about awareness among the downtrodden. The objective behind Dalit literature was to demonstrate the existence of an alternative culture, one that opposed established Marathi literature of the time. It touched upon the worst suffering of the downtrodden and Dalit writers made them conscious of their identity and served as a source of militant movement. Their relentless criticism of the essentially middle class nature of existing Marathi literature and their call for the creation of a new Dalit literature was a bold venture that sent shock waves to the Marathi literature. By their espousal of the ideas of equally and self-respect, the Dalit Sahitya exposed the hypocrisy of the caste based Hindu principles and brought into light the actual conditions of the Dalits. Dalit literature sprouted with the radical Mahar writers who protested against the faction ridden, self-seeking corrupt and aging leaders of Republican Party. It captured and captivated the minds of the Scheduled Caste youth.

A radical political organisation was born in Bombay on July 9, 1972. But it was only during the January 1974 riots that it shot into nation-wide prominence; by its opposition to the aggressive Shive Sena and by its participation in working class struggle. Its leaders argued that the old leadership that encouraged caste-based political protects like Maharashtra agitation, have no ideological base to stand upon. It was the united struggle which characterised the Dalit protests from 1972 when it was set up to 1974 when the split occurred. For instance, in the year 1972 in Bhugave of Harelli Taluk which was about ten miles from Poona a Dalit girl by name Kamala was raped and murdered by a Maharashtra Caste fellow. About 600 Dalits armed with weapons marched towards the village and threatened to burn the village, if the culprit was not brought to book.

In 1973, at a function held at Hastha Path in Poona, Shankaracharya, speaking in defence of the Caste system, was interrupted by about 200 Dalit youths leading to the cancellation of the function. So also in 1974, when Indira Gandhi visited Poona her way was disrupted by a massive group of Dalits near the Agricultural college in protest against government indifference to Dalits problems. In 1977 about 400 Dalits stopped and then Prime Minister Morarji Desai's visit to Poona, in protest against the government's reluctance to provide adequate educational facilities to the neo-Buddhists.

In the beginning, the ideology that guided the Dalit Panthers, was radical in nature and based on the ideology of Dr. Ambedkar. The organisation tried to unite and combine all oppressed sections of the society on the basis of Ambedkar's principles an uncompromising attitude to the superstructure combined with a radical policy towards an egalitarian society. Before the split occurred in 1974, the Dalit Panthers declared the manifesto of Dalit panthers in 1973. Though the document does not represent the views of all who identify themselves with the Panthers, it does represents important themes in the thinking of activists' in a variety of Dalit organisations. The manifesto therefore, became one of several points of controversy within the panthers organizations, even after it was both fragmented and dispersed across the country. It was one of the most powerful documents to have out since the death of Dr. Ambedkar. True, like any other Dalit organisation and Dalit and despite the fact the manifesto seems well-worn, old and therefore innocuous, a carefully examination of its contents reveals that it still has some lasting value and relevance.

The Dalit Panthers are disillusioned with conversion to other religious (most of the them are neo-Buddhists) and participation in parliamentary politics. Notwithstanding their continued allegiance to Ambedkar, at least part of their ideological kit is drawn from Marxism. They consciously opt for confrontation a total revolution, at the same time they do not attest the Marxian understanding of the Indian reality in its entirely as they think it over emphasizes the economic factors and practically ignores other dimensions of the social reality. It is significant to note here that the Dalit Panthers count not only scheduled castes and tribes and neo-Buddhists as Dalits, but the entire toiling masses — industrial workers, farm labourers landless tenants, poor peasants — not all of whom are drawn from scheduled castes. The Dalit Panthers should be credited with an appropriate diagnosis of the problems confronting the Dalits. Similarly their including the poor and oppressed from the non-scheduled castes in the Dalit category provides an adequate base for collective mobilization and action of the deprived. And yet, their appeals remain unheeded and no collective action work the name has been piloted by them so far. The reason for this non-performance should be located in the structure of deprivation in Indian society. As the Dalits are subjected to cumulative dominations and victims of multiple deprivations. Their experiential reality is not authentic to and shared by others who are simply economically poor. Small wooder, then, that the clean caste poor do not share their 'fraternity' with the Dalit poor.

Study is reveals that neither the activities or the reformist RPI nor the radical verbiage of the Dalits Panthers can deliver the goods for the Dalits. Even if the argument that the Dalit Panthers have potential to trigger off a universal protest enveloping all the Dalits of India (as Dalit Panthers define them) is accepted, they are nowhere near the achievement of this target as even the ideological appeal of the Panthers remains a sectarian enterprise confined to certain jatis in specific regions. On the other hand, the policy of protective discrimination remains equally ineffective. Inspite of the representation of the Dalits from the national parliament to local panchayats, their participation in the decision-making process remains peripheral and perfunctory. Even their free and unfettered participation in routine elections does not take place with ease. They are physically assaulted, politically intimidated, socially humiliated and economically threatened in the exercise of the constitutionally guaranteed universal adult franchise. It is necessary to understand the reasons for this predicament, which brings us to the point, namely the economic identity of the Dalits and the nature of class consciousness.

In the formal legal sense the Dalits are no more subjects but citizens. But the official guarantee does not automatically lead to the authentic exercise of their political rights we have mentioned above. The most important constraining factor in this context is the incognisance between their official political status (citizens) and actual economical predicament (slaves). It is on knowledge that the vast majority of the Dalits live in India's vast country side enmeshed in traditional master — slave relating: they are not yet a free-treating proletariat.

Dalits and Indian Economy

In order to the Dalits in the economy of India it is necessary to understand the source of their livelihood. Broadly speaking, we can categorise the sources of livelihood into three: First, those who depend on the investment of their wealth and assets — the capitalists, re-entries and landlords. There are, if any, only a handful of the scheduled castes in this category. Second, those who invest capitalists and expertise skills simultaneously — the traders and entrepreneurs and owner-cultivators. There is small sub-stratum of the scheduled castes in this category. Third, those who are exclusively dependent on their expertise or labour-power for their livelihood, the majority of the Dalits belong to this category. However, there are at least three broad sub-categories of this last category: *(i)* Those who are in the top professions (Medicine), law engineering, university teaching etc.) and the upper echelons of the civilian borers and the defence services. Understandably a few scheduled castes are in these occupations, thanks to the policy of reservation, *(ii)* Those who are in the middle level occupations (school teachers, nurses, clerks, army, jawans etc.). An increasing proportion of the scheduled castes find their placement in this category due to the governmental policy of protective discrimination. But their representation in these services remains much smaller than what is warranted by their size in the general population. *(iii)* Those who are in the lowest rung go the occupation ladder earning their livelihood through selling their skilled labour power. The overwhelming majority belong to this category. Even here, their preponderance is in the disadvantageous sectors—agricultural workers in the rural areas, labourers in the unorganized, informal, water paid urban sector. Thus it is clear that Dalits are economically the most disadvantaged and they are located predominantly in the rural and un-organised urban or forces.

It cannot be denied that a small section of the scheduled castes, particularly those from the dominant groups among them (the typical examples are the Chamars, teachers and the pulayas etc.), have experienced an upward mobility in the secular context through the state government measures have the following unanticipated consequences. According to Prof. P.K. Oommar: (1) The acceleration of a class polarization among the scheduled castes and the emergence of a bourgeoisie among them. (2) Crystallization of enmity and envy towards the well-off section among the scheduled castes on the part of the clean castes, particularly the poor among the latter. (3) The alienation of the scheduled castes elites, particularly the urban elite, from their antecedent social base. At the same time they do not easily get absorbed into the clean groups, leading to an identity crisis. (4) The emergence of a leadership from the well-off scheduled castes which often acts as political brokers and spokesmen of the Dalits, with the top leadership roles as the political resource, to further their carrier interests and material prospects, in the process endangering the wider interests of their less fortunate Dalit brethren.

Although slavery was formally abolished in India a century

ago, its current incarnations with minor modifications about in contemporary India, forced labour, bonded labour, patron-client system. Once again, legally all these practices stand abolished but the utter economic dependence of the Dalits on their rural employers who are drawn from the upper or intermediate castes, render it difficult for them to wriggle out of their substantive slavery. The non-Dalit agricultural workers do not suffer from this socio-cultural disability. This makes the organisation of the rural poor on a common platform nearly impossible. The Indian agrarian proletariat has not yet emerged; they are fractionated caste-wise and since caste operates in a regional-cultural context there is a scarcely any possibility of mobilizing the Dalits on an all-India basis. This is evident from the fact that while in certain pockets of India Dalits revolts and protests are visible, even virulent adjacent regions there may not be any overt manifestation of mobilization, that is conflict, with their oppressors.

Even in those areas where Dalit consciousness has crystallized on class lines are political parties have met the prospects of their universal mobilization. The Dalits were left out from the purview of mobilization even by the Communist parties of India. A.K. Gopalan, the Veteran CPM leader, remarked thus — "We have to make them (the landless labourers) the hub of our activities. Reluctance to take up their specific demands, fearing that this will drive the rich and middle peasants away from us, will have to be given up. This means that agrarian proletarian constituted mainly by the Dalits were not the focus of 'Peasant' movements in India. The other thing to be remembered is that those Communist parties in India (CPI and CPM) which are caught in the vortex of electoral politics, have to ponder to the caste sentiments of the Dalits to gain electoral support contrary to their doctrine that caste consciousness is false, and the only authentic consciousness in class based.

Ambedkar's Views on Dalit — Emancipation

In the early days of his struggle criticised the then ruling bureaucracy as conservative, repressive and irresponsible. He mostly emphasised the self-respects and self-elevation of his caste men. In one of his speeches he quoted Shakespeare's words to awaken his men: "There is a tide in the affairs of men, which taken at the flood, leads on to fortune."

In all his speeches, writings and letters he asked the depressed classes to be united to work in combination for their liberation. He said without unity among them they cannot at in real liberation from the Hindu society a point which is true even in present day India. Diversity among the downtrodden, lack of unity is their real enemy. That is why Dr. Ambedkar repeatedly stressed this aspect of unity.

Ambedkar made a distinction between social reforms in the sense of reforms of Hindu family and social reforms in the sense of reconstruction and reorganisation of Hindu society. According to him "the social movements inaugurated by reformers like Ranade and his organisation social conference, related to remarriage of widows, women's right to property, education of women, child marriages and other matters. While the later type related to the abolition of caste system and the reconstruction of Hindu society on the basis of equality, but this began at the top from the bottom." Pioneers like Chatrapati Sanu and Sayaji Rao Gayakwad and leaders like Karanveer Shinde toiled untiringly for the uplift of the untouchables. Despite these high souled services to the cause nor could stir in the heart of these suppressed people an emotion of confidence, hope and aspiration for own salvation. A feeling of independence, a sense of guardianship and an impression of patronage had grown among them. The untouchables knew this but could not express the difference between help and self-help. Self-help is their basic desire which is the best help.

So indifference and callous was the attitude of the vast masses of the caste Hindus, to the problem that they thought the fate of these suppressed untouchables Hindus was to be determined at their leisure and pleasure. The intention of Hindu reformers was good, but its execution was worse. Their isolation carried more gestures than active struggle for breaking the shackles that bound the depressed classes. Politically rigorous, valiant untouchability, socially most of them wished to whitewash a delayed house. It meant for Ambedkar Hindu society as a decayed house. It had to be totally destroyed and reconstructed. Minor changes like reforming Hindu family would not help. They forgot the truth that white-washing does not save a dilapidated house. You must pull it down and build a new. These were the observations made by Dr. Ambedkar on Hindu social reform oganisations. The case of Ambedkar was quite different. He spurn from amongst the untouchables. He was a leader who thought as they and felt as they felt. He has seen much, suffered much and also studied much. He was a man who regarded the woes and miseries of these classes as a personal humiliation and therefore, he had taken a vow to make self-respecting citizens out of those virtual slaves.

Ambedkar hated the sense of dependency and abhorred the feeling of partonage of the caste Hindu reformers. He held in utter contempt the organisations and movements that prospered or reared in the name of depressed classes where in untouchables were treated for functional occasions. Ambedkar was a believer in the divine principle that self-help is the best help. He diagnosed the disease correctly. He knew sufferer himself does away with it by his own exertions and actions. 'As long as the conscience of a slave does not fill with hatred for his slavery, there is no hope for his salvation.'

"Tell the slave he is a slave and he will revolt", was the slogan raised by Ambedkar. He exhorted the untouchables to fight for self-elevation. Self-help, self-elevation and self respect was the symbol on the standard he unfurled. It was the trident with which he goaded his people to action. The leader of the untouchables talked to them in a very caustic manner. He remonstrated with them in a tone, there was once tearing, carping and goading. He cried out, "my heart breaks to see the pitiable sight to your faces and to hear your sad voices. You have been goading from time immemorial and yet you are not ashamed to hug your helplessness as an inevitability. Why do you not perish and sadden the picture of sorrows, poverty, slavery and burden of the world with your deplorable, despicable and detestable miserable life? You had better die relieve this world if you cannot rise to a new life and if you cannot rejuvenate yourselves. As a matter of fact it is your birth-right to get food, shelter and clothing in this land in equal proportion with every individual, high or low. If you believe in living a respectable life, you must believe in self-help which is the best help.

Role of Education

Ambedkar awakened his people by quoting the great words of Ruskin, "That" doing is a great thing, as Carlyle says that the end of a man is action. He also says that action is the governing character of all makers of history. Reiterating his views after Mahad's struggle he said that untouchability must be condemned and abolished not only as the need of hour but also as the command of true religion, not only as a policy or as an act of expediency but also a matter of justice, not only as a matter of obligation but also as a service to humanity. He said that notion of purifying oneself with animal urine was more ridiculous and desirable than the notion of defilement at the human touch.

Ambedkar held that equality meant raising the level of lower classes to the level of higher classes as regards the agency which imparts education, he said in an editorial that no real progress could be made in education if education was entrusted to the teachers coming from the Brahmin community whose minds conceived an abhorrence for the lower classes and showed callous disregard for the intellectual uplift of any other class, treated human beings worse than dogs and never treated them with equality and kindness. He declared that teachers are the Charioteers of the nation. There is no question more important from the stand point of social reform than the selection of proper persons in this teaching profession.

He also stated that education is a noble, national and enlightened work. This work should not be entrusted to Brahmins. Ambedkar argued government would be able to achieve genuine progress by weeding out self-centred, nation destroying agencies. The progress of the nation, he added, would be stronger on such a broader base. The base is not to recruit narrow-minded teachers. He warned depressed classes that nothing could be achieved, if they did not adapt an aggressive attitude and prove by their thoughts, words and deeds that they would not now tolerate insult and disabilities any further. Ambedkar replying on Satyagraha said that "mere spread of education and exposition of scriptures would not be able to root out the age long disease of untouchability and caste system. The disease he said, was deep rooted and mere dressing it with bandages of knowledge or ingenuous schemes would not cure it. Deadly disease required drastic remedies."

Although Ambedkar defended individual development and creativity, he rejected the aggressive, self serving individualism of western capitalism as something guaranteed to perpetuate Dalit subordination. He devoted most of his life searching for radical social democracy but also remained convinced that the rid and inherently impermanent world of legislation and law courts would never be enough to create a necessary sense of community.

His answer was an attempt both to harness and tame the psychological power of religions by developing a modern activities atheist Buddhism, stripped or all belief in super natural forces and committed to the struggle for social economic equality. According to him there are two aspects of conversion, one social the other religious material as well as spiritual. The atrocities on SC's have nothing to do with the virtues and vices of an individual. This is not a feud between two rival men. The problem or caste system is a matter of struggle, between rival groups Hindus and the untouchables. This is not a matter of doing injustice against one man. It is one involving injustice being done by one group against another.

He started that this struggle is related to social status. He also explained that caste system is not a temporary feature of Indian society. To put it straight, it can be said that the struggle between the Hindus and the untouchable is a permanent phenomenon. It is eternal because high caste people believe that the religion which has placed Dalit at the lowest level of the society is itself external. Those who live a life of self-respect will have to think over this. Ambedkar contended that Hindu religion was nothing but a multitude of commands and prohibitions, it does not recognize man as man, Hindu religion for him, was a display or force and mockery. It also does not teach how individuals should behave with each other. He said that religion is for man and not man for religion. He urged that for proper human treatment, one must convert oneself, convert for getting organised, convert for becoming strong, convert for getting equality and liberty. He wondered why people should remain in a religion which prohibited them from entering a temple. Why remain in a religion which prohibited one from getting a proper job. Here he quoted Buddha "Take refuge in reason, do not succumb to others. Be truthful. Take refuge in Truth. Never surrender to anybody."

He laid stress on the need for Dalit's education as well as for adequate political representation. He believed in the power of political bodies to win freedom for the masses and endeavoured to fight for the same. His approach to religion was ethical, social and secular. The Buddhist conception of mains anthropocentric. Everything is related to man and society. Ambedkar's religious views combined empiricism and rationalism and he found Buddhism as a way of life for Dalits to acquire moral a generation and social emancipation. Religion to him was the driving force for human activities. It must be judged by social standards based upon social ethics. His religious attitudes were the manifestation of a political man, who desired freedom for the untouchables.

A Dalit Vision of Gandhi

Gandhi designate the untouchables as "Harijans".

'Harijan' means 'man of god'. Gandhi started using and popularised the term with the good intention that the change of name might at least spare the use of a 'reproachful' term although it might not bring about any change of status of the ex-untouchables. However, Ambedkar in those days and very recently Mayavati objected to the use of the term 'Harijan' as they believed it had derogatory implications.

The term had only trebled human agony as the Dalits and outcasts are socially ostracised, stigmatised as untouchables and lastly, they are basterdised. Gandhi had not only presumed, but toed the very tradition that preceded him. It was sincerely believed in our tradition that if God had created a problem for man, only God could solve it. As for the fate of the outcastes, that divine authority was seemingly delegated only to the upper most caste. By this tradition, if the redesignation of Harijan is treated as hallowed that cannot be so just because Gandhi believed that to be so.

Modern Indian History's most acrimonious debate had taken place between Gandhi and the Congress on the one side and B.R. Ambedkar on the other, on the most sensitive question of separate electorate for the Scheduled Castes. Both Gandhi and Ambedkar had taken exclusive stands sitting across the Round Table Conference when the former pledged to resist the demand with his life and to negate Macdonal's offer of separate electorate. Gandhi indeed went on a fast unto death in 1932. When two persons take seat across the table to argue for and against on issue that is Dalit and one suggesting that he would resist the proposition with his life, both cannot be God saviour to the same cause. It is evident that the idea of fast untodeath after ordering a new denture was to live at the cost of lives of the untouchables.

In a country where millions die of compulsive hunger every year, Gandhi's weapon of fast untodeath throws a new light on its caste-preordinated existence — the inequitous price the Dalits have to pay for their life. By calling upon the dying millions to forfeit their political demand in order to save his life was an extraordinary dispensation of the Dalits by Gandhi. The Dalits only saved his life in the bargain and an upper-caste only cut his life short is also a significant fall-out of a dubious understanding of truth and the philosophy of non-violence.

It is a text book of historical truism that the much publicised "Gandhian Harijan work seems to have been a bid to establish a hegemony over the potentially more radical pressures from below." Sumit Sarkar has added: "Like so many of Gandhian programmes, the Harijan campaigns (of Gandhi) were richly ambiguous in motives and significance. Radical nationalists like Nehru felt it to be a harmful diversion... Gandhi deliberately confined the Harijan to social reforms (like pond entry, etc.) refusing to attack caste as a whole. He advised caution on inter-dining, inter-marriage and went on defending the original *Varnashram* — which was non-existent. The people who copiously adore him for his 'high thinking and simple living' — may not know that Sarojini Naidu was worried that Bapu's visits to Sevanagar were costing lakhs of rupees for arrangement of cleanliness of the venue of his prayer meeting. Those who really think high and not the ones who live in simplicity. Those who work, are only the persons who have perforce to lead a simple life.

Ambedkar, knowing Gandhi's cosmetic treatment of the Dalits, posed 14 questions to Gandhi. (*What Congress and Gandhi have done to Untouchables, pp. 237-39*). There he had enumerated the various points where Gandhi failed to respond to the tasks and targets set by Gandhi himself for the much-publicised upliftment of the Dalits. Those who are sincere enough to know about Gandhi, may like to have a glance at these documented incidents. Many of their doubts may be dispelled as to why the Dalit vision of Gandhi is not bright.

Gandhi had performed as many as 22 fasts to press for some issue or the other but never fasted once for the Dalits. The one he wanted to perform in support of the entry of the untouchables into Guruvayur Temple did not take off. Ambedkar was against any superficial charting of course or acceptance of any superficial cosmetic treatment of the Dalit wart. He wanted a firm structure, not a fashionable penthouse, whereas the society was only accustomed to giving aims to the badgers during gorgeous festivals. Gandhi was not able to see the logic particularly with his orthodox inclination, for the charmed caste order. He succeeded to stall the demand of separate electorate by the Dalits, which became part of mythology. But it is not a myth any longer and Ambedkar was right in saying that this gave them no real political power and made them dummies in the hands of political power-manipulators.

With the passage of time, the political moves of Gandhi

became acute and so full of incongruities that even his trends and followers doubted them as honest. But the fact remains—he succeeded. In lionising Gandhi, Nehru also paid a rich tribute on his fire-fighting game-plan saying, "Bapu had a curious knack of doing the right thing at the psychological moment and it might be that his action — impossible to justify as it was from my point of view -- would lead to great results."

Gandhi evidently succeeded but left many historical paradoxes for the posterity to unravel as otherwise if would be a total injustice to the epoch to which he belonged.

The Dalit contact with Gandhi had an extra-terrestial significance. In our vested traditions, the saviours come from the sky. Gandhi's dramatic appearance in the socio-political scene of India with a semi-nude rustic outfit had, to the underdogs, no pretension or falsity about it. They had readily accepted him as their saviour. Precisely on the same type of tenuous background many a successful actor with little or no political credentials to start with ended up by earning the inescapable reputation of the "saviour" in this country.

Mandal Commission and New Dalit Movement

After the adoption of the Mandal Commission Report by the National Front Government the New Dalit Movement in India is emerging, or seems like emerging. Dalit politics draws its weight not simply from numbers and vote bank politics — roughly 52 per cent of the population are OBCs. The number of the desperately poor is staggering too — poor whose caste or religion is irrelevant in the face of the threat of material extinction. But the poor have not organised. They have not in part because they do not have a non-secular flag to march under. Hunger, illiteracy and ill health are uncompromisingly secular sufferings. That, and social ostracisation, was the fate of all scheduled castes and tribes for two thousand years. Which is why affirmative action for them has a rationale even in enlightened capitalism, as there is for blacks in the United States.

The dalit consciousness is by no means limited to the scheduled castes. It has begun to symbolise a much broader spectre of the oppressed and hitherto excluded social strata. It is based on an attempted though by no means still realised solidarity of the poor and the discriminated classes of the people, long held back and frustrated, its leadership divided and bought over, distanced from the masses and co-opted within the mainstream and in establishment structures and positions, were it not for a systematic and continuing onslaught by the rural upper castes and the real and deadly fear of a political kind held out by the emergent brahminic party (the BJP) and its arrogant cultural expression in the form of the VHP which in turn allowed a gradual alignment and realignment with major minorities (the Muslims in particular), the dalit phenomenon would not have emerged with the power and confidence that it did in 1993. Even then it is no more than a beginning for what has happened is somewhat unexpected even as it has happened. It will continue to remain weak until its main thrust is merely in terms of demands made on the state for jobs and positions instead of undertaking transforming the nature of civil society and thereby transforming the nature of the state, and until the pressure put on its own leadership from the grass roots is not strong enough. Also, there are continuing divisions both within the dalits and *vis-a-vis* the backwards and there is continuing to be disproportionate dependence on personalities most of whom happen to be unreliable in the long-run. All the same, in rolling back the threat of fascism combined with fundamentalism the role of the dalit movement is likely to prove historic.

For the past few years the reservation issue has been raised with the regularity of a ritual by all the political parties. However, this invocation has not been all that sacred. It has entailed political turmoil, casteist hatred mindless bloodshed.

But reservation *vis-a-vis* the Indian socio-cultural context has sadly enough not been analysed. The so-called messiahs of the scheduled castes, scheduled tribes and the other backward classes such as V.P. Singh, Kanshi Ram, Mulayam Singh Yadav and Laloo Prasad Yadav have unfortunately used reservation and social justice to retain the existing socio-political and socio-cultural institutions and the orthodox and backward system as a whole.

Not once has the reservation plank been used to change the existing social structure. Though the present day social and political institutions in India have originated under the influence of half baked industrial production relations which came to the country during the post-independence Nehruvian euphoria, their operations are facilitated by backward, feudal mechanisms which are embedded deep in the cultural matrix of our society.

Social justice is an attempt to secularise and modernise a

society mired in such primitive stratifications as caste by introducing the marginalised to job opportunities and pushing society to a more advanced stage of historical-material development. But in India the attempt has had just the SCs, STs and the OBCs have used reservation to strengthen the bureaucracy and the polity by infiltrating it with people who, despite belonging to the backward sections, operate as per the prevailing rules of these so-called modern institutions. A case in example is the idea of having reserved constituencies for election to legislative or executive bodies which run on the wheels of feudalism.

As a consequence feudal backwardness is perpetuated despite providing ample opportunities to the marginalised. What these messiahs do not understand or pretend not to understand is the fact that pro-marginalised struggles can be waged through yet another path, the path of pitting a subaltern discourse (read SC, ST, OBC) against the dominant, "Elitist" discourse.

On the other hand the Mandal Commission and the reservation issue have seen the emergence of kulak peasantry and neo-elites form among the SCs and the OBCs in the Hindi heartland. Upper caste private armies such as the Bhumi Sena of the Bhumihars and Sunlight Sena of the Rajputs now have their backward parallels in the Lorik Sena of the Yadav in Bihar. SC and OBC student politics has also had its dose of upper caste characteristics and traits. The newly emerging student leaders form among these sections operate like their upper caste compatriots — in a very athoritation style. They have even appropriated the political vocabulary of feudal upper caste politics, *Mathadhisha* — chief of a clannish institution — being an example.

There is a problem, however, in trying to base a movement on a fringe discourse contrary to the dominant discourse as far as the OBCs are concerned. OBCs such as Yadavs, Kurmis, Gujjars, Lodhas and so on, since they occupy the lower rungs of the upper caste feudal order, do not historically possess their own, distinct subaltern discourses. But as can be gathered from Karl Marx's writing on the first Indian war of Independence in 1957, suppression always lead to the formation of a marginal discourse of the oppressed different from the dominant one of the oppressor.

In these writings Marx tries to analyse why a major mutiny broke out under the British East India Company, when India had been invaded and ruled by foreigners — Turks, Mughals and

Afghans — many times in the past. According to Marx the reason lies in the fact the British, with their wealth of industrial capitalism, were the first foreign rulers who disturbed the fundamental organisation of Indian society — the Indian village — and thus attempted to create a hierarchy of discourses by using brute power and all that was at their disposal.

Dalits and Left Movements

As with the liberal democratic movement and the new social movements the Left Movement too has failed to produce a basis of real social change. There are many reasons for this. First, the Left movement ceased to be a 'movement' long back. The assumption that the politics of the Left would in turn utilize a mass movement that would in turn utilize institutional spaces within the system has happened: legislative and electoral spaces have utilized and manipulated the mass movements. Second, even as a movement to the extent rank and file parties and continuing concern with ideological issues were still there, it failed to provide the kind of para is that socially oppressed populations needed. It was at once fragmented and monolithic ('democratic centralist') riven by multiple divisions yet providing no real pluralism, on vibrant democratic proves in its organisational framework. It was for too long — and still is — dominated by upper castes, brahminic in both style and intellectual grasp. It provided no real fresh alternative to the nationalist secular credit to which it is still wedded. In terms of the development paradigm too it is a prisoner of western progressivism-cum-technologism, seeking credibility not from a mass movement but by joining the parliamentary democratic and nationalist-secular framework, wholly failing to provide an alternative to it. Worse still, the main parties (CPI and CPI(M) never really got out of the Congress-Communist honeymoon (every after the emergency experience) in the making of which Marxist intellectuals and academics of the CP variety played a leading part; for most of them crumbs of office and influence proved too seductive. Even later, after full disillusionment with the Congress, whenever they have been faced by a challenge from the Right, they have tended to slip into an opportunitistic alliance with the Congress as against building a viable and long-term Left alternative within the system, not to speak of a major revolutionary alternative to it.

As for the Naxal groups too, after waging some heroic

struggle in various micro and regional settings, most of them have shown signs of exhaustion and have sought entry into the legislative-electoral arena, mostly fielding upper and middle caste candidates.

Even the more Maoist groups committed to 'annihilation of class enemy' are driven by caste bickerings arising form domination by brahmin and brahminic individuals. Some of the M-L individuals and groups did join radical movements of the regional self-determination and ethnic-federal types (*e.g.* in Punjab, Kashmir, Assam and the North-East) leading to a collaboration between two types of militancy, but failed to address themselves to the burning social issues. If anything, they have tended to ignore the truly oppressed and out-caste social groups, as for instance in Punjab where the SC and other 'majhabi" elements have continued to support the Congress.

Dalit-Bahujan Alliance

Against all this experience of continuing, let downs and reactions comes the latest stream of non-Left radicalism, namely, the dalit-bahujan alliance of SCs and OBCs, offshoot of the Mandal slogan but couched in terms not just of achieving social justice (which is still based on the idea of making the existing state and its power-holders more just and accommodative of the lower social strata) but of the dalits and the OBCs grabbing political power. There are problems with this too. First, the SCs and OBCs have little in common, socially and organizationally. While the SCs are, relatively speaking, structurally homogeneous, the OBCs are internally highly differentiated and heterogeneous. Many of the latter are found to be perpetrating terror on the former in the rural areas. Second, provoked by the phenomenon of co-optation over such a long period, there has emerged a tendency among the details to insist on 'autonomous', exclusives identity and membership, striking a discordant attitude towards movements and intellectuals and political activists that are committed to them but belong to other castes. The recent Mayavati assault against Gandhian, Lohiaite and leftist efforts to serve the Dalit cause highlights just this. Paradoxically, all this is precisely what can be used by the ruling class and particularly by the Congress Party by *(a)* inducting dalits, backwards and others in the establishment thus giving them, especially the educated among them, a sense of triumph but then *(b)* working out concessions of various kinds and co-opting and corrupting them. The BJP too is in the process of devising a strategy that will cash in on such divisions.

The current permeation of this exclusivist notion of identity and struggle in grass roots, struggle-oriented movements on the Left is undermining their radical socio-economic striving and making them (including the Left parties) concede and co-opt. All this is producing a new crisis of identity of left and radical politics. Coming on top of the larger crisis of identity of the Left movement, following the collapse of socialism in the global political arena and acute questioning of the marxist ideology and of Marx (and Lenin) individually, this kind of aggressive posturing by the dalits will only put the Left further on the defensive. But nor would it provide the dalit cause the necessary political base for it to be a catalyst of history. Unless the new consciousness aimed at bringing about radical transformation also see itself as part of a larger social and global movement opposed to both capitalist and imperialist designs and fundamentalist and fascist social forces, both of which are on the upswing (despite the latter being held back as a result of the dalits and the Muslims defeating the BJP in UP), they are bound to face the pincer mentioned above, of backflash on the one hand and co-optation on the other. The Dalit Movement must emerge as a movement for genuine emancipation, aligning with all social action groups engaged in a politics of transformation, mobilising them all for a fundamental defeat of the brahminic social order. Where it should seek a change is with respect to the present economistic definition of such transformation and ask for a fundamentally socially redefinition of the same. Even the battles against imperialism and the 'new world order' should be socially defined, within and across nations. but there is no need to be exclusivist either in terms of caste identity or any other social categorization. There should be no compromising in any such broad-basing but there should be no fear or sense of insecurity either.

Perspective for Dalit Movement

There is no shortage of sensitive and committed people in castes and classes occupying the middle spaces in the country. One has only to watch the deeply moving plays and films, read the highly unnerving reportage on social oppression and state terror, gauge the string of the depths of our consciousness through literary and other humanistic efforts alongside the dalit poetry, the highly disturbing "feminist" exports, the moving appeals of citizens on the march protesting against the agonizing reports on atrocities, rampages and rapes, the inspiring chronicles of micro-movements of tribals and other 'indigenous' people struggling to retain and enrich their land and forests, their ancestral heritage and their holistic world views. What the Dalit Movement needs to do is to take all this in and to provide a new vanguard of social change. In the process, broad-base and deepen the social and cultural terrain of the 'dalit movement'.

2

Policy and Approach: National Policy on Education

1. EQUITY, SOCIAL JUSTICE AND EDUCATION

Education and Women's Equality Access to Water, Fuel and Fodder

There is a crucial link between the easy access to water, fuel and fodder and schooling of girls. This understanding needs to be explicitly reflected in the policy of Government and be concretised in operational designs. (4.1.10)

'Local Area Planning', as envisaged in the 'Approach to the Eighth Five Year Plan' document, must take into account the above linkage while planning for programmes relating to forestry, drinking water and greening of common lands. (4.1.10)

The Department of Education should coordinate with the other concerned departments and secure adequate resource allocation for the above mentioned programmes based on parameters which indicate the status of girls education in a given habitation/village. For instance, priority needs to be given to the habitations/villages having enrolment and retention rates for girls in schools below the average rates of the States. (4.1.10)

To achieve the above purpose, planning for educational development of any given region would have to be necessarily conducted at the Block or sub-Block level. This task would be facilitated

Note: The number given in brackets at the end of each recommendation is the paragraph number of the Report of the Review Committee under which that recommendation appears.

if it is undertaken through the proposed Educational Complexes in which there will be Block-level representatives of the various agencies/departments concerned with social welfare and development, along with teachers, Anganwadi workers and representatives of poor women's groups and Panchayati Raj Institutions. (4.1.10)

Teachers, Anganwadi workers, village-level functionaries of other departments, and representatives of women's groups and community-level organisations should play an important role in making micro-level information available to the Educational Complex for prioritisation of action in this regard. (4.1.10)

Early Childhood Care and Education (ECCE)

The policy framework on women's education must bring out the criticality of the link between ECCE and girls' accessibility to elementary education (4.1.13)

Comprehensive and effective ECCE services should be provided in proximity to every primary and middle school and be programmatically linked with elementary education. (4.1.13)

Priority should be given to child-care programmes catering to the 0-3 age group, particularly among the under-privileged sections of society. (4.1.13)

The timings of the ECCE centres should include the school hours so that the girls in the 6-14 age group are relieved from the responsibility of sibling care. (4.1.13)

While the Anganwadis (ICDS) should continue to be given importance, other models which are sensitive to local needs should also be encouraged. (4.1.13)

The management of Anganwadis and other ECCE programmes should be decentralised and be made participative, as recommended in the chapter on ECCE. (4.1.13)

In order that child-care facilities and pre-school and primary education of girls are prioritised in the village and the community, the Anganwadi workers and poor women's groups should be represented on the Village Education Committees. (4.1.13)

Regional Disparities

The issue of regional disparities needs to be incorporated into the operational design for universalising girls' access to elementary education. (4.1.16)

Any effective strategy for raising the educational status of women in India would have to give priority to the educationally backward districts. (4.1.16)

Educational planning at the level of Educational Complexes will depend on block-level or sub-block-level profiles. These profiles should be based on micro-level information collected from habitations/villages. Teachers, Anganwadi workers, other village-level functionaries and representatives of poor women and other community level organisations should be involved in making such information available. (4.1.16)

Decentralised and participative mode of planning and management offers an effective basis for responding to the challenge of regional disparities in education, including girls' education. Diverse strategies and disaggregated time-frames, worked out locally, constitute the twin instrumentalities to achieve the goal of universalisation. (4.1.16)

Content of Education and the Gender Bias

The curriculum in schools should include :

— Increase in the visibility of women and projection of a positive image of the role of women in history, their contribution to society in general and the Indian context in particular. For instance, social history should project the contribution that women have made in the national movement. All such issues should be carefully incorporated in the training and orientation of teachers, educators and administrators.

— Special efforts should be made to strengthen mathematics and science education among girls. Girls' schools should give greater importance to mathematics and science than at present.

— Undifferentiated curriculum for boys and girls.

— Elimination of negative stereotypes and biological and social concepts which have a sexist bias. This has been dealt with in greater detail in the Section that follows.

— Outmoded traditions and myths that hinder positive development of women and their role in national life should be objectively discussed in the class-room in a gender perspective. Similarly, the portrayal of women in our ethics and mythology needs to be critically examined in the classroom.

— Basic legal information including protective laws regarding women and children and extracts from the Constitution to make the children aware of the fundamental rights and other basic concepts therein.

— Specific measures to improve the participation of girls in physical training and sports should be undertaken. (4.1.19)

Stereotypes in Text-books and the 'Hidden Curriculum'

It is recommended that all school text-books, both by NCERT/SCERTs and other publishers, be reviewed to eliminate the invisibility of women and gender stereotypes, and also for the proper incorporation of a women's perspective in the teaching of all subjects. This review should also cover all the supplementary reading material and library books being recommended for schools, particularly those supplied by Operation Black-board. (4.1.22)

As an immediate step such an exercise should seek the active participation of different groups and individuals, such as Women's Studies experts, Women's Studies Centres of the Universities and Research Institutes, and women's organisations working at grass-root level, rather than exclusive dependence on NCERT/SCERTs. (4.1.22)

A similar exercise should be undertaken for the university curriculum and text-books in all disciplines. This should be initiated by University-based Women's Studies Centres and individuals already working on these issues. (4.1.22)

Role of the Media

All media channels, both in the public and private sectors should take serious note of the crucial role that the media can play in promoting gender equality and empowerment of women as enunciated in NPE. (4.1.23)

In the specific context of gender, advertisements displaying women as sex symbols and using them for sales promotion should be seriously dealt with. (4.1.23)

Media should project positive images of women. Women should also be shown in professional roles, for instance as doctors, engineers and scientists, so that they can serve as role models. (4.1.23)

An awareness of the need for Women's education, especially elementary and vocational education, should also be spread. (4.1.23)

The information and Broadcasting Ministery should evolve a network to monitor the projection of women, and evolve a code of ethics with regard to the presentation of women in all types of media (similar recommendations are also made in the Shramshakti Report, 1988). (4.1.23)

An Inter-Ministerial Committee, comprising representatives of the Departments of Education, Women and Child Development, Culture and Information and Broadcasting, should be constituted to monitor and ensure that the policy guidelines emerging from NPE and POA are being supported, rather than being violated, by the media, particularly Radio and TV. Representatives of women's organisations and Women's Study Centres may also be included in this Committee. (4.1.23)

A National Policy on Communication, giving a gender perspective to all forms and processes of mass communications, should be formulated urgently. The National Commission on Women should play an active role in this exercise. (4.1.23)

Vocational Education

Vocational Training for women should be planned and implemented at the State level, partly through the proposed Educational Complexes. (4.1.27)

Vocational Training for women should be encouraged in non-traditional occupations, following an undifferentiated curriculum. (4.1.27)

Concerted efforts should be made towards discouraging the existing biases in vocational courses for women. (4.1.27)

Vocational training courses for girls at 'Plus Class VIII' level (*i.e.* secondary stage) in order to expand the social base of vocational education. Opportunities should be especially given to dropouts after middle school. (4.1.27)

Diversification of courses and trades to match with the job potential at local level is important. For encouraging access to technical or craft-and-skill-training institutions, increased stipends, fellowships, and a system of placement is recommended. There should be at least one women's polytechnic in each District. (4.1.27)

Training of Teachers and Other Educational Personnel

Teacher training programmes in general require a critical evaluation and re-orientation within which the incorporation of the women's perspective should be a key dimension. This would include sensitivity to women's issues and awareness of the problems in the education of girls (4.1.30)

Teacher educators, Women's Studies researchers in universities and institutes including those in the Women's Cells, as well as representatives of women's organisations and development groups, and not just a handful of Central or State level agencies, should be involved in this process of evaluation and re-orientation of teacher training programmes. (4.1.30)

The *'core'* elements of a restructured teachers' training programme should emerge from the above exercises. Subsequently at the level of the State (or region), the DIETs and Educational Complexes alongwith educational institutions, Women's Study Centres, educators and grassroot level organisations should participate in evolving the actual curriculum of the teacher's training programme. This kind of decentralisation in curriculum planning, and later even in its implementation, allows for greater flexibility and meaningfulness. (4.1.30)

Teachers' training institutes should adopt the revised curriculum so that all teacher trainees, male and female, are exposed to the restructured training programme. (4.1.30)

A separate training and sensitisation programme for the teacher educators would have to be undertaken on a priority basis. (4.1.30)

Simultaneously in-service training programmes should be conducted to sensitize teachers who are already in schools. The DIETs in consultation with the Education Complexes should take the initiative in organising these in-service programmes. (4.1.30)

The actual form that the in-service training programmes will take, should be left to the DIETs in consultation with the Education Complexes. For instance, one school can serve as the training school where teachers' training will include practice teaching. The 'intership model' referred to elsewhere can be explored. (4.1.30)

Administrators and planners in education (including Heads of institutions) can be sensitised to women's issues through the diffusion of information, holding of workshops and frequent interaction with resource persons in the area of Women's Studies. This is particularly crucial when exercises involving decision-making in education are undertaken. (4.1.30)

Research and Development of Women's Studies

Women's Study Centres should be organised in all the Universities and recognised social science research institutions within the Eighth Plan. (4.1.32)

Women's Studies research findings should be incorporated into curriculum revision and development, and teacher training programmes at all levels of education. At the university level, representatives of the Women's Study Centres should be included in all official bodies concerned with curriculum and syllabus development in all disciplines (4.1.30)

A close linkage in the work of the University-based Women's Study Centres and Educational Complexes should be encourage with a view to widen participation, decentralise and diversify sensitisation and curriculum evaluation. This will also which the work of the Women's Study Centres themselves through feedback from the field. The Women's Study Centres of a university should play a key role in introducing a gender perspective in school education within the Education Complexes of the region that they serve. (4.1.32)

Women's Studies Courses

The foundation courses introduced by the UGC should be reviewed and revised to incorporate women's dimensions. This should be part of the students' overall assessment at the undergraduate level. The course should be carefully structured with the active involvement of Women's Studies research and development organisations and women's organisations working at the grass-roots level. Adequate representation of women's issues, from all sections of society, their concerns and living conditions should be incorporated. (4.1.33)

Existing courses should also incorporate the gender perspective, as suggested in the POA. This must apply to all courses, including science and technology, medicine, law, agriculture and veterinary sciences. (4.1.33)

All issues related to curricular revision and development on Women's Studies should be extended to the orientation of teachers as well. (4.1.33)

Extension Services

Women's Development Centres, such as the ones existing in some University Colleges should be extended to all colleges and higher educational institutions. (4.1.34)

These Centres should also be given funds to conduct awareness workshops, seminars etc. at both the school and community levels. (4.1.34)

Representation of Women in the Educational Hierarchy

The proportion of women teachers in Primary, Middle and High Schools should be increased to at least 50 per cent. For the success of this measure it would be desirable if the woman teacher is selected from within or near the habitation where she is to teach. In case a local woman teacher cannot be found, it would then be necessary to —

(a) provide living quarters with certain minimum amenities to women teachers on a priority basis,

(b) locate the living quarters within the habitation in order to ensure security, and

(c) wherever possible, provide living quarters to all women functionaries, apart from women teachers, in close proximity to each other. (4.1.36)

While an increasing number of women should be recruited at different levels of education, there should be promotional avenues also within the educational hierarchy. Special measures would have to be devised to ensure that women are fairly represented in decision-making bodies in teaching and educational administration. (4.1.36)

Special provisions to take care of women's needs should be built into the recruitment and service procedures, evaluation criteria, guidelines for promotion, etc. An example of such procedures is association of women in Selection Committees and Departmental Promotions Committees. This will ensure that women are not prevented by socio-cultural factors from rising in educational hierarchy. (4.1.36)

Women and men in positions of planning and decision-making within the educational hierarchy and public administration should be sensitised to women's issues so as to adequately discharge their leadership roles. (4.1.36)

Empowerment of Women

Develop *Mahila Samakhya* in a decentralised and participative mode of management, with the decision-making powers developed to the district or block-level and ultimately to the poor women's groups themselves. (4.1.40)

Implement *Mahila Samakhya* in such a way as to establish organic linkages with the ECCE programme and the efforts towards universalisation of girls' elementary education. (4.1.40)

Build a component of closely working with men in the community also, as part of the process of women's empowerment. (4.1.40)

Along with the means for economic independence for women, the issues of women's health, including reproductive health and sexuality, should be included in the parameters for empowerment of women. (4.1.40)

Adult Education

For imparting adult education to women and thereby empower them, the *Mahila Samakhya* model should be tried out. (4.1.40)

Resources

Fifty per cent of the elementary sector allocation for measures to increase girls' participation and be earmarked this allocation be made non-divertible. (4.1.42)

A share of all developmental allocations for secondary, vocational and higher education be earmarked for measures to improve girls' access thereto and the quality of education in these section be improved.

There should be special earmarking for girls within the Special Component Plan for Scheduled Castes and Tribal Sub-Plan. (4.1.42)

Management

Continuance of all Centrally Sponsored Schemes relating, in part or in full, to women's education may be treated in terms of the detailed recommendation given by the Committee in regard to Centrally Sponsored Schemes as a whole in the chapter on Decentralisation and Participative Management. (4.1.44)

The responsibility for planning, implementing and internal monitoring of all school-based programmes for women's education be handed over to the Educational Complexes in the Panchayati Raj framework. At the institutional level, the Head of the institution (Primary, Middle, Higher Secondary Schools) should be made fully responsible for micro-level planning and ensuring universalisation (not just enrolment) of girls' education and their access to high school or vocational education, according to disaggregated strategies and time frames. (4.1.44)

Education for the Schedule Castes, Scheduled Tribes and other Educationally Backward Sections

Incentive Schemes

A series of studies should be instituted to investigate into the impact that the various incentive schemes implemented in different states have had on enrolment and retention of SC/ST children in the schools. Community profiles of educationally backward communities should also be prepared based on study of their current educational status. With reference to these profiles and the findings of the impact studies, on a disaggregated basis, appropriate and logical strategies should be established for the educational development of the backward communities. (4.2.5)

Status of Access to Education

The Fifty All India Education Survey shows that a number of habitations predominantly populated by SCs and STs are not served by schools within walking distance. There should be a programme for the coverage of these unserved habitations with schools as per norms before the end of the Eighth Five-Year Plan. (4.2.6)

Improvement of Capability and Educational Environment

The scheme of remedial coaching should be re-organised such that on a phased basis, majority of the schools introduce the same. Instead of coaching being confined to two or three months of pre-examination periods, the same should be offered in a sustained way throughout the academic session in the concerned classes. (4.2.7)

A strategy to enrich learning environment and the socio-economic conditions in the tribal regions as district from mere remedial coaching should be evolved and brought under implementation. (4.2.7)

In the backward areas including SC, ST habitats, a network of school linked libraries should be established. For reaching out to smaller habitations without schools, a dynamic programme of bicycle-borne mobile libraries or para-school-based libraries should be brought under implementation. These libraries need to be enriched with creative children's literature. While the children's literature would be primarily in the regional languages, efforts should be made to increase the availability of children's books in the local dialects or languages spoken in educationally backward areas. (4.2.7)

In order to nurture all kinds of talents and aptitudes in children, ranging from academic subjects to co-curricular and socio-cultural spheres as may be identifiable. Educational Complexes should organise a wide-ranging programme of specific theme-based workshops/work camps, using the best available resource persons in the area. This programme should *encourage school drop-outs* as well to join and contribute in this collective endeavour towards excellence. (4.2.7)

In the curriculum of the educationally backward the following should be emphasised at all stages of education:

(*a*) Science and Mathematics;

(*b*) Expression, both oral and written, and creative writing;

(*c*) History and Sociology of the Scheduled Castes, the Scheduled Tribes and other backward sections of society;

(*d*) Contribution of these communities to national life and development, including the freedom struggle; and

(*e*) Role played by women belonging to these communities in national life and development.

(in fact, matters covering under (*c*), (*d*) and (*e*) should also be included in the National Core Curriculum). (4.2.7)

Above all else, in order to bring about universalisation of Elementary education among girls in backward areas, including those belonging to SC/ST communities, a network of ECCE centres should be established on a primary basis, with linkage to primary schools. (This has also been dealt with in the Chapter on ECCE). (4.2.7)

Recruitment of SC/ST Teachers

It should be ensured that in Government and Government-aided schools teachers from SC/St communities are invariably in the order of 15 per cent and 7.5 per cent respectively. Recruitment to reach these levels should also be closely maintained. (4.2.8)

Curriculum and Tribal Culture

The rich diversity of the tribal cultural identities should be included in the common cultural heritage which is one of the elements of the Core Curriculum envisaged in NPE/POA. (4.2.8)

Special Component Plan and Tribal Sub-Plan

Special Component Plan and Tribal Sub-Plan should be specifically exhibited in the budget document, schemewise. (4.2.9)

To the extent feasible, schemes meant exclusively for the Scheduled Castes and Scheduled Tribes should be prepared and included under SCP/TSP. (4.2.9)

Wherever exclusive schemes cannot be formulated, specific physical targets for coverage of Scheduled Castes/Scheduled Tribes under the schemes generally applicable to all should be indicated. (4.2.9)

A more effective monitoring mechanism should be established in the Department of Education itself for the purpose of periodically following up the progress of implementation of SCP/TSP. (4.2.9)

Intensive Area Approach

The Ministry of Welfare, according to the Business Rules, is expected to do coordination in the implementation of programmes relating to SCs/STs. While they have given a list of blocks identified as tribal blocks they have not given, with reference to 1981 census, a list of blocks identified as those of Scheduled Caste concentration. This Ministry should, therefore, provide lists of blocks with SC concentration. With reference to such lists the Department of Education should get feedback from the States regarding their coverage under the various educational programmes. (4.2.10)

All the educational programmes should be implemented to the extent feasible conveniently in the same blocks of SC concentration/

tribal blocks so that impact of educational development is felt in a demonstrable and balanced way in the respective areas. (4.2.10)

Monitoring

A single focal agency in each State should be identified for the purpose of reporting to the Government of India comprehensively on all the educational programmes. (4.2.11)

Minorities

Government of India should establish a standing machinery to closely monitor issue of detailed guidelines by the States for the purpose of granting recognition to minority managed educational institutions; to review the pace of disposal of applications for recognition of these institutions; and thereby to secure quality of education in institutions so recognised (4.2.12)

All the educational programmes that are now under implementation should be concurrently implemented, to the extent feasible, in these districts on a priority basis after conduct of bench mark surveys as envisaged in POA.* (There is no evidence of implementation of education programmes in these districts based on initial bench mark surveys to assess the status of literacy therein and to build programmes therein for further improvements). (4.2.12)

The twenty-five districts which have not yet been covered under the community polytechnics should also be brought under their coverage before the end of the Eighth Five-Year Plan. (4.2.12)

The orientation programmes for the Principals/Managers and teachers of minority managed educational institutions should be organised on a decentralised basis through SCERTs at the State level and DIETs, CTEs & IASEs at the sub-State levels. (4.2.12)

Special coaching should be organised through reputed and progressive voluntary organisations, particularly those operating for the benefit and welfare of the minority communities. (4.2.12)

Open universities including the IGNOU should establish distance education programmes for imparting special coaching. (4.2.12)

---

* Note: The forty-one districts identified in the POA as being of minority concentration.

Education of the Handicapped

People should be made aware of the problems of the handicapped, in terms of the magnitude and types of handicaps. The media should be effectively used for this purpose. (4.3.6)

Every family with a handicapped child should be provided support through incentives, dialogue and periodic training and evaluation. Parents' groups and community education groups should be formed. (4.3.6)

The educational system for the handicapped should be flexible. It should offer a range of education provisions—special schools for those who cannot be educated in general schools, special classes in general schools, and integrated education for the disabled of the type already in existence. Education should be through different options—formal, non-formal, open schools, home day schools, vocational centres etc. (4.3.6)

Educational packages should be offered for hearing impaired children in a differentiated way—

* Pure orally oriented programmes for profoundly deaf children.
* Combined oral-manual programmes for some of the profoundly deaf children for the education of whom pure oral programmes will not be adequate.
* Segregated programmes for those children for whom such programmes are essential.
* Integrated programmes for those whom this modality promises better emotive, cognitive, social and linguistic development. (4.3.6)

For making the boys and girls of impaired hearing economically independent, vocational training has to be specially organised. Vocational training which is job-oriented and matched to the abilities and aptitudes of the hearing impaired, should be organised in a significantly diversified way making a departure from the earlier practice of confining to a limited number of vocational training programmes like in drawing, painting, tailoring, knitting, embroidery, book-binding, etc. These diversified courses also relate to industrial operations such as sheet metal works, printing, turning, fitting, welding, electrician's trade, carpentry, etc. (4.3.6)

Bharati Braille has been developed, thanks, inter alia, to the special effort made by the National Institute for the Visually Handicapped. Based on this, teacher training and book production programmes have also been launched. These production programmes should be intensified by their scales of operation being enlarged and diversified to cover wide range of subjects and in-school and out-of-school needs. (4.3.6)

While work has been initiated for development of Braille notations for mathematics and science, not much progress has been made. On account of the growing emphasis on science and mathematics teaching a comprehensive and effective code for use in the area of mathematics and science should be developed. (4.3.6)

For the moderately mentally retarded, special curricula should be developed and standardised—not merely for the purpose of basic education in 3 R's but for training in self-care skills like motor integration, perceptual and motor skills, language, communication and conceptual skills. It should be clearly understood that for the mentally handicapped, academic achievements are relatively unimportant in comparison to social adaptation and vocational training. (4.3.6)

Vocational schools for the mentally retarded adults are not too many. For their benefit jobs in sheltered workshops, farms and industries should be provided as they are not capable of receiving open employment. The idea is that after receiving training they can work on sub-contract basis. (4.3.6)

In pre-service teacher training programme, education of the handicapped, should be made part and parcel of the pedagogy and methodology. (4.3.6)

A programme of sensitization should be implemented for in-service teachers as well. This should include various components, namely, Non-Formal Education, vocationalisation of education and distance education. (4.3.6)

Teachers' training colleges should have special courses for teaching the handicapped children; a special component on the education of the handicapped should be included in the B.Ed. courses as well. (4.3.6)

At least one resource faculty should be provided in each DIET to provide teacher training inputs in the context of education for the handicapped. (4.3.6)

The role of the special schools should be clearly redefined as spelt out below:

(i) Early identification of children with handicaps and formulation of stimulation programmes for them and the community in their catchment areas;

(ii) Education of the handicapped children who cannot be educated in general schools upto the point when they can be integrated—thus breaking the insulation between the general and special schools.

(iii) Service as resource agencies for implementing the integrated education programmes in general schools so that they feel as a part and parcel of the educational system.

(iv) Bringing about mutual reinforcement of the pedagogies of special and general education. (4.3.6)

A lot of development is taking place in the application of technology for the benefit of the handicapped. Several technological aids are already available like for example. Brailleix produced by Federal Republic of Germany which facilitates recording of whole encyclopaedia on cassettes, printing conversion devices like 'tactocon' which facilitate presentation of printed material in vibrotactile form so as to enable the blind persons to read, devices facilitating mobility of the blind persons etc. The technologies and techno-aids available for meeting the special needs of the handicapped children should be reviewed and measures for dissemination of information should be formulated. (4.3.6)

Sustained researches should be undertaken to determine the needs of the physically handicapped and produce technological aids capable of helping in overcoming handicaps. The Indian Institute of Technology and other technological institutions in the area of higher education should be given specific responsibilities for undertaking these researches. (4.3.6)

Common School System

The first step in securing equity and social justice in education is the building up of a Common School System. Specific actions required in this context are the following:

— Provisions of significantly increased outlay for elementary (particularly primary) education. This would help in the building up of the required levels of infrastructure and quality of education, thereby transforming Government, local-body and aided schools into genuine Neighbourhood Schools.

— Provision of special allocations for improvement of school system in backward areas, urban slums, tribal areas, hilly tracts, desert and marshy areas, drought and flood-prone zones, costal belts and islands.

— Ensuring instruction for all in the medium of mother tongue at the primary level, particularly for linguistic minorities; active encouragement of teaching in the regional languages at the secondary level; and discontinuance of State aid to the schools imparting education otherwise than in the medium of mother tongue/regional languages.

— Phased implementation of the Common School System within a ten year time frame, and essential minimum legislation, particularly to dispense with early selection process, tuition fee, capitation fee etc.

— Exploring ways of including the expensive private schools into the Common School System through a combination of incentives, disincentives and legislation. (4.4.8)

Navodaya Vidalayas

The Committee, having considered the strong views expressed by the members for and against the Navodaya Vidyalaya Scheme and after taking into account all aspects of the scheme in terms of the concept, philosophy, design, its implementation and future, recommends that the Government may decide from out of the following three alternatives:

(i) *No Further Navodaya Vidalaya need be opened.* The existing 261 Navodaya Vidyalayas may be restructured and continued with provision of adequate resources. The scheme may also be reviewed at the end of 1992-93. The terms of reference for this review may be—

— Whether the objectives for which the scheme was established have been achieved-in terms of nurturing of talents, reservations for the SCs/STs, girls, representation for rural children, pace setting functions and national integration through migration of children.

— If the objectives have not been achieved what are the reasons for the same?

— Restructuring, if any, of the scheme with reference to:

* redefinition of the concept of special talent or aptitude such that the selection takes into account the entire cognitive and affective domain as well as the psychomotor skills;
* broadening the process and canvas of selection with a view to make provision for the vast potential of talent in different attributes of life that exists among rural children, but is not identifiable by conventional academic tools;
* changing the present life style and value orientation of the Navodaya Vidyalayas such that the alienation of the campuses from rural life, particularly that of the underprivileged sections, is guarded against.

(ii) All the existing 261 Navodaya Vidalayas may be transferred to the State Sector for the States to run them as residential centres on the Andhra Pradesh model.

(iii) The Navodaya Vidalaya scheme may be transformed into a Navodaya Vidyalaya programme of broad based talent nurturing and pace-setting. (A day-school each under the Common School system can function in the premises of the Navodaya Vidyalayas). (4.5.10)

2. EARLY CHILDHOOD CARE AND EDUCATION

Scope of Article 45 of the Constitution

The scope of the Constitutional directive (Article 45) of providing, within a specified time-frame, free and compulsory education for 'all children until they complete the age of fourteen years', should be enlarged to include ECCE. (5.1.6)

Operational Design

Since ECCE is a cross-sectorial programme, addressing the inter-secting needs of children, women and girls, ECCE as a component should receive due attention in all dimensions and stages of education, such as women's education, education of Scheduled Castes and Tribes, elementary education, vocational education, content and process, teacher training, higher education etc. (5.2.0)

Priority

ECCE should be included in the Minimum Needs Programme. (5.3.0)

Role and Responsibility of Various Departments

The Department of Women and Child Development in the Ministry of HRD at the Centre (and the Departments of Social Welfare in the States) should be held accountable for the implementation of ECCE *in all aspects* of its operational design, as recommended in the POA. (5.4.4)

This Department must also accept the model role of stimulating, co-ordinating and monitoring the ECCE work undertaken by other agencies/departments, such as Labour, Works and Housing, Tribal Welfare, Agriculture, Irrigation, Rural Development, Forest etc. (5.4.4)

The Department of Women and Child Development (and its counterparts in the States) should seek the setting up of an Inter-Ministerial Committee (and its equivalent in the States), comprising representatives of the Departments of Labour, Health and Education to assist it in planning, co-ordinating and monitoring the ECCE programmes. (5.4.4)

At the same time, the Department of Education cannot, under Article 45 give up its basic responsibility for the education of children from birth to six years, and must ensure that this continuing concern is reflected in action in all dimensions and stages of education. (5.4.4)

Strategies and Models

The principles of diversity, flexibility and decentralised funding and management must be incorporated into the policy framework, with a view to widen coverage and improve retention, especially with reference to remote habitations and most underprivileged or migrant communities. (5.5.4)

These principles must be reflected in the operational design for developing a country-wide network of ECCE programmes, linking a rich diversity of models and strategies. (5.5.4)

Provision should be made for Statutory Cretches and Day Care Centres for both the organised and unorganised sectors and for strict implementation of all labour laws dealing with child care services. These laws should also be reviewed to facilitate easier implementation. (5.5.4)

Wherever possible, ECCE centres should be linked physically as well as programmatically with the primary school (5.5.4)

ICDS

In order to broaden access and improve quality, ICDS should move in the direction of becoming a participatory network of decentralised ECCE centres managed by local groups, preferably poor women's groups, under the umbrella of Panchayati Raj Institutions, with the Government providing support through essential funding (may be, on a per child basis), training, monitoring and guidance. (5.6.2)

Other Models and Strategies

Concrete provisions should be made in financial and programmatic terms for decentralised and community-based implementation of the various models and strategies mentioned in POA, such as—

(i) Strengthening and upgrading all existing models.

(ii) Promoting innovative and experimental models.

(iii) Developing special programmes for specific underprivileged or migrant communities and for remote habitations, and

(iv) Developing and promoting media support on a massive scale (as is being done at present for the adult literacy campaign) for generating public awareness and understanding regarding issue relating to care and education of children in the 0-6 age group. (5.7.4)

Comment and Quality

The basic principles of curriculum and content of ECCE should be translated into localised content. (5.8.4)

Effective field strategies, buttressed by a systematic media campaign (as is going on at present for adult literacy), need to be urgently implemented in order to discourage formal teaching methods and early introduction of 3 R's in ECCE programmes, both in the private and the Government sectors. (5.8.4)

Appropriate and acceptable ratios of adults to children in ECCE programmes for different age-groups and models should be worked out as guidelines for agencies implementing ECCE and adequate provision be made to proportionately augment the staff of the centres. (5.8.4)

Personnel and Training

Recognising the skilled nature of work in ECCE and the links between programme quality on the one hand and wages, job satisfaction, social status and motivation on the other, the policy for remuneration of ECCE workers spelt out in POA must be implemented with immediate effect. (5.9.9)

The overall responsibility for teacher education and personnel training for ECCE at all levels must be accepted by the Departments of Education, both at the Centre and the States/UTs in close co-ordination with the Department of Women and Child Development at the Centre and their counterparts in the States, while developing mechanisms to respond to the needs and perceptions of the users and programme implementers, such as the Departments of Labour, Forest, Irrigation, Works and Housing, Rural Development etc. as well as the private sector. For the other components of ECCE (health, nutrition etc.), a close co-ordination with the nodal and other related departments/agencies would be necessary. (5.9.9)

Working through Educational Complexes (as proposed elsewhere), DIETs should assume responsibility for training in ECCE and establish a *field-based* networking relationship with ECCE programmes. For this purpose DIETs should build up their own training capability. (5.9.9)

Building up on the base of available training pattern a network of modular training programmes for ECCE must be developed at all levels (grass roots, para-professional, professional and supervisory) through a diversity of models and strategies, with content to meet the holistic goals of ECCE and a participatory methodology using the basic principle of internship with different degrees of field placement. (5.9.9)

A system of accreditation of training programmes and agencies in ECCE must be developed as indicated in POA (this would also promote diversity and decentralisation). (5.9.9)

Action should be taken soon to develop Vocational Education of ECCE at the +2 level in the States/UTs. The feasibility of organising ECCE training following Class VIII should be examined on a priority basis with a view to which the social base and availability of ECCE workers. (5.9.9)

Measures should be initiated to re-structure the training programmes of elementary school teachers all over the country to integrate and emphasise the child-centred and non-formal approaches of early childhood education in the primary schools, especially at the early stages, with a view to improve schools' capability to receive and retain children. (5.9.9)

Decentralisation

The ICDS and other related Centrally Sponsored Schemes for ECCE may be shifted to the States/UTs following the completion of the present phase. The State/UT Plans should then be proportionately augmented with additional funds with conditionality of non-divertibility and accountability. (5.10.3)

The management of Anganwadis and other ECCE centres should be fully handed over to voluntary organisations and/or local community groups, preferably poor women's groups, through the Panchayati Raj framework. Village-level and/or Mohalla-level Committees may be constituted by local bodies, with at least half of the members being poor women and with suitable representation of Anganwadi workers, for planning, coordinating and monitoring of a cluster of community-based centres in a village or town. Needless to add, the principle of community control over ECCE programme would carry with it the principle of full public accountability to the community. (5.10.3)

In order to ensure diversity, flexibility and responsiveness to local needs and socio-cultural conditions, the community groups and or village or mohalla-level committees, would be fully responsible for designing the model and strategy for the local ECCE centre, while being expected to ensure the minimum programme recommended by the State Government. Experimentation and innovation in approach to training, recruitment of personnel and management would be encouraged and be provided for. (5.10.3)

The Village or Mohalla-level Committee or the community group responsible for managing the ECCE centre would also be free to mobilise additional resources, in addition to the State resources, while subjecting itself to both financial and social audit. (5.10.3)

ECCE should be included in the charter of responsibilities of the Educational Complexes proposed in the school education sector. Women and other community groups managing ECCE centres and Anganwadi workers may be suitably represented on the executed bodies of the Complexes. (5.10.3)

The role of the Educational Complex would be to develop a perspective plan for ECCE for the region covered by it and to assist the local committees and groups by arranging for training (through DIETs), supplying educational and other materials (not locally available) guidance in budgeting, coordination, promoting mutual exchange of information and, most importantly, monitoring. (5.10.3)

Since the ECCE centre would be accountable to the community it is serving, the monitoring role of the Educational Complex as also of the State Government assumes special significance. While the Educational Complex would make its report on individual centres available to the community/village as an input in the awareness-raising process, the State Government would monitor the Complex as a whole and release its report for public action at the Block or district level. In this framework, supervision as a means to control and improve performance becomes superfluous. (5.10.3)

The role of the State Government may be confined to:

(a) ensuring essential funding (may be, on a per child basis) for ECCE through the Panchayati Raj Institutions/ Educational Complexes;

(b) spelling out policy imperatives and broad guidelines;

(c) providing training through SCERT DIETs;

(d) supplying materials not available locally;

(e) promoting *lateral* exchange and analysis of information and experiences amongst Educational Complexes;

(f) co-ordination;

(g) monitoring; and

(h) raising public awareness and giving media support (5.10.3)

The State Government should also ensure that representatives of the user agencies and programme implementers (*e.g.* Departments of Labour, Irrigation, Forest, etc. and voluntary organisations) are included in the State-level structures set up for planning, programme formulation, designing curriculum, and development of training models and strategies, so that their needs and perceptions find adequate expression. (5.10.3)

Resources

A Central Fund for child care services should be set-up at the national level. (5.11.0)

The Government should provide a substantially higher allocation for ECCE, spelling it out as a percentage of GNP, keeping in view the estimated requirements of Rs.4900 crore per annum even for achieving the POA targets to be reached by the end of Eighth Plan in a phased manner. (5.11.0)

A 10-year action and resource allocation plan for building-up a national network of child care services be prepared, such that at least 70 per cent of the children below six would be covered by an essential package of services by 2000 AD, as suggested in POA. (5.11.0)

Funds for the national network may be drawn from five sources as given below:

(a) Government: As per Article 45 of the Constitution, the Central and State Governments would have to bear the major responsibility for funding the programme. These funds may be drawn by pooling together the provisions made in the respective budgets of the Departments of Education, Women and Child Development, Health and Labour for this purpose. To facilitate this, an *Inter-Ministerial Committee* may be constituted. The Government Departments which employ labour (*e.g.* Irrigation, Rural Development, Forest, Works and Housing etc.) should henceforth be required to make a proportionate provision for expenses on child care services and contribute this money to the Central Fund.

(b) Employers: A special welfare cess for the Central Fund should be levied on all employers, whether in the private or in the public sector, regardless of the sex of the workers employed. No distinction need be made on the basis of the type of employment—salaries, daily wage or some other form.

(c) Local Bodies: Panchayats, Municipalities and Corporations may be encouraged to raise additional funds for ECCE through special local cess/taxes.

(d) Parents: With community control, it should become possible for the Village/Mohalla Committee to raise a certain fraction of the needed resources from the parents at the local level, as a

voluntary contribution on a monthly basis. In the organised sector, this contribution could be collected through the trade unions.

(e) Donations: Tax incentives may be given on contributions to the Central Fund. (5.11.0)

A special allocation of additional funds, say Rs.100 crore, be made for 1991-92 to undertake preparatory work consisting of an awareness-raising media campaign, upgradation of the existing ICDS and other centres, developing decentralised structures at the grass roots, building up training programmes and promoting action research in alternative models. (5.11.0)

Monitoring and Evaluation

DIETs and Educational Complexes, rather than any higher level structures, should have a major role in both planning and execution of the system of *internal* monitoring and evaluation. (5.12.0)

The State Government should also organise an independent system of monitoring and evaluation of the programme at the level of Educational Complexes only (*ie.*, not at the level of individual centres) and make its reports available for open and public consideration at the District or Block level. (5.12.0)

One major objective of these exercises should be to use the findings as a direct input for renewal/strengthening of the programme at the local level. For this, it would be necessary to foster lateral interaction and exchange of findings (complex to complex or centre to centre or centre-complex), rather than the exclusive vertical and upwards flow indicated in the POA. The reports from monitoring and evaluation exercises should also be released for open interaction at both the formal and informal fora with a view to build up public pressure for programme efficiency. (5.12.0)

The Index of Human Development should be a dynamic concept and be made public as a means of monitoring as well as community intervention in the programmes. (5.12.0)

3. UNIVERSALISATION OF ELEMENTARY EDUCATION

Right to Education

The Right to Education should be examined for inclusion

amongst the fundamental rights guaranteed under the Constitution of India. All the socio-economic measures, without which realisation of this right will not be possible, should be taken. (6.1.3)

Thrust Areas

The Policy Statement in para 5.5 of NPE should be modified to incorporate the following three areas of concern as thrust areas:

(a) convergence of services,

(b) linkage between the school and the community, and

(c) decentralised and participative mode of educational planning and management. (6.3.2)

Formulation of strategies for UEE must take into account the three thrust areas listed above along with the two areas already included in para 5.5 of NPE. (6.3.2)

Lacunae in NPE 1986

The policy has certainly done well by emphasising child-centred approach to education and by pointing out that it is the best motivation for the child to attend school and learn (NPE Para 5.6). The Committee's perspective in this regard is presented below:

(i) although implied in the warm, welcoming and encouraging approach mentioned in NPE, it would be better if the policy would explicitly refer to the elements of joy, fun, exploration and play as integral to learning in the early stages of primary education.

This explicit mention is required because the prevailing educational practice in the school system not only excludes these elements, but seems to consciously resist their introduction in the learning process.

(ii) similarly, the policy statement should emphasise the role of singing, drawing, clay-modelling, games and particularly all forms of folk-art and folk-lore in enriching the learning process.

(iii) it is not clear why the benefit of being allowed to set their own pace and be given supplementary remedial instruction is restricted only to the first generation learners.

By implication, the policy would deny the other children the advantage of setting their own pace.

(*iv*) the policy emphasises the need to increase cognitive learning and the skill component with the growth of the child. In the same spirit, the policy should have emphasised the role of the affective domain and psychomotor skills at the earlier stages.

(*v*) whereas the Committee endorses the declaration of retaining the policy of non-detention at the primary stage, it is presented in the negative framework of detention *versus* non-detention. Instead, a positive concept of continuous, disaggregated and comprehensive evaluation as a means of improving the quality of learning should have been emphasised, with a clear understanding that the concept of a *terminal examination has no place in child-centred education* (the widespread antagonism amongst the teachers to the non-detention policy in vogue in several States probably has its roots in this negative presentation and teachers lack of appreciation of the tool of continuous evaluation for quality improvement).

(*vi*) the policy declares that corporal punishment will be firmly excluded. While welcoming this assertion, it may be noted that corporal punishment is already excluded on paper in most of the States/UTs. Yet it persists in most parts of the country. Therefore, the policy would have done well by emphasising measures to control the socio-cultural, psychological and educational factors that justify corporal punishment in the minds of the teachers.

(*vii*) similarly the policy declaration to adjust school timings as well as vacations to the convenience of children has been made time and again from several public fora. The policy should have, instead, spelt out its strategy to mitigate the reasons that have not allowed this to happen so far.

The policy Statement on Child-centred Approach in para 5.6 of NPE should be modified in order to remove the inconsistencies and/or lacunae, as pointed out above. (6.3.3)

While giving due importance to the provision of additional

facilities to the schools, the Policy must also stress the role of the teacher, the community and the social environment as key factors in improvement of the quality of school education. (6.3.7)

Since the present enrolment data are not reliable the policy should stress a continuing concern for improving both enrolment and retention, as distinct from enrolment to retention. (6.3.7)

The curriculum at the +2 level should not be allowed to determine the content and process of education at the primary and middle school levels. The curriculum development for the primary and middle school stages should aim at evolving a self-sufficient model of knowledge, skills and attitudes so that the majority of children who would not proceed to the high schools would be fully equipped to enter the 'world of work' and continue self-learning throughout life. (6.3.7)

NPE's 'Resolve' in para 5.12 should be modified to:

(a) emphasise both enrolment and retention in the school;

(b) relate fixing of targets to ground-level realities through a decentralised and participative mode of disaggregated planning, rather than fixing targets in an *ad-hoc* fashion; and

(c) integrate non-formal and formal education systems over a period of time such that their cadres, infrastructure and management structures would form an organic whole (6.4.9)

Non-Formal Education

Over a period of time non-formalise the formal school in the following ways:

(a) shifting of the school timings to early morning hours, after-noons or late evenings, as per the convenience of the majority of children and in consultation with the Village Education Committee and the Educational Complex;

(b) adjusting school calendar to agricultural activities, local cultural engagements and the weekly markets with a view to optimise school attendance;

(c) introducing child-centred approach with concomitant *reduction in school hours*, but an *increase in the learning hours*. This would come about through utilisation of improved pedagogic practices involving elements of inquiry, play-

way, activity, creative writing, peer group learning, experimentation etc. Creative use of singing, drawing, story telling and particularly of folk-lores and folk-arts would enrich the pedagogic practices;

(d) linking at least one day care centre, providing holistic services for children in 0-6 age group, with the school in both physical as well as programmatic terms; the school should adopt the play-way and activity-based approach of ECCE from the day care centre; the Anganwadi workers may be viewed as associates of the school staff;

(e) wherever required and feasible, holding of classes twice in the day — mornings for the written tradition and evenings for oral tradition, games and cultural action;

(f) introducing 'ungraded class room' which would encourage all children at different levels of learning to set their own pace;

(g) relating content and process of learning with environment and life of the community; and

(h) allowing all working children, particularly the girls, to *drop-in* the school at any time of the day or the year they want; also encouraging the children of migrant families from other villages/habitations/towns to similarly *drop-in* (this flexibility becomes possible as a direct consequence of the 'ungraded class room' approach). (6.5.11)

For the purpose of non-formalisation of the school, it would be essential to restructure the appointment, placement and training of teachers in the following ways:

(a) in addition to the regular teaching staff, empower the Head Master/Head Mistress to recruit 'para-teachers' (*Shiksha Karmis*)* for the early morning or evening classes and/or habitations/villages/*mohallas* still unserved by a school;

* The concept of a 'para-teacher' is somewhat similar to the concept of Shiksha Karmis practised at present in Rajasthan on an experimental basis with a view to reach-out to unserved habitations.

(b) although the appointment of the 'para-teachers' would be probationary for a period of two to three years, she/he shall be paid a respectable emolument, which in no case shall be lower than one-third (preferably, it should be one-half) of the salary of the school teacher or the local minimum wage level whichever is higher;

(c) as far as possible, the 'para-teacher' should be recruited from the local community, with preference being given to women; if necessary, young persons with commitment and aptitude for working with children having even less than minimum qualifications could be recruited, provided they are willing to upgrade their educational qualifications within the probationary period through the open school system;

(d) the regular school teacher and the 'para-teacher' shall be inter-changeable in terms of teaching responsibilities;

(e) at the end of the probationary period, the 'para-teacher' should be absorbed as a regular school teacher provided she/he has been able to upgrade her/his educational qualification to a certain minimum level (say, Class XII) and ensure a concrete move towards enrolment and retention of all children in the community who were earlier outside the ambit of the school; and

(f) organise the training of the 'para-teacher' along the lines of the 'Internship Model' wherein the training emerges from and is integrated into the empirical experience of the class room; a sandwich programme of internship and in-service training would be evolved by the DIET in consultation with the Educational Complex; the training staff would comprise of the senior teachers of the local school as well as the Educational Complex and also the DIET personnel. (6.5.11)

In order to non-formalise the formal school, the following package of measures would have to be adopted as a *'pre-condition'*:

(a) handing over the effective control of the school, including the appointment, posting and promotion of teachers, to a

co-ordinated management system involving the school, Village Education Committee and the Educational Complex;

(*b*) empowering the local community, especially under-privileged sections of the society with assignment of specific role to women groups, to monitor and support the school;

(*c*) develop the school into a community school which would take active interest in social and cultural life of the village and welcome contribution by members of the community in both the planning and the teaching process; the school would also act as a nucleus of multiple social welfare services provided by the Government, including health, early childhood care and education, women's education, adult education etc. (6.5.11)

Modern technological aids should be introduced only when their role is established on the basis of the class room experience through a participative mode involving teachers and teachers-trainers; any hasty measure to introduce such aids (*e.g.* radio-cassette player, TV or VCR) would only lead to waste of valuable resources. These should be introduced only where teacher asks for the same based on full needs.

Operation Blackboard

The question of continuance of Operation Blackboard as a Centrally Sponsored Scheme may be treated in the light of recommendations made by the Committee in regard to Centrally Sponsored Schemes as a whole in the Chapter on Decentralisation and Participative Management. (6.6.6)

The State Governments should devolve all decision-making powers concerning Operation Blackboard to the Educational Complexes which would seek consultation from DIETs on the one hand, and the concerned school and the Village Education Committee, on the other hand, for planning and implementing the scheme. (6.6.6)

The schools and the Village Education Committees, made fully responsible for UEE in their respective areas, should undertake a micro-planning exercise for working out their requirements under Operation Blackboard and be accountable for its implementation. (6.6.6)

Operation Blackboard must be given the status of one of the priority strategies for UEE, but, at the same time, it should be ensured that investment is made only on those items whose need has been established by the teachers and other related persons on the basis of micro-planning and class room requirements. (6.6.6)

For posting women teachers in the villages, it would be best to select them locally, wherever possible, or else make provision for their accommodation, security and other support services. (6.6.6)

Measure to 'Reach Out' to Children

Provide each habitation with a population of 300 or more with at least one Primary School by the year 2000 (this implies an additional 1.22 lakh schools as per 1986 data). In the meantime, each such habitation may be served by a 'para-teacher', linked to the nearest Primary School. (6.9.0)

Provide each habitation with a population of 500 or more with at least one Middle School by the year 2000 (this implies 2.5 lakh additional schools as per 1986 data). In the meantime, each such habitation may be served by a 'para-teacher', linked to the nearest Middle School. (6.9.0)

A network of 'para-schools', linked to the nearest Primary School, should be started such that all unserved habitations with population of less than 300 would be served by at least one 'para-school' by the end of the Eighth Five Year Plan period. (6.9.0)

A network of 'para-schools', linked to the nearest Middle School, should be started such that every child has access to a 'para-middle school' within one km. of residence by the end of the Eighth Five Year Plan period. (6.9.0)

In starting 'para-schools', whether at primary or middle level, priority should be given to the habitations having enrolments and retention rates for girls below the State average. (6.9.0)

In order to reach out to the children who are engaged in the workforce during the day time or the girls engaged in domestic chores, it would be necessary to organise 'para-schools' either early in the morning, afternoons or late in the evening, depending upon the convenience of the children. These 'para-schools' may be run by the school teachers who reside in the same village or nearby. Alternatively, the school may recruit fresh 'para-teachers' even for the habitations which have a school. (6.9.0)

For children who are engaged in wage labour in organised or unorganised sectors for durations extending beyond the stipulated eight hour period and especially for those children who are engaged in hazardous industries, it would be necessary to go *beyond* the measure of opening 'para-school' within the habitation or in the evenings. For this 'hard-core' measures involving provision for opportunity costs and mid-day meals may become necessary. In addition, strict implementation of child labour laws in such 'hard-core areas' would become an essential 'educational' task. (6.9.0)

Strategies and Measures for Achieving UEE

Make each school, primary or middle fully responsible accountable or formulating and implementing strategies for UEE in villages/habitations/*mohallas* in the area under its coverage. For this purpose, vest the school with the necessary authority and autonomy to decide upon their mix of strategies and measures (*e.g.* adult education, para-schools, Operation Blackboard). Provide each school through the avenue of the Educational Complex adequate funds and intellectual resources to implement its programme of universalisation. (6.13.0)

Authorise the school Head Master/Head Mistress to recruit 'para-teachers' *(Shiksha Karmis)* for reaching out either to unserved habitations or to those children who cannot attend the school in the day hours. The issues of emoluments, rules governing their probationary period and eventual absorption in the school, and their training in an 'Internship Model', have already been dealt with in this chapter. (6.13.0)

Encourage innovation by teachers themselves in building up diverse models of child-centred approach to education and create mechanisms for collating, integrating and disseminating the growing experience of the teaching community within and among Educational Complexes. (6.13.0)

In order to increase the relevance of education from the standpoint of working children, especially girls, it would be necessary to emphasise vocationalisation of the entire educational process upto Class VIII level. (6.13.0)

The goal of universalisation of education may be viewed in two phases — the first phase of Universalisation of Primary Education (UPE) and the second phase of UEE. While the school shall be expected to undertake micro-planning for UPE in association with the Educational Complex in the first phase itself, UEE may be allowed to grow organically out of the development of Primary Education. In the second phase, after achieving the goal of UPE, micro-planning for UEE would also become necessary and viable. (6.13.0)

Adopt the principle of differentiated or disaggregated targets and pluralistic educational strategies for achieving UEE. This mode of decentralised and participative planning provides scope for gender-specific, community-wise, Block-level and District-level, and regional parameters to inform the planning process. The national and State targets of UEE as well as resource allocation shall emerge from collection and integration of the disaggregated targets. (6.13.0)

Monitoring of the move towards UEE shall be integral to the planning process and may operate at three independent but co-oriented levels—

(a) within the Educational Complex, of individual schools;

(b) within the district, of individual Educational Complexes; and

(c) within the State of individual District Boards of Education.

The reports of monitoring shall be made available publicly and discussed at specially organised fora with a view to build up public pressure for achieving UEE within this century. (6.13.0)

Express the learning outcome expected of schools and other educational programmes in concrete and easily communicable forms such that these would inform the public criteria and process of monitoring, questioning and intervening in the system. This may take the shape of monthly or yearly community functions in which the general public may participate in collective evaluation of children and the school, and also offer concrete support, financial and otherwise, for the improvement of the school. In this way, create community-based mechanisms and structures for organising a nation-wide process of community empowerment and thereby build a countervailing pressure on the school system to perform and achieve UEE. (6.13.0)

Monitoring and Data Gathering

In order to monitor progress towards UEE, it is essential that we move beyond the state of enrclment and retention. Data must be gathered on actual attendance in class rooms, attainment in learning and equally, if not more importantly, or aptitude towards productive work and attitude towards society. It is only by perceiving UEE in terms of such attributes of education that the whole exercise would acquire as social significance.

4. ADULT AND CONTINUING EDUCATION

Adult Literacy as a Felt Need

Imparting of literacy should be placed in the context of the developmental needs of the adult. Adult education programmes should be accompanied by a wide range of measures relating to health, nutrition, housing, and employment needs. They should also address themselves to issues of fundamental rights, laws, secularism and democracy. After creating awareness in respect of these essential needs and issues the adult learner himself should be expected to ask for adult literacy as a felt need. Instead of starting with adult literacy, the start should be in respect of creation of awareness for essential needs and from there work backward to adult literacy. (7.9.0)

Mass Campaign Strategy and Mahila Samakhya Model

While the mass campaign strategy may be tried out further, the alternative model being employed by the Department of Education through Mahila Samakhya may be closely monitored and its application for adult literacy examined — considering that the objective of this project is to create awareness regarding issues of survival and thereby generate felt needs. (7.9.0)

The mass campaign strategy as well as the Mahila Samakhya model may be objectively evaluated to look for meaningful lessons for the future. (7.9.0)

Voluntary Efforts

On most of the developmental problems and matters relating to fundamental rights, social justice etc., the majority of the illiterates more often than not find themselves in positions of conflict with the official authorities. Therefore, genuine initiatives for adult education programmes by voluntary agencies, community groups, political parties and their mass organisations should be facilitated. (7.9.0)

Evaluation of NLM

While NLM goes ahead with its planned literacy campaign in the Eighth Five Year Plan period, an independent study group should be commissioned to evaluate the programme, particularly with a view to arrive at an understanding of what may be appropriate strategies to remove adult literacy in the quicker possible time. The evaluation may also look into the various alternative models and study their relevance with respect to diverse socio-cultural and political conditions in different parts of India. The minimum objective of this study should be to find out on objective basis what approaches do not yield results, so that, five years later, at least those models may not be encouraged. (7.9.0)

Imparting of Vocational Skills

The Department of Education should coordinate with the Department of Rural Development and Ministry of Labour and organise programmes for vocational skills for the adult illiterates — facilitating flow of funds from programmes like TRYSEM (Training of Youth for Self Employment). Community Polytechnics should also be involved in a large scale in imparting vocational skills amongst the adult illiterates. (This will enhance the employability of the adult illiterates and thereby create awareness regarding basic needs and issues of life, in the process generating demand for adult literacy as a felt need. (7.9.0)

Continuing Interface with Literacy

The neo-literates should be placed in an environment in which they have constant interface with the challenge of the written word. (7.9.0)

UEE and Adult Education Programmes

Illiterate adults are those who have either not had access to education or having had access, have been unable to complete their schooling. A person has to remain in school atleast for a minimum of four years to attain a relatively irreversible level of literacy. Literacy should be a form of basic training making it possible for the adult to acquire some knowledge as may be necessary. It is imperative that Universalisation of Elementary Education is given top priority in educational planning and resource allocation. The objective should be to ensure that no child in the early nineties shall grow into an illiterate adult in the next century. (7.9.0)

5. EDUCATION AND RIGHT TO WORK

Scheme of Vocationalisation of Education

As of now, the State Governments do not furnish, at the time of presentation of proposals for Central assistance, specific deadlines within which they will undertake the various activities for implementing the vocational education scheme — activities such as production of teaching/learning materials, formulation/modification of curriculum/syllabus, completion of civil construction, procurement of equipment, positioning of man-power including teachers etc.

So long as the scheme in the present form is implemented, Government may insist that the State Governments should furnish deadlines for each of the above mentioned activities to be undertaken before funds are sanctioned. Reportedly, in Karnataka State, before seeking Central assistance, the State Department of Education gets all the necessary clearances internally within their Government. This practice may be commended to the other States. (8.4.8)

Work Experience/Socially Useful Productive Work

Work Experience/Socially Useful Productive Work should be integrally linked with various subjects both at the level of content and pedagogy. (8.6.0)

Integrated Design of Vocational Education

An integrated design of vocational education to be operated for classes IX to XII may be established as presented in the following model — with a general core and vocational core and flexible mixes of academic and vocational subjects:

Classes IX to XII

Compulsory			*Core General* *Core Vocational*	
Optional	Academic	Vocational	Academic	Academic
Groupings	Academic	Vocational	Academic	Vocational
	Academic	Vocational	Vocational	Vocational

Flexibility should be provided for children to opt for different mixes of academic and vocational subjects as per the pattern exhibited above. (8.7.0)

Structural Changes in Secondary Education

In order to make vocationalisation a success, substantial structural changes may be introduced in secondary education along the principles of modular courses and credit accumulation, at the same time providing flexibility for multiple exit and entry points for the students. In other words, students opting for any particular vocational course should have the facility of acquiring credits for specific modules of courses, go out into the world of work and come back later at their convenience for earning further credits by pursuing further modules. This would make it possible for the schools to offer vocational courses in varying combinations with subjects such as Languages, Mathematics, Sciences and Social Studies. No doubt vocational and non-vocational subjects should be inter-woven both at the level of content and pedagogy. For those students taking up vocational courses at the secondary stage leading to direct job placements, provision should also be made for further education in those vocations or other fields and, if necessary, bridge courses may be provided. These arrangements are necessary in the expanding world of knowledge and technology, which requires continuing and updating of education for all. What is required for long-term viability of vocationalised education is to make provision not merely for specific skill training but also for necessary theoretical background to enhance transferability of well planned and logically designed open learning and distance learning programmes at the school and university levels should be established as the same would be a good support system for vocationalisation of education. (8.7.0)

Vocational Programmes in NFE

For those who do not go in for formal secondary education in the school system, vocational programmes should be organised in non-formal stream like through TRYSEM and community polytechnics and in the formal stream through the ITIs. Rural Institutions etc. (8.7.0)

Removal of Anomalies in Vocational Courses

Several vocational courses get sex stereotyped. That is, they are considered predominantly relevant in the domain of women. This stereotyping should be carefully availed; and girls given access to increasingly diversified courses not discriminated in terms of relevance to men or women. (This subject has been referred to in the Section concerning Education and Women's Equality.) Access for Scheduled Castes and Scheduled Tribes to vocational courses should be enhanced too. (This has also been referred in the relevant section of the Chapter on 'Equity, Social Justice and Education'.) (8.7.0)

Work Benches and Practice Schools

In order that the process of vocational education is enriched by a meaningful combination of teaching of theory and practice and effective linkages are established with the 'world of work', 'work benches' and 'practice schools' may be identified, accredited and involved as described below:

— 'work benches' and 'practice schools' are work situations selected for the purpose of giving vocational training and direct experience to students within production units or developmental activities of the official agencies. This arrangement offers a more effective educational strategy for providing vocational experience to students than what can be arranged within the four walls of the 'classroom'. Here the training would revolve around real problem—solving and on-the-job development of skills. Whereas 'practice school' is a more institutionalised arrangement with larger units in the organised sector, 'work benches' can be carved out of smaller units from the unorganised sector as well within the neighbourhood of the school. In both cases, the school would not be required to make any substantial investment on skilled personnel or equipment, the same being contributed by the 'world of work', with or without a mutually worked out fee.

Education at these work places would be through student involvement in work activities which would be clearly identified against different areas and levels of work. Further, information would be available to the students in regard to how, under a given work area, one could move from one level to another (vertical mobility), and skills could be transferred from one work area to another (horizontal mobility). A tested evaluation system would be identified to assess students attainment in the work activity and its inter-relationship with nature and society. Based on this assessment, certificates would be awarded by the accredited 'work benches', whether in private or public sector, government or voluntary organisations, and these should be acceptable for employment in any part of the country. Of course, this would call for devising of proper accreditation guidelines and procedures, as well as periodic review by authorised bodies, and this task will have to be done carefully, so as to ensure that this educational innovation does not degenerate into unhealthy social and educational practices. Further, special attention should be given to identify and accredit 'work benches' in the rural sector, especially from economies built around activities such as farming, forestry, animal husbandry, dairying, fisheries, watershed management and ecological conservation.

— Personnel in the 'work benches' and 'practice schools' are not merely to engage themselves in teaching process but are also to be involved in the planning and designing vocational courses, preparation of text materials and evaluation—in a sense in the entire process of education. (8.8.4)

Redesigning Teacher Education Courses

Teacher education courses for vocational education at both the secondary level and post-secondary level should be re-designed in order to prepare teachers who would be equipped, besides general theoretical background and skills, with the necessary interest and attitude for preparing students to meet the requirements of a developing society. Technologists, foremen, skilled craftsmen and other trained personnel from the 'world of work', when recruited as teachers for vocational courses, should be given specially designed bridge courses in areas such as Psychology, Pedagogy, Evaluation, Content Planning etc. (8.9.0)

Decentralisation of Planning and Management

The management, planning and implementation should be decentralised to the level of individual high schools or school complexes, as well as colleges universities, thereby involving actively, the Heads of institutions in decision-making, alongwith representatives of local enterprises from both the industry and agriculture as well as those of official development agencies and voluntary organisations. This would necessitate shift from the present practice of designing vocational courses under centralised initiatives at the national level. Courses have to be designed at the institution levels (schools/colleges) to the extent possible, drawing upon the resources of DIETs. This would also call for greater autonomy at the institutional level in order to fully exploit local and/or regional industrial agricultural, commercial and development potential in framing courses and curriculum. This will further facilitate matching of manpower needs at different stages of development planning. The criticality of institutional autonomy for ensuring success of vocationalisation calls for redefining of roles of various central or state-level agencies under the Department of Education (NCERT, SIE, SCVE etc.), so that these agencies would play only catalytic and resource-sharing roles, rather than directing, determining and detailing all processes. (8.9.0)

The existence at present of multiple and parallel authorities implementing and supervising vocational education, no doubt, is to be seen as a major contributor to ineffective implementation of vocationalisation. This has been brought out by the POA also. Hence, vocational education should be the responsibility of the Department of Education, though other Departments/agencies must collaborate and be even involved in the planning of vocationalisation. (8.9.0)

The concept of National and State Councils of Vocational Education should be re-formulated in the framework of decentralised planning, management, evaluation and accredition in order to involve the 'world of work', private or public, in expanding the reach of vocationalisation of education to the masses. (8.9.0)

Above all else, the Department of Education should coordinate with the concerned agencies under the Central and State Governments for the establishment of appropriate wages and income and employment policies without linkages to which vocationalisation of education, however carefully designed, will not be a success. (8.9.0)

— Ensuring equivalence of the diplomas awarded by rural universities/institutes with university degrees in order to facilitate horizontal and vertical mobility for its graduates.

— Coordination for involving the rural institutes with the district-level rural development programmes.

— Facilitating affiliation of rural institutes with State level universities/Agricultural Universities according to their choice. (9.14.2)

Agricultural Universities

So Agricultural Universities may diversify their education programmes, particularly in areas closely connected with agriculture. The State Agricultural universities should be encouraged to set up centres/institutes for rural development. (9.14.3)

National Council of Higher Education

The Programme of Action under NPE, 1986, envisages establishment of a National Apex Body. Action has been initiated by the Department of Education, in this context, for the establishment of a National Council of Higher Education to bring about coordination between the UGC, the All India Council for Technical Education, Indian Council of Agricultural Research, Medical Council of India and Bar Council of India. In specific terms, the objective of establishing this body, as reflected by the POA, is to deal with policy aspects of higher education and to undertake integrated planning and to reinforce programmes of post-graduate education and inter-disciplinary research. Functions envisaged are tendering of advice to Government on policy, coordination of activities of the various bodies in different fields, encouragement of inter-disciplinary and promotion of interfaces amongst different areas, allocation of resources, establishment and management of common infrastructure and coordination of policy concerning external academic relations.

Going by these objectives and functions of the apex body, it does not seem necessary to create another institution at the national level to function as a super body, as it were. These objectives can be achieved and functions performed by an appropriate coordination mechanism that could be brought into existence by a mere Resolution of Government. This mechanism, in the opinion of the Committee, could have a two-tire structure—*(i)* a Council of Ministers of Higher Education, the Ministers being those holding portfolios relating to education, agriculture, health, law and science and technology; and *(ii)* a Council of Secretaries dealing with these subjects and Heads of the concerned institutions apart from Finance

Secretary to Government of India and Secretary, Planning Commission. Being a high powered body, the former Council may be presided over by the Prime Minister. One of the concerned Ministers may be the vice-chairman by rotation. The Council of Secretaries and Heads of Institutions together may basically formulate the policies and submit the same to the Council of Ministers for approval. (9.15.0)

Grievance Redressal

The recommendation of the Law Commission in regard to tribunalisation of justice in centres of higher education is pending decision. Early decision on this may be taken by the Government. (9.17.0)

6. HIGHER EDUCATION

Maintenance of Standards in Higher Education

Pressures for opening new colleges and universities being very intense, and the political system reacting to such pressures in different ways, in different states, it would only be appropriate for the Government to re-examine the feasibility of national level statutory mechanism for strongly discouraging non-standard/substandard colleges and universities being established. In the process of this examination, no doubt, the Central Government should have necessary prior consultations with the State Governments. (9.4.0)

After NPE, 1986 was formulated and brought under implementation, and though discouragement of proliferation of universities has been specifically mentioned in the Programme of Action, Government of India themselves have passed laws in May, 1989 and October, 1989 respectively for establishing Assam and Nagaland Universities. Steps of this nature may not help in the process of bringing about discipline in the establishment of universities at the State-level and should be avoided. Therefore, Government of India should themselves set an example by not establishing more Central Universities without genuine justification for the same. (9.4.0)

Restructuring of UGC

The UGC has not been able to function effectively in the face of expansion of the higher education system in terms of increasing number of colleges and universities. Workload in terms of development programmes of the universities to be scrutinised by the Commission has been on the increase and their scrutiny and clearance by the Commission suffer in quality as well as on account of delays.

Therefore, restructuring of the UGC is called for. In the opinion of the Committee, the Commission should consist of at least five full time members apart from the chairman and vice-chairman, with specialisation in specific areas—teaching, research, extension, management and finance. The Commission should also have regional offices for decentralised disposal of the problems relating to higher educational institutions in the respective regions. Structural decentralisation would be meaningless unless adequate decentralisation of authority and functions is effected and accordingly this should also be effected. (9.6.0)

Selectiveness in Admission

The universities have come under severe strain on account of the load of administering examinations at the bachelor's level. They should be relieved of the responsibility of holding these examinations so that they can concentrate on post-graduate doctoral and post-doctoral studies, apart from research. (This matter has also been separately dealt with under the subject of Examination Reforms). (9.6.0)

If in a college M.A. and M.Sc teaching is to be continued, it must be made mandatory that there are adequate facilities for research in those subjects. (9.6.0)

Autonomous Colleges

The UGC has already appointed a Committee to review the programme for establishing autonomous colleges. This review should be expedited and modalities should be evolved in this review for introducing a regime of autonomy by securing the participation of all. (9.7.2)

New Management for Universities

Government, should facilitate early decisions on the report of the Gnanam Committee, the same having been received as early as January, 1990. (9.7.3)

Curriculum Development

For the redesigning of courses the UGC has set up twenty-seven Curriculum Development Centres in different disciplines. The emphasis is on modernising and restructuring courses in modular form. Reportedly, twenty-two Curriculum Development Centres have given the reports and they have been circulated to universities and colleges for consideration and implementation. One important question that arises for consideration, in this context, is whether this centralised arrangement does not militate against the autonomy of the universities and colleges on which much emphasis has been laid under NPE, 1986. One view that has been expressed is that these courses are only recommended to universities and colleges which are free to adapt themselves with such modification as they deem fit. The chairman of the UGC, in the course of interactions with the Committee, had occasion to observe that though UGC may be only issuing guidelines on various subjects from time to time, the higher education system as a whole has come to look upon such guidelines as iron-bound mandates and this by itself has introduced a certain rigidity in the system.

Viewed in the light of this observation, the Government and UGC should examine whether the whole process of Curriculum Development and designing of courses cannot be decentralised—the respective universities and colleges seeking the assistance of UGC and panels of experts suggested by them for the purpose of designing courses according to the locally felt needs. (9.8.0)

Decentralisation

The UGC should immediately conduct a study on the extent to which conditions going with the revision of pay scales of the University and College teachers have been actually implemented and fulfilled. (9.9.0)

Teacher Training

In order to enhance the quality of the teachers in the university system, pre-induction training for a period of one year after recruitment should be organised. This training should be organised on a decentralised basis by the respective universities themselves. (9.9.0)

Research

In basic research it may not be really worthwhile to pursue and promote everything that seems interesting, important or feasible. The important criteria for the choice of areas should be promise of achievement of excellence and existence of special advantages that India or Indian scholars possess. (9.11.0)

Where there is a potential for exploitation in the near or foreseeable future in the context of national needs and priorities, special efforts should be made by supporting agencies, (in addition to encouraging basic research in relevant areas) to ensure possible exploitation of these results through establishing proper linkages with user (Economic Ministries or Industry) and undertaking programmes jointly with them. (9.11.0)

In certain selected areas of research all efforts must be made to identify a few educational institutions where talented students and faculty could be attracted for pursuing well-planned advanced courses so that these institutions become the centres of excellence for teaching and research. Such centres should be well-publicized and well-equipped so that the best of talent knows about the challenges and opportunities available to them. At these centres, criticalized research groups should be established around outstanding scientists and engineers. Such centres of excellence should receive support from the Department of Education and the UGC as well as from other agencies for carrying out research. Resources available for such facilities should be adequate. Facilities of national laboratories located in the vicinity should be made fully available to workers in the universities, who together with the scientists of these institutions should take up joint post-graduate programmes and research wherever possible. (These centres are envisaged differently from the University Departments for which the UGC gives special support to turn them into Advanced Study Centres). (9.11.0)

Science and technology agencies must support universities not only in the form of time-bound research projects but also in the setting up of sophisticated research facilities in educational institutions and providing such other infrastructural facilities which will attract the best of minds from all over the country: S and T agencies should provide certain proportion of overheads (say 20 per cent) to the institutions as part of the research grants. Without such overheads, the institutions will not be able to provide the infrastructure for high-quality research (9.11.0)

It is important that research in humanities and social sciences is directed towards contemporary realities in the country. There is also need to initiate research which takes the Indian intellectual and cultural traditions seriously, not necessarily to accept them without question, but to learn from them in order to understand ourselves and to develop the composite culture of India envisaged in the Constitution. (9.11.0)

We have to pay attention to those who aspire for careers in specialised areas of science, humanities, etc. Since we do not have many undergraduate institutions imparting instruction of the highest quality, a few select ones should be provided high-level support by the states and the UGC in order to enable talented and motivated students to get proper training and opportunities for learning. (9.11.0)

Extension in Universities

Universities should involve themselves in development issues in the concerned regions. They should become instruments of development in the respective regions. Consistent with this concept, curriculum, course development etc. should undergo significant changes. To be specific, for example, university teachers could involve themselves in improvement of rural schools so that they become the real 'living link' between the universities and school going population in the regions.

The school experience gained should be built into the content and pedagogy of university education. For this purpose, the universities, so to say—as stated elsewhere—should affiliate themselves to educational complexes engaged in the improvement of the whole system of school down to the elementary level. This way the universities would also come to contribute to enrichment of knowledge. This would develop a cycle of overall development from content of education of competence building. In the process, students coming into the universities would also improve in quality and standards. There will be consequent overall improvement in the environment prevailing in the university system—teachers looking upon their work as of interesting social relevance and better crops of students by themselves, contributing to the quality of university education. In the opinion of the Committee, the slogan of the university system should rather be *Vishwa Gyan Gaon mein Dhyan*. (9.12.0)

3

Educational System and Grassroots Democracy

Although India had made a choice in favour of a democratic political set-up much earlier, the constitutional stamp on the decision was put in 1950. Since then there has hardly been an open demand for its reversal. But the country is not free from individuals who have fascist and totalitarian proclivities. And even in countries where democracy is well-est..blished and has long traditions, the educational system has to be constantly geared to strengthening democratic thinking and process. Therefore, in a country like ours where democracy is yet to strike roots, where obscurantist thinking and economic distress are endemic, there is much greater need for democratic education.

The first prerequisite for the success of democracy is literate electorate. Speaking to the Association for Education in Citizenship in 1937, Bertrand Russel said, "You certainly cannot work a democracy when your population is illiterate.' A compatriot of his, Lowe, had given similar advice much earlier in 1860, when he said in Parliament "We must educate our masters".

One of the foremost concerns of education in India should be liquidation of illiteracy. By any criterion, the effort in this direction has been meagre and its outcome move disappointing. Literacy in India, according to the census of 1971, was 29.34 per cent and the rate of progress in literacy declined during a decade from 7.6 per cent to 4.35 per cent. At this pace 100 per cent literacy may be achieved in about 140 years. Out of 19 crore in the age group 15 to 25 years about 12 crore are completely illiterate and about four crore semi-literate. The Eighth Five-Year Plan gives top priority to schemes to reach this age group.

Why literacy drives started with much fanfare have failed is not difficult to explain. The reasons are well-known. A most serious one is the absence of felt-need for literacy among adults. They cannot be expected to take interest in literacy only in order to prove better voters. How to make them want education?

A study completed in Rajasthan shows that among the four top 'reasons for drop-out' given by the adults themselves are: 'got tired during day's work', 'sowing time', 'irrigation time and animal husbandry work.' Among the four top reasons for persistency given by adult learners are: 'to be able to write letters', 'to be able to sign', 'to read labels on fertilisers and pesticides'. There will be a demand for literacy if it has relevance to the life of adults. Increasing mechanisation of agriculture and methods of production in general may in course of time enhance the value of literacy. Should literacy be made a condition for employment or grant of increment at some stage for all jobs? This may help too.

Countries with poor economy will find it difficult to finance literacy campaigns on a massive scale. Should beneficiaries of higher education, which is no doubt heavily subsidised from public funds, be required to work for adult education in return under some compulsory social service scheme? Will compulsion for this service in the interest of democracy itself be incompatible with individual liberty.

Cleaning the aegean stables of illiteracy will be of no avail if the provision of schooling for the new generations remains as inadequate as it is today. Article 45 of the Indian Constitution required provision of free compulsory education for the age group 6-14 by 1960. It was not attained for the age group 6-11 even. From the point of view of democracy more disturbing is the disparity in the figures for boys and girls, for rural and urban areas, and for one state and another. "While 70 per cent of the boys and 66 per cent of the girls in Kerala see their way through from class I to class IV in primary schools, only 27 per cent of the boys and 15 per cent of the girls do this in Bihar." One survey showed that the fall in enrolment from class I to class II was 19.42 per cent in rural areas and 7.84 per cent in urban areas. To what extent is wastage a consequence of economic backwardness and primitive farming?

Again the disadvantaged groups have much less representation as they go up the educational ladder; so that knowledge and leadership for the elite is reserved. Is this conducive to the growth of democracy whereas Radhakrishnan Commission observed, "Education is a universal right, now a class privilege."?

Should expansion of university and higher education be held up to release funds for expansion at lower stages, and also to rectify the existing imbalances? The average cost of educating an undergraduate in art and science for one year and that of 22 students in a primary school is the same. The corresponding figures for one M.A. and M.Sc. are 41 and 89 pupils in primary schools. The important question is: if the water supply is limited and the land to be irrigated vast, should the scanty resources be used to create cases here and there, or be spread over the whole land in the name of equitable distribution?

Restricted admissions in higher education are resented as curbs on boys and girls from traditionally backward sections who are striving for better status. At the same time open-door policy is wasteful. Yet no political group, not even the avowedly leftists, for fear of the middle class voting strength, has had the courage to oppose expansion of higher education. The right to have highest education is the right of the privileged to have further study at the cost of the inarticulate underprivileged, who have little nuisance value in Indian politics today. How to meet this antidemocratic attitude of a class that has a dominant voice in the democratic decision-making process? Should the unacademic type be given consolation prizes in the form of diversified vocational type courses at the secondary stage? In any case to make the soporific work it would be necessary to absorb these school leavers in jobs. In the long run the wage structure will have to be drastically modified to make these school-avenues to employment more respectable and attractive. How?

A number of investigators have arrived at the same conclusion about returns from different stages of education. While the individual gets better returns from higher education, it is from primary and secondary school education that society obtains higher gains. Whose interest should be the prime concern, the individual's or that of society? Freedom of the individual, it has been held, is the essence of democracy. Nevertheless, in recent times, all over the world the interest of society is becoming a more important desideratum. Even ardent champions of individuality, like the English, speak more and more about 'social individuality' in education, especially after World War II.

In affluent and advanced societies even people feel that for higher education received by an individual, and principally financed from public funds, the individual is indebted to society, and he should require in one way or another. Will a student-loans scheme replacing the scholarships scheme by and large be in the interest of social justice? In 1971, Lord Robbins advocated student loans on the ground that "university students were a privileged minority presented with the means of increased individual earnings at the expense of the community in general", and so he approved of a loans system in which "repayment would be a fixed proportion of income paid each year to amortize the advance."

For democracy, 'how much' education is as important as 'what type' of education. C.E.M. Joad described education of the few as "ample, intense, dignified" and education of the many as "scanty, cheap, and nasty". What was the result of this disparity in England? In mid-nineteenth century, and sometimes till much later, many Englishmen said, "We are still two nations." The difference in the quality of education one getting in exclusive schools and the other in ordinary schools in India is not conducive to the growth of democratic thinking and attitudes in the country. Should such expensive schools be abolished? Or instead of trying to have one highway for all, will it not be better to maintain the existing alternative paths and to provide ladders in the form of scholarships to make transfers possible? In any case, is it possible to wipe out the great disparities in the quality of education for various groups as long as the glaring disparities in wealth exist? In a democracy the privileged rich also are entitled to *freedom* to choose, and buy, the type of education they want for their wards. How can you prevent the rich from buying expensive education for their children?

Democracy stands for *equality* as well as for *freedom.* No individual is truly free if he denies freedom to others. The democratic man not only tolerates dissent but also respects it, even encourages it. Variety of views leads to enrichment. But there are ancient authoritarian traditions in Indian education. Only democratic teachers can promote democratic attitudes among the taught. The reading material, the administration and control, and the general atmosphere in Indian schools are not favourable to the growth of democracy. Institutions supported liberally from public funds are dominated by people who use these to spread parochialism, communalism, and for downright material gains. To what extent and in what form, can educational institutions be controlled nationally so that the nationally accepted ideals, democracy, socialism and secularism, etc. can be realised?

Education is a large word and there is more sense in speaking about the aims rather than the aim of education. Among these the vocational aim is second to none in importance although it has been denigraded for long by starry-eyed thinkers who have harped on the 'liberating' function of education. The most 'liberal' education too was not free from a vocational bias. The recent vociferous demand for job-oriented education is based on the naive belief that if the economy does not create more employment, job-oriented education will.

Unemployment is not a new phenomenon in India. Too much preoccupation with problems created by the articulate organised educated unemployed pushes into oblivion the misery of the silent uneducated unemployed who have no political nuisance value. If the present day educational system is a continuation of the one devised by a rapacious colonial power to arrest India's economic development and restrict employment avenues, then what changes do the economists and politicians propose in wage structure etc. to improve the situation?

Education for intermediate skills for which demand should be increased in urban as well as rural areas both may be one answer. Obviously, much will depend on the pace of industrialization and modernization of agriculture.

The grave economic problems in national life created by the defective educational system, no doubt, constitute a threat to the democratic set-up off and on by engendering a series of political crises. But education also impinges upon the non-material aspects of national life. These are vitally important for the success of democracy. For example, unless a wise language policy acceptable to people in our polyglot society is evolved and pursued the much deplored hiatus between the elite and the masses will remain. Education through a foreign tongue creates misfits in society. They form a parasitical class of middlemen who exploit the common man, especially, if he does not understand the language of the administration. How to give the regional languages the place they are entitled to in consistence with a democratic administrative set-up and at the same time build up an indigenous medium to serve national purposes will tax the ingenuity of Indian educationists, and is a challenge to imaginative and resourceful statesmanship.

At present education is producing self-centred careerists and efficient technocrats. They find it difficult to identify themselves with the privations and yearnings of the masses, for whom they have more pity than sympathy, and show more condescension than understanding. Will taking the centres of education to the people instead of requiring the people to flock to these urban centre make a difference? The reluctance of the urban educated youths to serve the people away from cities makes a mockery of the city-based education which is largely financed by rural India. To justify and defend such antidemocratic attitudes they invoke the spirit of democracy and freedom of the individual. Can a stint in the countryside be made obligatory for the university educated youths as a gesture of reciprocity towards rural India?

There is a welcome awareness in present-day India about the undesirable disparity between educational development of men and women. As in the case of other disadvantaged groups special efforts are called for as compensatory justice to educate women. But, in India, there is a serious paradox. The scarce funds marked for expansion of women education are appropriated by a tiny minority of the elitist class to the disadvantage of women folk in general. The robbing of the ignorant because they are ignorant goes on. It is in the interest of democracy to curb temporarily the influx of women from the privileged class to advanced specialized courses which have been for long the preserve of men?

Lastly, emergence of democratic leadership will largely depend upon how much democracy in action the students see around them in educational institutions and to what extent they are practised in democratic decision-making. From this point of view divisions into majority and minority and acceptance of the decisions taken by the former, are much better than a research for unanimity. Students who sulk, after the majority goes against them in school or college matters, will be reluctant to accept the verdict of the electorate later in life. Strong and earnest advocacy of one's stand and cheerful acceptance of the majority decision in the long run is the bedrock of democratic practice.

In which areas will students be associated with democratic decision-making? Campus disturbances all over the world for about a decade have highlighted students' dissatisfaction with the much too limited association. On the other hand, university authorities who panicked at the first explosion of student revolts in U.S.A., France, Germany, Sweden etc. and conceded student participation in the name of democracy on a scale unheard of before, are now veering round to the view that for the sake of good university administration students should serve on "selected committees" and keep off "reserved areas of business". Is all delimitation of this area reaction? In any case who will do it? How?

True democracy in action leads to much enlightenment of even illiterate people, and is an agency of education. But it has been misused also. History shows that freedoms solicited and enjoyed in the name of democracy were later used to destroy democracy *e.g.* by the Nazis in Germany. Appeal for freedom to run educational institutions proves often a comouflaged nefarious design to indoctrate the young in antinational and antidemocratic ways.

An enlightened electorate with a progressive out-look only will be able to eliminate the danger posed by fascist groups which demand the right to run separate educational institutions in the name of safeguarding some cultural particularism. Until schools are in one way or another controlled by the government or some national associations etc., even student participation may not serve the purpose of democracy, because students are likely to act as the vanguard of parochialism entrenched in educational institutions.

No democratic set-up will be stable if the students as they move up to more advanced courses become more remote from the concerns of the common people and of rural India, which stills is the real India. A realistic practicable scheme of compulsory social service, work experience and service in the country-side, should be well-thought out and pursued with utmost vigour.

Conclusion

In India, the sins of the political economists were visited upon the educationists. Not that the latter had no sins of their own to expiate. But, there was not much the educationists could really do to strengthen the democratic set-up if the paymasters who controlled education and shaped policies wanted to maintain the *status-quo* in their own interest. Giving illustration of equalization of educational opportunity, it has been stalled almost as much as transfer of land to the tillers. In both cases the reasons were similar; hold what you have. Educational backwardness of groups and regions is a continuation of their economic and social backwardness. Helpful as schemes of extra coaching, stipends, loans etc., are the real remedy for educational backwardness, in his opinion, has to be sought in the home background. Educationists in non-communist societies have realized it, *e.g.* even programmes adopted in post Plowden years in the United Kingdom.

The best defence of the democratic set-up lies in producing secular-minded citizens who believe in giving equal rights to people of all regions, castes and creeds. To produce such citizens it may not be necessary to nationalize all educational institutions. But the state must exercise effective control ever them, to make sure that nowhere education is imparted which curtails freedom of thought or embitters social relationships or spreads religious fanaticism. Persons who do not stand for toleration, dissent, freedom of thought and equality should be denied freedom to run educational institutions.

Ignorance is an ally of fanaticism and invites exploitation. Mass education is a national need. It is equally important to rid education of its too literary and bookish character. Much higher education is remote from the important concerns of the Indian society. Courses of study leading to positions of power and prestige are crowded with young persons who cultivate 'gentlemanly' manners and the arts of avoiding contacts with the common herd. Association of the teaching as well as non-teaching staff at appropriate levels with administration in schools as well as colleges may prove beneficial. Similarly, participation of students in educational matters concerning them directly may prove valuable training in the process of democratic decision-making. Too much authoritarianism puts a premium upon unquestioning acceptance of decisions. This does not promote democratic thinking. The usual reticence of the Indian students at question time after an address shows how limited scope the average Indian teacher leaves for enquiry and differences of opinion in the class room. Such atmosphere is not favourable to the emergence of democratic leadership in the country.

It has often been observed by professional educationists that people who know least about education talk most about it. Too many cooks like to have a finger in the pie, when a new educational system or set-up is being planned. Many never get an opportunity to spoil the broth; yet nobody suspects he is ignorant about the best recipe. No wonder in a gathering of senior and eminent educationists recommendations about Education for Democracy come in galore.

To begin with, educational changes seldom keep pace with the pressures of social, economic and political life. Education appears to be a most handy tool for social transformation; but its limitations are often lost sight of. To promote democracy which is striking roots in India, education could make a significant, even striking, contribution provided corresponding social changes were introduced *pari passu*.

Many experts argue in the same strain so much so that the discussion became a prolonged complaint against the politicians, economists, planners, etc. who had, the argument ran, by their poor performance taken the wind out of the educationists sails. Nevertheless, all agreed, that certain reforms in the educational set-up were overdue if the democratic structure in the country was to be strengthened. For example, English-medium or exclusive and expensive schools, often called 'public schools' were severely criticized by several speakers. From the speeches it was obvious that privately managed, aided, institutions also, especially the ones run by religious agencies and sectarian bodies, were no less an anathema. The former, it was pointed out led to perpetuation of vested interests. The rich bought the best jobs for their sons and daughters. Money power made a mockery of competitive examinations as well as interviews for selection; because it alone could buy the type of education and ensured the competencies and skills which mattered. The common people had access to common schools which produced persons for common jobs.

The privately managed institutions, it was repeatedly said, have proved breeding ground for parochialism and fantaticism which strike at the roots of national integration and democracy. In the guise of minority rights and civic freedoms, ostensibly put forward as legitimate demands in a democratic set-up, the most undemocratic forces are unleashed. Many educational institutions are virtually caste republics. Huge government grants are received by schools which are training centres for fascist cadres. Many participants demanded immediate take over of schools and colleges by the state.

Not only private and aided institutions but institutions supported wholly from public funds also were doing precious little to promote democratic thinking and attitudes. Outmoded curricula, authoritarian attitudes of teachers and educational programmes which rendered school leavers and graduates misfits in Indian, especially rural, society needed immediate and drastic reform. Teachers who belonged to the older generation and had themselves been brought up in traditional ways passed on to the new generations values and attitudes not conductive to the growth of democracy. Could something be done to imbue teachers with values desired to be instilled in the youths? The paternal control which the average Indian teacher demands, and other exercises, in schools as a descendant of the ancient guru leaves hardly any scope for enquiry, dissent and tolerance without which democracy cannot thrive.

Most educationists express their disappointment at the slow progress made towards equalization of educational, opportunity. In the name of 'pool of ability', 'merit', 'academic aptitude', 'peaks of excellence', 'need for leadership', 'open competition' etc. barriers had been put against which youths from disadvantaged groups and regions wage losing battles. Hardly anyone questioned the necessity of providing financial and other aids to deserving students who did not have the wherewithal to go for higher education.

Even this, it was argued, would be of little avail for the success of democracy if higher education continued to produce alienation from which Indian graduates suffer. Young men whose education was supported from public funds contributed largely by people in the Indian countryside turn their backs on the villagers. Even agricultural graduates are lost to the tribe. As a remedy a stint in the countryside, compulsory social service schemes, etc. were proposed by some. Others bemoaned how similar plans conceived and at times sincerely tried in the past fell through.

The threat to the democratic set-up as a consequence of mounting educated unemployment underlined, the need for 'job-oriented education'. But many participants dismissed it as an empty slogan, a shibboleth which will mislead no one. The real remedy these critics argued was to create jobs. Which again lay beyond the pale of education proper. Restrictions on admissions to higher education found favour with a few speakers. It smacked of 'railway compartment mentality' said many. Passengers scampering on the platform seldom are debarred by exaggerated warnings of discomfiture from those who were seated inside the train.

Should educationists feel apologetic about propaganda in favour of democracy even? Neutrality in the face of feudalism, communalism, fascism, obscurantism, exploitation, etc. is no virtue but unpardonable escapism. Indoctrination in favour of democracy is very much to be desired.

For this purpose, some experts aver formal schooling and conventional methods of education would be neither adequate nor very effective. It is in the interest of democracy that non-formal education, mobile libraries, information centres etc. are organised on a large scale.

Last, but in no way less important, was a mild warning that in our zeal to work for expansion of education in the conventional sense, we should not forget to think of education in much more important terms, *i.e.* adding new dimensions to the education of the individual person by giving it a spiritual base. This was needed as much by the student as by the teacher for his constant personal growth.

More often than not statements about the role of educational institutions and educationists in bringing about the desired changes in society are characterised by facile optimism. Of course, in modern times at least education is looked upon as an instrument of social change, which indeed it is in a way. No one would deny its role in future building on a national or universal scale. But it is far from an Alladin's lamp. In the past much of education was in one way or another related with religion. In modern times economic, social and political issues influence education. Although concern for the individual has always been a most significant determinant of education, more recently education has become closely community-oriented. In some societies education has been used for social transformation with spectacular effects. Here two important considerations should not be lost sight of.

Firstly, education has seldom initiated bold and far-reaching changes in the social and political set-up. Social change was inevitable as a result of developments in economy, modes of production, opening of new markets and trade routes, development of transport and communication. These impinged upon the political, and even religious set-up which was sometimes also affected by other historical incidents, actions of individuals, civil or military. There is no inevitability about the ways a society is influenced by such changes. In other words, societies' response is varied. The challenges a society faces set tasks to its system of education, and the destiny of the country or nation will indeed depend on what happens in its schools.

Secondly, the adjustments, modifications, and innovations necessitated or desired in the educational system seldom come as fast as people usually expect. The widely-spread disenchantment with the educational systems in developing countries is mostly the inevitable result of unrealistic expectations and hopes for quick returns. That much change is occasioned in education itself by forces outside education should not be forgotten. If steps are taken to introduce quick and drastic changes in the educational system, they produce distortions with the result that improvements are more apparent than real. The educationists are censured for their conservatism and traditionalism, if not condemned for obstinacy and inertia.

For instance, universalization of elementary education in India has a long history; but to many the extremely slow progress even after independence seems astonishing. This is because there was, and still persists, the false notion that it was all a question of opening more schools and reducing or eliminating fees. In fact, we have to think in terms of questions such as: Can the common people, say scheduled castes and tribes, make use of the education we offer? If the course offerings are tailored too closely to the present serial set-up and their ways of doing things, education may only perpetuate the *status quo*.

Expansion of higher education suffers from many shortcomings; but it has its own *raison d'etre*. Certain aspects must not be ignored. Higher education is also a national industry to produce the much needed expertise and skills. Of course, because of the unpredictable national economy now very much subject to influences from world markets also, and also because of lack of community involvement the programmes of education in general, higher education suffers from almost unavoidable imbalances and shortcomings.

4

Reservation as Social Equity Measure

Introduction

Today, concessions such as reserved quotas and lowered qualifying requirements for admission of persons belonging to ethnic groups and communities identified as disadvantaged, to institutions of higher education, figure prominently among the strategies for the promotion of equality. These concessions are provided in recognition of the fact that the students from these groups and communities experience serious difficulties in securing admission to higher education, not only because of the economic handicaps, the social constraints and social discrimination that they suffer, but also because they find it difficult to "measure up" to the performance levels required for admission through open competition. The latter consideration is rooted in the conviction that the educational advance of students from the disadvantaged sectors of society should not be inhibited or cut short because of their poor performance, specially at points that are critical in terms of entry into the higher echelons of education. It marks a brave new advance in the struggle against inequality. Nevertheless, it is being seriously questioned for several reasons.

Issues and Considerations

By a strange irony, the concessions based on this consideration are firstly criticized for negating the ideal of equality, as expressed in the principle of selection by merit, which has emerged as the governing principle for the differential allocation of positions in societies struggling to replace ascription with achievement as a more egalitarian basis for the determination of hierarchy. The criticism is that in as much as eligibility for concessions is defined in terms of "birth" in specific groups or communities, the concessions are ascriptive in character. Secondly, they are criticized for encouraging a disregard for "competence" and "standards", thus damaging the larger interests of society. Somewhat in the same vein, they are criticized for diluting one of the most important functions of higher education namely, that of ensuring that the younger generation is equipped with specified levels of knowledge, competence and skill for their occupational and other adult roles, and for confusing the related function of "screening", "selecting" and "grading" individuals by the level of their competence.

The lowering of performance requirements in favour of the socially disadvantaged is also criticized on pedagogic grounds. It is emphasized that the gap between the academic level of students admitted under concessions and the levels expected of the courses to which they are admitted is invariably large and difficult to bridge. It is pointed out that pedagogic techniques and strategies to bring these students upto the required level of competence have not yet been adequately developed and it is argued that the policy of granting concessions must be acknowledged to be unsound in the face of the existing state of pedagogic unpreparedness.

Finally, it is pointed out that concessions create problems in the administration of educational institutions. The practice of selection by merit functions as an effective mechanism for obtaining, at each level of education within an institution, neatly graded, and relatively homogeneous batches of students that are relatively easy to manage. In contrast, the provision of concessions makes for batches that are highly uneven and disparate in terms of their academic preparedness, and therefore difficult to manage, not only within the class room but in other situations as well. Critics argue that the dislocation that results is severely detrimental to the education system.

The ethico-moral issues of merit and competence seem substantial to start with, but they do not hold weight on careful examination.

A series of research studies into the factors responsible for the relatively poor educational performance of students from the disadvantaged sectors of society have clearly shown that the inadequacies of their socio-economic situation are primarily to blame (Coleman 1966, Jencks 1972, Sewell and Shah 1977, Berslein Floud and Halsey 1956, Douglas 1964 and Halsey 1980). It is universally acknowledged that this in fact means that the disadvantages into which these children are born pursue them through school and adversely affect their performance. Consequently, they cannot really be considered to have an 'equal chance' to perform meritoriously. In the face of these revelations, there has been a radical reconsideration of the entire notion of "merit" and a serious questioning of whether "meritocracy" as principle of social ranking is at all consistent with the ideal of equality.

Further, research into the structure of formal education indicates that syllabi, curricula, instruction, evaluation, programmes, schedules, as well as the variety of behavioural norms, values and expectations that constitute the structural framework of formal education are in tune with the lives of the relatively privileged sectors of society. Conversely, they are ill-suited to the kind of life to which the disadvantaged belong. (Bernstein 1975, Keddie 1971, Rist 1970, Rosenthal and Jacobson, 1968, Bowles 1977 and Gicourel and Kitsuse 1963). Thus, the dice are doubly loaded in favour of the privileged.

Finally, research suggests that social class considerations and vested interests seem to operate imperceptibly in the manner in which requirements for the several occupational positions available in society are defined. Requirements are not defined purely in terms of knowledge or skill required. Expectations regarding "suitable" manners, bearing, behaviour, values, style of life and functioning are subtly woven in such a manner that the nexus between social class/family background and occupational placement is retained. In equipping students for their occupational roles, educational institutions are expected to cultivate or at least to reinforce these qualities. Thus educational institutions do not fully function as melting pots and their effectiveness as instruments of even social mobility is restricted. What is even more relevant to the issue under consideration is that the evaluation of these 'qualities inadvertently creeps into the total evaluation of students with the result that what is considered to be a purely academic merit rating is in fact a rating that includes several non-academic factors as well.

Dissent and Exploitation

In the face of all this evidence, the thrust of the ethico-moral issues raised by way of criticism of concessions is weakened. Nevertheless the pedagogic and administrative inadequacies that have been mentioned remain. As may be expected, the dislocation they cause builds up into resentment against the practice of concessions and eventually into resentment against the beneficiaries of the concessions who come to be viewed as the "cause" of the dislocation. Sections of the erstwhile privileged population displaced because of the special support accorded to the disadvantaged exploit this resentment to regain the advantage that they have lost. They harness it to build-up pressure against preferential policies in favour of the disadvantaged and thus secure their own privilege. In fact, they seem to utilize the frustrations caused by the pedagogic and administrative inadequacies in coping with the consequences of concessions to play up the ethico-moral issue and to gain the sympathy of a public that is altogether unaware of the findings from research (Yagnik, 1981).

Under the circumstances, the implementation of concessions turns out to be a difficult task of handling vested interests, of containing the resentment of those who have been antagonized because of the dislocations caused, of coping with the pedagogic and administrative challenges involved, and of informing the public about the realities of the situation.

Meanwhile it is necessary to come to grips with the basic question that cannot really be waived, *viz.* the extent to which concessions should eventually be provided and whether they should be progressively reduced, terminated or increased. The answer to this question would differ from one society to another, or rather differ in terms of the ideological positions that those who answer the question take as well as the contextual realities of the society with reference to which they frame their answers. While some may reject concessions as short-term interventions that do not really solve the problem and find it necessary to formulate their answers in terms of a radical restructuring of society, others may yet be willing to look for answers within the existing structure.

Regardless of which of these two alternatives are preferred, the answer would have to take several ideological and practical considerations into account. Three of the most significant could be listed as follows:

(*i*) the character and the level of competence that educational institutions are expected to obtain in their students,

(*ii*) the extent to which a comparative evaluation of students and their "selection", "screening" and "ranking" in terms of required levels of competence is considered to be an essential function of formal education,

(*iii*) the nature and size of the gap between the performance level of those who are identified as disadvantaged and therefore deserving of concessions and the others.

It is hardly necessary to emphasize the difficulties involved in plotting any of these parameters with an adequate measure of clarity. We shall present some data on one of the six Indian Institutes of Technology in the country with a view to indicating how complex each of the three points listed above is and how different the implementation the policy of admitting Scheduled Castes/Scheduled Tribes students to apex educational institutions in the country has turned out to be.

The six Indian Institutes of Technology (IITs) are expected to function as guardians of high standards of scientific and technical skills and abilities. Consequently, their academic programmes are pitched at a level of excellence that is considered to be high even by international standards. The evaluation of students is rigorous and exacting. Partly because their courses are challenging, but even more so because they equip their products for well-paid and high status positions in industry and research, these institutions attract the cream of the student population in the country. Entrance is highly competitive and none but the best can aspire to get in.

Admissions are made on the basis of a Joint Entrance Examination (JEE) conducted jointly for all the six IITs in the country.[1] Approximately 30,000 students appear for this examination each year. Of these about 1,200 are eventually selected for admission. All those who have passed the school leaving examination in their respective States, with a score above 35 per cent are in principle, eligible to apply for admission and to appear for the JEE examination. However, the calibre of the applicants may be gauged from the fact that it is only those who have scored more than 70 per cent marks at their respective school leaving examinations who eventually qualify for admissions. On the whole, it could safely be said that the entrants to the IITs constitute the top 10 per cent of the students at the school leaving examinations at their respective centres.

The IIT from which data are presented in this paper was established in the year 1958. As with other institutions of higher education in the country, this IIT was subject to the general requirement that 15 per cent of the admissions should be reserved for the Scheduled Castes and five per cent for the Scheduled Tribes. However, until 1973 no special efforts were made to fulfil this requirement. Like the others, the SC/ST students had to appear for the JEE examination. "Other things being equal", they were admitted to the reserved quotas of admission. Data on the percentage of the SC/ST students actually admitted is not available for the period prior to 1973. However, data on another IIT in the country indicates that none of the students on the rolls between the years 1965 and 1970 belonged to the SC/ST (King, 1970). There is no reason to believe that the situation was any better at the IIT under observation.

In 1973, it was decided to *fill the entire quota* of reserved admissions, possibly due to pressure from the Government. Further, it was decided that in order to obtain the number of students required to fill this quotas, all those who appeared *in all the four papers* at the Joint Entrance Examination would be offered admission. In 1974, the provision to admit all those who appeared for all the papers at the JEE examination was replaced with a provision to admit all those who scored 10 per cent of the total marks at the JEE. This must be considered to be a massive concession in view of the fact that the JEE score of those admitted in open competition ranges around from a minimum of 70 per cent to a maximum of 90 per cent. In 1975, the requirements were further lowered. It was decided first to admit all SC/ST students who scored upto two-third or more of the marks scored by the last candidate to be admitted under open competition and then to fill the remaining quota "directly" by admitting as many as necessary from among all SC/ST applicants who have scored more than 50 per cent at the relevant school-leaving examination regardless of their performance at the JEE. This policy was continued upto 1978. However, the latter concession has been discontinued since 1978. Only those who score two-thirds or more of the score of the last candidate accepted through open competition are now admitted.

It may be observed that between the years 1973-1979, the policy for the admission of SC/ST students shifted from one of marginal concessions (prior to 1973, reserved admissions and "other things being equal") to progressively more extensive concessions (admission for all those who appeared in all papers for the JEE in 1973 and finally to a disregard for the JEE examination altogether and admission to all those who had scored more than 50 per cent at their school-leaving examination by 1975) and back again to somewhat reduced concessions in 1979 when the latter provision was stopped, and admissions were confined to those who scored at the JEE a minimum of two-third of the score achieved by the last candidate admitted under open admissions.

It is important to note that the full quota of reserved admissions had yet to be filled at the point that the concessions were reduced. Although about 54 seats are reserved for the SC/ST each year, the maximum number of students ever admitted was 42 in 1977, the year prior to the reduction of the concessions (see Table 4.1).

Table 4.1
No. of SC/ST Students Annually Admitted to the IIT between 1973 and 1980

Year	*Criterion for admission*		*No. of students admitted*
1973	(a) Appearance for all papers of JEE		15
1974	(b) At least 10% marks at JEE		37
1975	(c) At least 2/3rd of the ranks obtained by a normal candidate last on the merit list on JEE	3 }	27
	(d) Direct admission	24 }	
1976	(c) 9	—	27
	(d) 18	—	42
1977	(c) 9	—	
	(d) 33		
1978	(c) and (d)	—	N.A.
1979	(c)	—	N.A.
1980	(c)	—	21

Source : Report of the Committee appointed to be considered the problems of Scheduled Caste/Scheduled Tribe students, IIT, Bombay (1977) and JEE-1980 Report to Senate, IIT, Bombay (1980).

The marked increase in the number of admissions in the year 1974 as compared to 1973 clearly reflects the impact of the liberalization of concessions in 1974. The relative drop during the years 1975 and 1976 is difficult to explain, but it indicates that the quota remained unfilled despite sustained efforts to improve the enrolment of SC/ST students. It also gives an idea of the situation that prompted the IIT in 1975 to take the decision to disregard the JEE results and to admit *"directly"* all SC/ST applicants who had scored more than 50 per cent at their school-leaving examinations to the seats that remained after accommodating those who had scored more than two-thirds of the score of the last candidate admitted through open competition. It is evident that, in spite of this measure, the number of admissions in 1977, was closer to but not yet equal to the quota required. The fact that they dropped noticeably in 1980, obviously due to the discontinuation of the "direct" admissions in 1979. Since the quota of reserved admission had yet to be filled it would be pertinent to ask why "direct" admissions were discontinued from 1977 onwards.

Drop-out and Stagnation

A probe into the circumstances that led to the decision to discontinue the practice of direct admission reveals that the decision was largely influenced by the observation that those who were "directly" admitted were finding it extremely difficult to measure up to the academic level required.[2] The records pertaining to this decision show that when the IIT in question decided in 1975 to make its admissions policy as liberal as it could, by opening up a stream of direct admissions, it had done so on the basis of the assumption that SC/ST students directly admitted could be helped to bridge their "performance gap" with the help of courses specially designed and offered for the purpose. Experience between the years 1975 and 1978 proved that it was not really possible to do so. In spite of the special coaching that the SC/ST students were provided with, there was a heavy drop-out and stagnation among the SC/ST students admitted under the policy of reservations and particularly so among those admitted directly. The situation was so bad that responsible members of the academic community at the IIT began to question the wisdom of direct admissions. Table 4.2 describes the situation briefly. It indicates the number of SC/ST students admitted at the beginning of each academic year during the period 1973-

77. For each batch admitted, it indicates the number that were still studying at the IIT by the end of the academic year 1977-78. The number that dropped out can easily be calculated. For instance only five (33.3 per cent) out of the 15 admitted in 1973 had survived upto the end of 1977-78. None of these survivors were in their fifth year, as they should have been if they had progressed without any failure. Three out of the five lagged behind by a year while two lagged behind by two years. The percentage of dropouts from the batches admitted in the subsequent years is distinctly smaller, but nevertheless for each batch, it ranges from 15 per cent to 26 per cent in their very first year. Stagnation too is marginally smaller, but it continues to be quite high.

Table 4.2
No. of SC/ST Students Admitted and Retained during the Period 1973-77

1973-74	*1974-75*	*1975-76*	*1976-77*	*1977-78*	*No. of students at various stages of the 5-year B. Tech programme*	
15	10	9	5	5	IV yr.	3
(100.00)	(66.67)	(60.00)	(33.33)	(33.33)	III yr.	2
	37	32	26	26	IV yr.	1
	(100.00)	(86.49)	(70.27)	(70.27)	III yr.	6
					II yr.	19
		27	23	23	III yr.	3
		(100.00)	(85.19)	(85.19)	II yr.	8
					I yr.	12
			27	20	II yr.	10
			(100.00)	(74.07)	I yr.	10
				42		
				(100.00)		

Note : Figures within paranthesis shows the percentage of students survived at the end of each successive year.

Source : Report of the Committee appointed to consider the Problems of Scheduled Caste/Scheduled Tribe Students, IIT, Bombay: 1977.

Failure to Maintain the C.P.I.

At the IIT concerned, academic performance is evaluated on a 10 point grading system. A student is expected to maintain a minimum Cumulative Performance Index (CPI) of 5.5 throughout. If a student fails to maintain this minimum level, he or she is given a warning and is given a chance to improve his academic performance within a prescribed period; in other words, he or she is kept on probation. If the student fails to improve his performance within the prescribed period, he or she is advised to leave the Institute. Table 4.3 shows the different stages at which the SC/ST students were on probation or advised to leave the Institute.

Table 4.3
Number of Students either on "Probation" or "Advised to Leave" or "Withdrawn" at the End of Each Semester (upto July, 1977)

Year of admission	*Total No.**	*1st semester*	*2nd semester*	*4th semester*	*6th semester*	*8th semester*
(1)	(2)	(3)	(4)	(5)	(6)	(7)
1973	15	3	2	4	5	2
1974	37	—	2	10	8	—
1975	27	—	3	11		
1976	27	—	1			

Source : Report of the Committee appointed to consider the Problems of Scheduled Caste/Scheduled Tribe Students, IIT, Bombay: 1977.

* In the first row, the figures in columns 3, 4, 5, 6 and 7 add upto more than the total because the performance of some of the students on probation was not satisfactory and they were eventually advised to leave or withdraw. They have been recorded for each of these stages and therefore counted twice, or sometimes thrice over.

These data do not say anything about the actual performance of the SC/ST students, nevertheless a probe into the grades obtained by 106 SC/ST students admitted during the years 1973-1978 revealed that only 15 out of these 106 were able to maintain the 5.5 C.P.I. expected and required.

Socio-Economic Disparity

The foregoing data on the admission, retention, dropout and the C.P.I. scores of the SC/ST students at the IIT under observation clearly indicate that SC/ST students admitted under the policy of reservations find it difficult to bridge the performance-gap. They also suggest that the IIT concerned has been facing serious problems in "accommodating" these students. The problem is evidently so serious that there has been some reversal in the operation of the policy of reservations at this institution and serious doubts have been expressed about the wisdom of continuing with it.

At the same time, the meagre data available on the socio-economic status of the SC/ST students (Table 4.4) indicates that the disparity between the socio-economic status of the two categories of students is so large, and the situation of the SC/ST students is so heavily disadvantaged that it would be totally unrealistic to expect them to make it on their own. Positive discrimination in their favour is unquestionably required.

The three Tables 4.4 (a, b, c) offer a brief comparison of the socio-economic situation of the two categories, and illustrate the socio-economic gap.

The data on the basis of which comparisons between the two categories of students are made is not strictly comparable in that they relate to different periods of time, and are framed in somewhat dissimilar categories. Nevertheless, it is adequate enough to provide a rough idea of the nature and the scale of the disparity. Firstly, it indicates that the overwhelming majority (91 per cent) of the non-SC/ST students have studied at city schools whereas the majority (63.6 per cent) of the SC/ST students have studied at small town or village schools. To the extent that urban life in general, and urban schools in particular offer better facilities, and better opportunities for academic stimulation and growth, the non-SC/ST students are likely to have an edge over the SC/ST students. Secondly, the data suggest that this particular disparity between the two categories of students is likely to be further aggravated by the fact that a large percentage (25 per cent) of the SC/ST students are children of agriculturists and labourers and thus presumably lack the educational/occupational home background and influences that familiarize and informally equip a child for a career as a professional. None of them came from homes in which professions are practised. In contrast, as many as 33 per cent of the non-SC/ST students are

Table 4.4

	SC/ST students admitted in the years 1973-76			*Non-SC/ST students admitted in the years 1973-76*	
(a) Place of schooling before coming to IIT					
	N	%		N	%
Village	5	5		1	—
Town	53	58		19	8
City	33	36		208	91
Total	91	100		228	100
(b) Father's Occupation					
Agriculture	10	15	Agriculture	1	0.5
Service	40	63	Business	35	15.8
Teaching	7	11	Medicine	2	0.8
Labourers	6	9	Engineering	29	12.7
			Law	2	0.8
			Public/Government Service	114	50.0
			Private service	27	11.8
			Teaching/Research	16	7.0
Total	63	100%	Total	228	100%

(c) Parents' Annual Income

	(a) SC/ST students (%)		*(b) Other students (%)*	
Upto Rs. 2000	15	(19)	2	(0.8)
Rs. 2001 — 4000	13	(15.4)	1	(0.4)
Rs. 4001 — 6000	21	(25)	7	(3.0)
Rs. 6001 — 9000	18	(21.4)	10	(4.3)
Rs. 9001 — 12000	8	(9.5)	24	(10.5)
Rs. 12001 — 15000	1	(1.1)	29	(12.7)
Rs. 15001 — 20000	5	(5.9)	39	(17.1)
Rs. 20001 — 25000	3	(3.5)	30	(13.0)
Rs. 25001 and above	1	(1.1)	86	(37.7)
Total	84	(100.0)	228	(100.0)

children of professionals practising medicine, engineering or law. Thirdly, whereas a majority (59.4 per cent) of the SC/ST come from homes where the father's annual income is less than Rs. 6,000 per annum, a majority (67.7 per cent) of the non-SC/St students come from homes where the father earns more than Rs. 15,000 per annum. In fact, as many as 37.7 per cent come from homes where the father earns more than Rs. 25,000 per annum. Only one per cent of the SC/ST students belong to the latter category and barely 10.5 per cent come from the Rs. 15,000 per annum income group to which the majority of the non-SC/ST students belong.

In the face of this situation, the issue of providing reserved admissions for SC/ST students in institutions of advanced education, such as the IITs seems to be one of balancing the equally valid but rival claims of academic standards and professional competence on the one hand and social justice on the other. Both sets of claims are important and neither can be neglected without serious consequences to society. Decisions on how and where the dividing lines between the rival interests of competence and social justice are to be drawn depend again on several economic and political considerations. Moreover, it is not easy to determine the operationalization of social justice with respect to academic inequality.

As has been brought out in Turner's well-known distinction between sponsored mobility and contest mobility, it could legitimately be argued that it is "unjust" to "protect" and "sponsor" the disadvantaged all the way upto their completion of advanced courses in education and then abandon them to the ruthless selective mechanisms of the employment market. (Turner, 1961). Those who take this position would probably recommend that "deserving" and "talented" SC/ST students are selected in early childhood and carefully groomed through their early years to cope with open competition as the grow up. This preference for "contest mobility" may in turn be criticized for disregarding the fact that "talent" and "ability" do not necessarily reveal themselves full in a child's early years. Early selection may thus be considered as "unjust" for eliminating those who flower late, even before they have had a chance to show their worth. Some synthesis of contest mobility and sponsored mobility, of early selection and continued grooming is probably required. What form this synthesis should take needs urgently to be explored. Meanwhile, the ultimate question regarding the justice of any measure of selection remains to be solved in terms of ideological priorities and commitments.

REFERENCES

1. The Joint Entrance Examination is an All-India competitive examination conducted yearly to select IIT students. The student has to take examination in English, Physics, Chemistry and Mathematics. However, in English a candidate has to get only the minimum qualifying marks and the marks scored in English is not counted for one's rank, which is calculated on the basis of marks obtained in other three subjects. JEE is a very rigorous test of the comprehension, speed and originality of the candidates.
2. IIT, Bombay, "Report of the Committee appointed to consider the Problems of Scheduled Caste/Scheduled Tribe Students." 1977, p. 18.

Notes

Bernstein B., *Class, Codes and Control,* Vols. I, II and III, London, Routledge and Kegan Paul, 1973 and 1975.

Bowles, S., Unequal Education and the Reproduction of the Social Division of Labour in J. Karabel and A.H. Halsey (ed.), *Power and Ideology in Education,* N.Y., Oxford University Press, 1977, pp. 137-152.

Coleman, J.S., *Equality of Educational Opportunity,* Washington D.C., U.S. Govt., Printing Office, 1966.

Douglas, J.W.B., *The Home and the School,* London, MacGibbon and Koe, 1964.

Floud and Halsey, *Social Class and Educational Opportunity,* London, Heineman, 1956.

Gicourel and Kitsuse, J., *The School as a Mechanism for Social Differentiation,* in Karabel, J. and Halsey, A.H. (ed.), *Power and Ideology in Education,* N.Y., Oxford University Press, 1963, pp. 282-291.

Halsey, A.H., *et al., Origins and Destinations,* Oxford, Clarendon Press, 1980.

Jencks, C., *Inequality: A Reassessment of the Effect of the Family and Schooling in America,* Norwich, Fletcher and Sons Ltd., 1972.

Keddie, Classroom Knowledge, in M. Young (ed.), *Knowledge and Control*, London, Collier MacMillan, 7, pp. 133-160.

Rist, R.C., Student Social Class and Teacher Expectations: The Self-Fulfilling Prophecy in Ghetto Education, in *Harvard Educational Review*, Vol. 40 (August), 1970, pp. 411-450.

Rosenthal, R. and Jacobson, J., *Pygmalion in the Classroom*, N.Y., Holt, Rinehart and Winston, 68.

Sewell and Shah, Socio-economic Status, Intelligence and the Attainment of Higher Education in *The Power and Ideology in Education*, N.Y., Oxford University Press, 1977.

5

Dalit Movement and Politics of Reservations

The Constitution (85th Amendment) Bill to include the Tamil Nadu Reservation Act in the Ninth Schedule of the Constitution was passed by both Houses of Parliament in August, 1994. The Tamil Nadu Act ensures the continuation of 69 per cent reservation in educational institutions and jobs in the state, a matter that is sub-judice.

The Tamil Nadu quota system violates the existing Supreme Court ruling that the total reservations should not exceed 50 per cent. The Supreme Court expected the states to limit the reservations for all categories to a maximum of 50 per cent as laid down by a nine-judge Constitution Bench in the Mandal judgment on November 16, 1992. The apex court also ruled that 'creamy layer' should be kept out and that quotas should only apply to recruitment and not to promotions. The decisions of the Union Government to give assent to the Tamil Nadu Reservation Act and subsequently to move a Constitutional Amendment to take it out of the jurisdiction of courts seems to have opened a pandora's box, with one state government after another rushing through similar legislation.

Madhya Pradesh has raised the quota for other backward classes (OBCs) by 14 per cent, thus stretching the overall quota limit to 63 per cent. Andhra Pradesh also included 14 groups including Muslims and the Kapu community in the list of OBCs. But the high court admitted two writ petitions and put the government order on hold.

Bihar Chief Minister Laloo Prasad Yadav has vowed to raise

the ceiling of reservation to 80 per cent through an ordinance as against the existing 50 per cent. Uttar Pradesh has already made 27 per cent reservation for backward classes in addition to the 23 per cent earlier available to scheduled castes and scheduled tribes. The reservation of 27 per cent for OBCs sparked protests in the eight hill districts which have only a two per cent OBC population.

The Karnataka government raised the quantum of reservation from 68 per cent to 73 per cent in April this year. The state assembly on September 20 passed a bill seeking to provide 73 per cent reservation in employment and education and in a resolution called upon the Centre to include it in the Ninth Schedule.

Union Welfare Minister Sitaram Kesri has already signalled to the states wanting to increase the quota percentage that the Centre will not obstruct them.

At present, the reservation quota exceeds 50 per cent in Tamil Nadu, Karnataka, Arunachal Pradesh, Meghalaya, Nagaland, Madhya Pradesh and Gujarat. The quota touches 50 per cent in Bihar, Manipur, Punjab, Sikkim, Uttar Pradesh, Kerala, Orissa and Rajasthan.

Supreme Court Ruling

Within three weeks of Parliament amending the Constitution to place Tamil Nadu's Act for 69 per cent reservation in the Ninth Schedule, the Supreme Court has once again reiterated that the quota cannot exceed the ceiling of 50 per cent.

On September 9, 1994, the apex court directed Karnataka not to exceed the limit and also confirmed the stay of its 1986 notification which provided for 68 per cent reservation for the Scheduled Castes, Scheduled Tribes and Backward Classes.

The ruling comes at the time when several states, with an eye on the approaching elections, are making moves towards hiking quotas in contravention of the Supreme Court ruling.

The ruling has given rise to the apprehension that the apex court could even now strike down as unconstitutional the Tamil Nadu Act providing for 69 per cent reservation, which has been challenged before it. Normally, it is rare for Acts which are placed in the Ninth Schedule to be struck down but such an eventuality is not altogether ruled out; the Supreme Court can do it in case it feels that the basic structure of the Constitution is in any way altered.

The moot question now is whether the basic structure has indeed been altered in the light of the Supreme Court noting that the dictum of reasonable restriction on the fundamental right to equality ceased to operate if the quota exceeds 50 per cent.

While the laws in the Ninth Schedule cannot generally be challenged in courts, the Supreme Court has ruled in the past that the government cannot use this Schedule as a protective dumping ground for laws that may violate the "basic structure' of the Constitution. And this basic structure is enshrined, among others, in Articles 15 and 16 which protect a citizen from discrimination on grounds of caste and religion. These provisions, nonetheless, allow reservation for backward castes as an exception, to promote social justice. And it is on this that the Supreme Court has relied in fixing the 50 per cent limit.

Exceeding this is an obvious violation of the "basic structure" because the exception now becomes the rule. And the Supreme Court is unlikely to rule that the new quota is entitled to Ninth Schedule protection, according to some jurists. But if the reservation hikes are struck down, the politicians can always pass the blame on to the Centre and Supreme Court. If the hikes are not struck down, they have everything to gain politically.

Bill on Reservation

The Constitution (85th) Amendment Bill to save from judicial scrutiny the Tamil Nadu law on 69 per cent reservation, which is under challenge before the Supreme Court, was passed by Parliament at remarkable speed.

The Tamil Nadu Government desperate as it was to circumvent the Supreme Court's directive requiring it to adhere to 50 per cent quota limit in admissions to professional colleges, hit upon the rather dubious strategy of statutorily mandating, with retrospective effect, the 69 per cent quota scheme and then getting the law included in the Ninth Schedule of the Constitution under Article 31-B, a provision that affords protection against judicial scrutiny to certain types of enactments.

How exactly the apex court will view what prima facie amounts to defying its specific injunction against crossing the 50 per cent bar remains to be seen, although it chose to take a soft line in its interfere order by deciding not to interface with the admissions to professional colleges made this year on the basis of 69 per cent reservation and granting relief to the limited extent of accommodating the 62 'merit' students who had been denied seats as a consequence. A less objectionable option for the Government would have been to stick to the 50 per cent limit and create additional seats to provide for the prospective beneficiaries of the 'other' 19 per cent.

Doubtful Validity

In any event, the mere fact of inclusion of a law in the Ninth Schedule will not totally preclude judicial scrutiny, as the nature and scope of Article 31-B are subject to varying constructions. For instance, it is a moot point whether the 'protection' available under the Article is restricted to certain specific areas or is open to any and every law that may be passed by legislation and without any time bar. Above all, there is the larger and more vital question whether the Tamil Nadu Act does not seek to alter the "basic structure" of the Constitution to the extent that it provides for quotas at a level that far exceeds 50 per cent, the point beyond which, as noted by the Supreme Court, the dictum of reasonable restriction on the fundamental right to equality ceased to operate.

It is true that the apex court did say in its Mandal case judgment that "some relaxation on the strict rule (of 50 per cent ceiling) may become imperative" in certain "extraordinary situations inherent in the great diversity of this country and the people." But it seems very unlikely that the court had States like Karnataka and Tamil Nadu in mind when it spoke of the "extraordinary situations." Surely, these issues will be agitated before the Supreme Court and, as such, the last word is yet to be said on the much abused quota system.

The Central Government's decision to place the Tamil Nadu Reservation Act under the Ninth Schedule of the Constitution threatens to reopen once again the reservation controversy, reviving memories of those dark days when the Mandal report had split society and youths immolated themselves in a protest which had no precedent in North India.

The Centre's move is bound to upset the consensus the Supreme Court had evolved over the reservation issue. The apex court, in its famous judgment upholding the implementation of the Mandal report, had laid down the following principles.

Principles of Reservation Policy

1. Reservation for socially and educationally backward classes other than Scheduled Castes and Scheduled Tribes is constitutionally valid.
2. Reservation should not cross the maximum limit of 50 per cent, except in those areas where a extraordinary situation prevails.
3. The creamy layer among the other Backward Classes (OBCs) should be excluded from the reservation pool.
4. It implicitly recognized the principle of dereservation of those castes that cross the threshold of backwardness.

In the absence of a cogent Central policy on reservation, it was generally assumed that the Supreme Court judgment on the Mandal report would henceforth form the basis of any affirmative action that a government may decide to undertake. This view was buttressed not only by the government's unequivocal acceptance of the Supreme Court verdict but also because several intellectuals hailed the Justices to striking a fine balance between merit and social justice.

Sociologist Yogendra Singh explains. "The Supreme Court reiterated the constitutional position that while there is a case for reservation for the OBCs, this policy should not and cannot neglect merit." The Supreme Court thus laid down that reservation should not exceed 50 per cent, quoting Dr. B.R. Ambedkar who had wanted the government to reserve only a minority of seats and posts.

This created a piquant situation for those states that had reservations beyond 50 per cent. A Consumer Action Group petitioned the Supreme Court pointing out that the Tamil Nadu government was violating the 50 per cent ceiling. The Jayalalitha government in return gave a written commitment to scale down reservation to the statutory limit.

Such a step was obviously fraught with serious political consequences, and the Chief Minister got the Assembly to pass unanimously the Tamil Nadu Reservation Bill protecting 69 per cent reservations. The Bill became law when the President's assent was obtained following a meeting between former Chief Minister Ms. Jayalalitha and former Prime Minister P.V. Narasimha Rao.

Janata Dal ideologue Surendra Mohan says "The Centre's decision to place the Tamil Nadu Reservation Act under the Ninth Schedule is extremely short-sighted. Not only will the other southern states, which have reservation above 50 per cent, follow suit, but even states like Uttar Pradesh and Bihar are likely to raise reservations above the 50 per cent limit."

The Supreme Court has already admitted a writ petition challenging the Moily government's decision to increase reservations to a whopping 80 per cent in Karnataka (it is now down to 73 per cent again). Bihar Chief Minister Laloo Prasad Yadav, too, has announced his government's intention to raise reservation to 80 per cent.

These developments have predictably split the votaries of reservation into opposing camps. The political class finds nothing wrong in having reservation in excess of the Supreme Court limit. Says Mr. Surendra Mohan, "Why did the Supreme Court fix the limit at 50 per cent? It should have realized that reservation much above 50 per cent was already in existence in some states when the Mandal case came up."

Opposing them are those intellectuals who had unabashedly supported reservation for the OBCs, even dating to go against the popular anti-Mandal sentiments of those days. They feel the Tamil Nadu Act and the Karnataka experiment threatens to put the philosophy of reservation on its head. For instance, Mr. D.L. Sheth, a member of the National Commission on Backward Classes, said "This will render the whole policy absurd."

The moot question is: What does the reservation policy aim at? Reservation is essentially a socially affirmative action aimed at removing backwardness arising from historical disabilities and injustices which certain social groups suffer from. These disabilities create backwardness which, unlike those resulting from development processes, are structural in nature. These groups, when freed from historically debilitating conditions, are then expected to compete with others on equal terms.

Rajya Sabha Approval

In a rare display of unity, the Rajiya Sabha, on August 24, 1994 approved without debate the Constitution (Eighty-Fifth Amendment) Bill for inclusion of the Tamil Nadu Reservation Act in the Ninth Schedule under Article 31-B of the Constitution.

Mr. Chimanbhai Mehta (Ind), the lone dissenting voice, made a futile attempt to oppose the Bill and stood isolated on the subject alongwith Mr. Sharad Pradhan (Shiv Sena) when Rajiya Sabha Chairman K.R. Narayan ordered a division.

The division on the clause-by-clause consideration of the Bill, showed 148 members in favour and two members against it. At the end of the exercise, the Chairman declared the Bill, amid much thumping of desks from all sides, as adopted.

The 90-minute exercise was not without its share of drama with the members of the ruling party and the Opposition lapsing into a prolonged wrangle over Mr. Kesri's desire to make a formal statement on the rationale and philosophy behind the Constitution Bill.

Several Opposition members took exception to the statement from the Welfare Minister on the plea that since the Business Advisory Committee (BAC) of the Upper House had decided to adopt the Bill without any discussion. Mr. Kesri should not be allowed to make a formal speech and if he was given an opportunity to explain the Government new-point on the subject, the Opposition could not be deprived of a similar privilege.

As a result of the row over the ticklish issues, Deputy Chairperson Najma Heptullah adjourned the House for 15 minutes and invited the floor leaders into her chambers to sort out the problem. The issue was resolved with the floor leaders agreeing that the Ministry only make a statement on the 'statement of objects and reasons' for the Constitution Bill and drop his proposed speech.

A visibly disappointed Mr. Kesri had to content himself with this. The Welfare Minister traced the history of policy of reservations in Tamil Nadu and how it had to be increased to 69 per cent consistent with the needs of the majority of the people.

Mr. Kesri gave the sequence of events beginning with the Supreme Court observations in the Mandal case in November 1992; the direction of Madras High Court to the Tamil Nadu Government to stick to the 50 per cent ceiling prescribed by the Supreme Court from the academic session 1993-94; enactment of the Tamil Nadu Reservation Act by the State Government for continuation of the 69 per cent reservation and the subsequent Presidential assent to the Bill.

The Minister quoted from the July 22, 1994, representation of the Tamil Nadu Government asking the Centre to give constitutional protection of the Tamil Nadu Reservation Act, so that it was put beyond the jurisdiction of the courts.

As per the letter quoted by the Minister, "now it has been decided to address the Government of India for including the Act in the Ninth Schedule to the Constitution, so that the law cannot be challenged is violative of any of the fundamental rights contained in Part III of the Constitution, including Articles 15 and 16, and gets protection under Article 31-B of the Constitution."

Mr. Kesri informed the House that since the Union Government has already supported the Tamil Nadu Reservation Act, as a corollary to the decision it was now necessary to bring the Act within the purview of the Ninth Schedule.

Earlier, when the Deputy Chairperson called on Mr. Kesri to introduce the Bill, Mr. Chimanbhai Mehta rose to raise objections to its introduction under Rule 57 on the ground that Parliament was not competent to enact legislation which violated the very spirit of the Constitution.

Lok Sabha Assent

With the Lok Sabha approving the Constitution (85th Amendment) Bill on August 25, 1994, Parliament extended legal immunity to the Tamil Nadu Reservation Act.

However, several Opposition members were not sure whether the measure was "100 per cent" foolproof, as CPI leader Indrajit Gupta put it. His apprehension was that the Supreme Court could "intervene", if it felt "affronted" by Parliament's attempt to circumvent its ruling that reservations should not exceed 50 per cent. Wondering if the move was "really watertight", he urged the Government to tell the House what "exactly are we legislating."

His feares were shared by Mr. Buta Singh (Congress) and the Janata Dal (G) leaders Chandrajit Yadav and Syed Shahabuddin, who argued that the Supreme Court's ruling emanated from the case involving larger issues, some of which were still pending before it. The legal dimensions of the legislation needed to be considered, lest it later be struck down by the court, they pointed out.

After a nearly two-hour discussion, during which the Opposition demanded a comprehensive constitutional amendment on reservations for all states, the House approved the Bill without a single dissenting voice. The impressive voting figure — all the 348 members present at the time of the division voting for the Bill — did not reflect the misgivings expressed by almost all Opposition members about the Government's "intentions" to give social justice to the weaker sections.

The Welfare Minister, responding to the points raised during the discussion, hinted that if under similar conditions other states came forward with legislation on the lines of the Tamil Nadu Act. — envisaging more than 50 per cent reservations — the Centre would seriously consider them. Indirectly, he let it be known that other states could successfully emulate the Tamil Nadu "model". He told the more vocal supporters of "social justice" that instead of concentrating all their fire on the Floor of the House, they should raise their voice outside to mobilise opinion in support of measures intended to help the weaker sections.

Earlier, the Opposition, while supporting the Bill, used the occasion to accuse the Government of not being serious about raising the status of the disadvantaged sections. The political will needed to give them a share in power was lacking, the Government should formulate a more coherent policy for the uplift of the backward classes, and "piecemeal" measures such as a Constitution Amendment Bill would not do in the long run.

Janata Dal leader Ram Vilas Paswan told Mr. Kesri to "stop dangling lollipops" and come forward with a comprehensive bill. He suggested amendment to Articles 15(4) and 16(4) of the Constitution, thus allowing each state to fix its own reservation quota depending on its perceived need. Such an amendment would settle all the problems relating to reservations, he said, echoing the known position of the various Janata Dal factions.

Mr. Nitish Kumar (JD-G) said the amendment was only a "limited measure" restricted to one state and did not address the needs of other states. It was simply an attempt to "defuse" tension in Tamil Nadu and indicated that the Centre did not have a clear-cut policy. The Left parties sharply differed on the question of amending Articles 15(4) and 16(4).

Mr. Indrajit Gupta, while extending "whole hearted" support to the Tamil Nadu Act, opposed the proposal to allow every state to fix its own quota. If such a principle was accepted there would no longer be "one India", he said. His CPI(M) colleague Saifuddin Chaudhury too qualified his party's support to the Tamil Nadu Act. His party was supporting it because the level of reservations in

Tamil Nadu exceeded 50 per cent before the Supreme Court imposed the ceiling. His party did not want to give the impression that it favoured taking away the rights which people already enjoyed.

Quota Raj

Parliament's seal of approval on Tamil Nadu's bid for constitutional safeguards to its Act on reservation has once again pushed the issue to quotas to the top of the country's political agenda.

With assembly elections in 10 states round the corner, several other states are queuing up to step on the plank of social justice by hiking quotas for backward classes.

Andhra Pradesh, which goes to the polls in December, 1994, along with Karnataka, is the latest to announce inclusion of more communities in the BCs list. Karnataka has already enhanced reservation to 80 per cent with a Bill to give effect to its resolve, just as Tamil Nadu did.

In the North too, chief ministers are going all out to woo the OBCs. In Bihar, Mr. Yadav, who is expected to face a tough fight in the elections due next year, was spoken of 80 per cent quotas. Uttar Pradesh is on the boil with the forward castes taking to the streets against the state government's decision to provide 27 per cent reservation in the eight hill districts.

In such a scenario, the passage of the Constitution (85th Amendment) Bill is considered significant as it has thrown up several legal and political questions.

For instance, what happens to the Tamil Nadu Act if is struck down by the Supreme Court? And will the Centre oblige other states if they come up with similar legislation? Or will the Centre be forced to bring amendments to Articles 15(4) and 16(4) of the Constitution to allow the states to vary quotas ignoring the apex court's ceiling of 50 per cent?

Constitutional experts are of the opinion that normally courts do not strike down those Acts which have been included in the Ninth Schedule, but they refuse to rule out such a possibility. They cite the Keshavanand Bharti case to buttress their point.

Says Mr. Shanti Bhushan, "If the Supreme Court feels that the Tamil Nadu Act is in some way altering the basic structure of the Constitution, it could choose to strike it down. But if it does not, it will be very difficult for the court to strike it down, especially in view of the universal consensus behind the Bill."

It is not as if the legal questions did not bother the Centre, but political compulsions proved too strong.

While the crisis over the so-called reservation tangle may have blown over, the inclusion of the Tamil Nadu Reservation Act in the Ninth Schedule has serious implications at both the political and Constitutional levels.

Implications

The move, which is intended to provide the Reservation Act with immunity from judicial review under Article 31(b) of the Constitution, raises two fundamental sets of questions.

Among the first of political questions is whether this will lead other states, which want to enhance reservations over the maximum 50 per cent, to enact similar legislation. What will be the political fallout of such demands? And how will the Centre react to them?

The constitutional question is what impact the Tamil Nadu Reservation Act will have on the distributing legislative system. The Act is a unique piece of legislation in asmuch as it is based on the premise that a State Government may, under Article 31(c), enact legislation aimed at implementing the Constitution's Directive Principles.

So could it set a precedent by leading other state governments to make laws under Article 31(c) on issues other than reservation and justify them on the ground that they are directed at securing any of the Directive Principles?

The possibility of other state governments enacting a similar quota bill is real, Karnataka Chief Minister Veerappa Moily's recent attempt at increasing the reservation level to 80 per cent was stymied by the Supreme Court. The state assembly on September 20 passed a bill providing for 73 per cent reservation. The Bill had originally sought 80 per cent reservation. Mr. Laloo Prasad Yadav too has proclaimed his intention to raise the reservation limit.

The implications of the Tamil Nadu Act for the distributive legislative system, are very important. Those who had doubts about the legal validity of the legislation argued that the scope of Article 31(c), under which the Act was passed, was limited to securing or implementing Articles 39(b) and (c) of the Directive Principles, which deal with the distribution of property and wealth. Also, more generally, that a State Government was not empowered to legislate or reservation.

Legal proponents of the legislation maintained that it could be used to secure any or all of the articles in the Constitution's Part IV (Directive Principles of State Policy).

Andhra Pradesh Policy

Election year compulsions have finally caught up with the ruling Congress Party in Andhra Pradesh. The state joined Tamil Nadu and Karnataka in hiking the reservations by including Muslims, Kapus and 12 other castes and communities in the list of Backward Classes on August 25, 1994.

Since the government made it clear that these newly included communities would not cut into the existing quantum of reservations, the total reservations after this announcement may exceed 70 per cent, bringing the state at par with Tamil Nadu.

Speaking to newsmen after the meeting of the State Cabinet, which ratified the hike, Chief Minister Vijaya Bhaskara Reddy said the state government had considered legal and all other aspects before taking the decision and added that, if necessary, the existing law would be amended to uphold the Government decision.

The communities included in the backward castes list by the latest Government order are Muslims, Kapus, Balijas, Telegas, Ontari, Ayyakaras, Kasi, Kapidi, Patra, Ajulabalijas, Nagaralu, Pondara, Kurakalas, Quresh and Palaekari.

According to official estimates, Muslims comprise 12 per cent and Kapus account for 17 per cent of the state's population, whereas the remaining 12 cases account for 8 per cent of the State's populace. So today's order brings an additional 37 per cent of the State's population under the reservation category.

The decision would have wider political ramifications. It is noteworthy to mention that the Kapus are the most vocal group in coastal Andhra Pradesh and play a decisive role in as many as 60 Assembly constituencies in the state. They have been demanding, for quite sometime, their inclusion in the BC list.

The Government had asked the State BC Commission headed by the Mr. Justice Puttuswamy to give its interim report early so as to facilitate a decision in the matter. As the commission expressed its inability to submit its interim report in such a short time, the Government decided not to wait but include them in the BC lists.

The Government order stated that the commission would

decide about the percentage of reservations and economic criteria subsequently.

It further stated that the order would have no bearing in respect of admissions in education institutions for the academic year 1994-95 or selections to services for which the process had already been started. As regards the demand of other communities and castes for inclusion in the BC list, the statement said that the commission would examine them separately.

The decision regarding inclusion of Muslims has come as total surprise for the community leaders. Though there had been demands from time to time there was no immediate provocation as in the case of Kapus. They felt that the decision was clearly aimed at winning over the Muslims, who had deserted the Congress after the Ayodha episode. Andhra Pradesh, incidentally, became the third state in the country after Utter Pradesh and Karnataka in extending BC status to Muslims.

The Andhra Pradesh High Court granted an interim suspension of the Government order including Kapus, Muslims and 12 other communities in the backward classes list. The court granted the interim suspension while admitting two writ petitions on August 29 filed by the Andhra Pradesh Backward Classes Association and an advocate.

Madhya Pradesh Quota

The Madhya Pradesh Government's decision to reserve an additional 14 per cent of vacancies for the other backward classes (OBCs) in Government service has taken the total percentage of reservation in nine tribal districts of the state of 64.

Asked if the state government directive raising the total percentage of reservation to as high as 64 would not violate the Supreme Court ruling restricting it to 50 per cent, an official spokesman said he could not say whether it was violative of the apex court's ruling. "If anyone went to the court, the latter could decided upon it. The grounds for reservation have been already been listed in the notification," he added.

Tamil Nadu

The 69 per cent reservation applies to all educational institutions in Tamil Nadu, but it is the medical and engineering seats which have been the subject to controversy. The reason is that arts colleges are a plenty, with the availability of seats more or less equal to the demand.

A statement filed by the Advocate-General in the Supreme Court shows that of the 300 students admitted against the open competition quota (OC) of 31 per cent this year, the candidates belonging to backward classes, most backward classes and scheduled castes are 213,29 and two respectively. The number of students not belonging to any of the reserved categories admitted against the OC quota is 56, that is, less than six per cent of the 970 seats available.

The Supreme Court judges said, "This shows and affirms the trend disclosed last year — a trend both heartening the highly significant. The candidates belonging to Backward Classes are getting 80 per cent of the seats in merit quota on the basis of their merit alone. In addition, they are getting 50 per cent of the total seats (excluding All India Merit Quota) under the rule of reservation."

The Supreme Court has also directed the Tamil Nadu government to release 52 extra seats under the merit quota. The reason is that had the Government scaled down reservation to the 50 per cent limit, these students would have been on the merit list.

Even those in the Backward list have to get 90 per cent or more to be in the reckoning for professional courses. There is much talk in academic circles that parents manipulate marks to ensure admission for their wards to engineering or medical colleges. The manipulation is done at the university level, with the amount to be paid linked to the increase in percentage.

This year admissions to engineering and medical colleges were held up until the President gave his assent to the Tamil Nadu Reservation Act. Subsequently, the list of selected candidates was announced under the 69 per cent quota.

Uttar Pradesh

UP Chief Minister Mulayam Singh Yadav has announced a 27 per cent reservation in jobs and in educational institutions for the OBCs in the state. Initially, the UP government had said that even if the reserved seats meant for the backward classes were not utilized by them these would remain vacant. However, under mounting public pressure the state government has had to amend this. Mr. Yadav has also announced a two per cent reservation in state government services for the people of the hill districts. But these steps have failed to pacify the agitating people in the hilly region of Uttarkhand. In fact, the agitation is spreading both in intensity and the area affected.

The grievance is not against the reservation policy as such as against the implications of what will happen when the quotas are enforced in the hill areas. It is believed that in this region the OBCs constitute not more than two per cent of the total population. And the 27 per cent reservation for such a tiny population would be unfair for the other sections who have remained backward in terms of other considerations. If the composition of the backward classes in the region is really so, the grievance of the agitating people has substance. People in different parts of the country have varying characteristics. Casteism of the plains may not be a sure winner of votes in Kumaon or Garhwal. The OBC politics of the plains of Bihar and UP cannot be replicated in all parts of the country. Regional differences should have been taken into account. But, unfortunately, instead of admitting this, the UP Chief Minister has taken a tough stand. He is reported to have threatened that the agitation in the Hills might produce another agitation in the plains.

Legal Issues

The Tamil Nadu Backward Classes, Scheduled Castes and Scheduled Tribes (Reservation of Seats in Educational Institutions and of Appointments or Posts in the Services) Act 1993 (Tamil Nadu Act 45 of 94) providing for 69 per cent reservation in educational institutions and appointments in the services raises certain important legal issues.

The Supreme Court in its judgment in the Mandal case, delivered in November 1992, *inter alia* laid down that the reservations should not exceed 50 per cent.

At the same time the Court observed that "while 50 per cent shall be the rule, it is necessary not to put out of consideration certain extraordinary situations inherent in the great diversity of the country and the people. It might happen that in the far-flung and remote areas the population inhabiting those areas might, on account of their being out of the mainstream of national life and in view of conditions peculiar to and characteristical to them, need to be treated in a different way, some relaxation in this strict rule may become imperative. In doing so, extreme caution is to be exercised and a special case made out."

A legal question that arises is whether the Tamil Nadu Act is in accordance with the apex court's ruling in the Mandal case (on the limit of reservation). In this connection reference might be made to Articles 142 and 144 of the Constitution. Article 142 deals with enforcement of decrees and orders of the Supreme Court throughout India, while Article 144 says that all civil and judicial authorities in the country shall act in aid of the Supreme Court.

Another issue is whether the 'relaxation' in the matter of reservation (of 69 per cent) is in conformity with the observations of the apex court in the Mandal case.

A question is whether the Tamil Nadu Act is in conformity with the "equality clauses" in the Constitution namely, Article 14 (equality before Law), 15 (prohibition of discrimination on grounds of religion, race, caste, sex or place of birth) and 16 (equality of opportunity in matters of public employment).

The total percentage of the population of SCs, STs and BCs in Tamil Nadu is reported to be around 88. The question is whether the reservation of 69 per cent in Tamil Nadu, having regard to the socio-economic conditions of the SCs, STs and BCs in the state, can be described as being on the 'high side'. Should the percentage of reservation in favour of specified classes of citizens bear reasonable proportion to the total population of the classes of citizens concerned in the context of the public interest and public purpose underlying public services and higher education?

The apex court, in its interim orders made on August 18, 1994, in the Tamil Nadu reservation case, *inter alia* noted that the candidates belonging to BCs had got 80 per cent of the seats in the medical colleges in the 'merit quota' during 1993-94 and 1994-95. In addition, they were getting 50 per cent of the total seats (excluding all India quota) under the rule of reservation. The percentage of candidates "not belonging to any social reservation categories" who got admission in the "merit quota" this year was not even six per cent of the total seats. Should not policy planners and state authorities examine this aspect and do justice to those not belonging to any of the social reservation categories?

The Tamil Nadu Act contains a 'declaration' that it is giving effect to the policy of the state for securing the principles laid down in Part IV of the Constitution, namely. "Directive Principles of State Policy" and in particular, Article 38, clauses (b) and (c) of Article 39 and Article 46 of the Constitution.

Article 46 deals with the promotion of educational and economic interests of SCs, STs and other weaker sections by the state.

Article 38 deals with the obligation of the State "to secure a social order for the promotion and welfare of the people", clause (b) of Article 39 says that the state shall, in particular, direct its policy towards securing "that the ownership and control of the material resources of the community are so distributed as best to subsecure the common good." According to clause (c) of Article 39, "the operator of economic system does not result in the concentration of wealth and means of production to the common detriment."

Under Article 31 C, no law giving effect to the policy of the State towards securing any of the principles in the "Directive Principles of State Policy" shall be deemed to be void on the ground that it is inconsistent with any of the rights conferred by Article 14 (equality before law) or Article 19 (personal freedoms).

An important question that arises is whether the subject matter of the Tamil Nadu Act bears reasonable and rational "nexus" with the specified Directive Principles of State Policy.

Palkhivala Opinion

According to noted Constitution expert Nani A. Palkivala, an appropriate petition should be filed in the Supreme Court to declare the latest constitutional amendment void. It is well settled that an amendment of the Constitution which purports to affect its basic structure is void; and the insertion of the Tamil Nadu Act in the ninth schedule does impinge upon the basic structure of the Constitution. Reservations of the type sought to be made in Tamil Nadu can be allowed to prevail only by scrapping what Chief Justice Mahajan called "our sublime Constitution" and promulgating a backward Constitution for a backward nation.

Mr. Palkhivala said there are five important reasons in support of the view that the insertion of the Tamil Nadu Act in the Ninth Schedule violates the basic structure of fundamental law. First, the basic structure of the Constitution envisages a cohesive unified, casteless society — in which Casteism, petrified and ossified for centuries, should become merely the dust on the shelf of Indian history. The right to equality before the law and to the rule of meritocracy was allowed by the majority judgment to be encroached upon only to the extent of maximum reservations of 50 per cent. In other words, even according to the majority view which stretched the law to bursting point, it is not permissible to cross the limit of 50 per cent when caste is given precedence over merit and calibre. It is common knowledge that already reservations in different states have resulted in the substandard replacing the standard and the reins of power passing from meritocracy to mediocrity.

"Do we intend to re-enact the pre-independence tragedy with the roles reversed — the erstwhile under-privileged now becoming the privileged? (The desperate tale of the forward caste woman in Kerala who, merely with a view to gaining admission for her son in a medical college, deposed before a magistrate in the presence of her husband that the son was her illegitimate off-spring by a harijan, does not seem to have attracted the attention of our lethargic and indifferent citizenry)," Mr. Palkhivala said.

Secondly, the Supreme Court is the final arbiter of constitutional issues and every executive and legislative authority has to respect the Supreme Court's verdict. It is absurd beyond words to suggest that a state legislature can sit in judgment over the Supreme Court. If the Supreme Court lays down that 50 per cent reservations on the ground of caste represent the ultimate constitutional limit of reservations, which state government can claim the right to revise that limit? In the words of studied moderation, the Tamil Nadu Act represents the ultimate in contempt for the Supreme Court. There is already a scramble among state politicians to vie with one another in prescribing large reservations, Karnataka and Arunachal Pradesh are taking of 80 per cent reservations for the backward classes. The backlash in the U.P., hills and the move in Karnataka to give OBC status to two advanced castes, are 'grim portents of the chaos to which Casteism has already reduced this benighted country." Mr. Palkhivala said.

Thirdly, flexibility is available to the states to decide what percentage should be reserved on the basis of caste, but only subject to the overall ceiling of 50 per cent which is not to be exceeded in any case. If the latest amendment to the Constitution is valid, every state would be entitled to ignore the overall ceiling and have its law specified in the Ninth Schedule prescribing any percentage of reservations for its backward castes. India has already become the laughing stock of the civilized world as the only country which has reservations for the majority of its citizens, while in the rest of the world reservations are known only for minorities.

Fourthly, the unity and integrity of India is one of the prime objectives of the Constitution, as expressly set out in the Preamble. This basic objective would be set at nought by laws like the Tamil Nadu Act.

Fifthly, the preservation of the sovereignty and security of India is again one of the paramount aims of the Constitution. If the state can ignore with impunity the express ruling of the Supreme Court that reservations should not exceed 50 per cent in the aggregate, with far greater impunity would it feel emboldened to ignore the mere "advice" of the Supreme Court that the armed forces and some higher civilian posts should be outside the purview of caste reservations.

The Mandal report envisages not only reservations in civil service on the ground of caste but also reservations in the armed forces on the same ground. Further, not only appointments but even promotions are to be reserved for the privileged (euphemistically called "backward" class). Mr. Palkhivala said the country's armed forces are the pride of the nation — the only institution which has not been devalued and degraded. "What kind of an army, navy and air force shall we have when field marshals and generals, and admirals and air marshals, have secured admissions and promotions on caste considerations? This raises the most momentous of all issues — the security of the state. If the bitterest enemy of India were to be in charge of amendments of our Constitution, he could do no more disastrous job than to put laws like the Tamil Nadu Act in the ninth schedule and ensure the crumbling of the fundamental law of India."

Wiser Framers

"The framers of the Constitution were infinitely wiser than our so-called leaders of today. They forbade reservations based exclusively on caste — as if a poor Brahmin or a rich Dalit is a contradiction in terms. They harkened to the reality that there are no backward castes but only backward individuals. The only known solvent of casteism is a change in the national consciousness: harmony among, and social intermingling of, the anachronistic castes," Mr. Palkhivala said.

During the 207 years of its existence, the U.S. Constitution has been amended only 27 times; while the Indian Constitution has been amended 76 times in 44 years. "Let us ask ourselves in despair the question — Do we deserve our noble Constitution."

6

Drop-out Dilemma in Education

Since factors impinging on drop-out situation are predominantly related to the child's family background and school environment, it is only proper that we should examine in more detail the role of both, the home and school in the child's educational life. It is equally important to analyse the contributions, if any, of the child's community which includes his immediate neighbourhood, caste groups and also the village settlement as a whole. Community pressures for or against education can vitally determine the schooling prospects of younger generations. In a sociological perspective, all the three institutional units *i.e.* family, school and the community have a strategic concern with the level of educational advancement of the children. School drop-out is a manifestation of failure or non-fulfilment of the basic objectives at the hands of one or more of these units. Do they perform their role satisfactorily? What are the limitations or drawbacks which they encounter in their task of meeting the basic obligations in the field of education? In the present paper, we will deal with these apparently simple but basic questions.

Role of the Harijan Family

By now, enough is known about the social and economic conditions of the Harijan households. We may recapture some major strands to keep a link in the discussion here. The Harijan child, we have seen, has often inherited a social and economic legacy of which he could hardly boast of or conceive as helpful to future prospects. Economic hardships in some quarters, abysmal poverty in others, might have undermined the honest and determined efforts of many a schooling child. Added to these were the social and cultural factors, parental unconcern and carelessness and child's own apathy towards school education. All these forces, acting singly or in unison, were responsible for the child's exit from the school. We must, however, bear in mind that it would be an error of judgment to view Harijan families as universally irresponsible or careless with regard to the studies of their children. Such a sweeping generalisation would certainly do injustice to the Harijan homes, which have displayed affection, care, sympathy and some degree of involvement in the child's schooling.

We may recall, to provide a backdrop to further discussion, major aspects reflecting the involvement of the child's family in his educational activities. Despite the fact that most of the Harijan parents were illiterate, it is they who had taken a major initiative in sending the child to school. Enrolment decision regarding the child's schooling was made by the parents in most cases. Besides, a large majority of them were careful in admitting their child in school at the right age *i.e.* six years. Harijan parents were fairly well-informed about the child's progress in school, his likes and dislikes in respect of the outer world. It was, however, an enigmatic finding that out of 300 Harijan parents, only 53 per cent had visited the school, while the rest did not visit the school at all. When the school teachers were asked to give their definite opinion in this respect they too came out with identical responses in Table 6.1. A majority of them stated that the parents, visit to the school was limited to one or two occasions at best. Normally, these occasions related to the admission efforts, enquiries relating to the child's performance in annual examinations and the like.

Table 6.1
Question: Do the Harijan Parents Visit Your School?
(School Teacher's version)

Answer	*No. of Respondents*
Rarely	9
Just once/twice a year	22
On quite a few occasions	6
On most occasions	3
Total	40

Comparatively speaking, parents from other caste groups were reported to be somewhat more particular in this respect. They used to visit the school oftentimes, enquiring from the teachers about the child's requirements, behaviour in the class and his performance in studies. School teachers, in turn, visited the homes of these children and, in the course of general discussion, kept the parents informed about the child's development in school. Some of the teachers belonging to upper castes were reported to be giving private tuitions to the children of caste-Hindus. Harijan children were not fortunate enough to enjoy such privileges. They had no means to engage the services of school teachers for private coaching. Some Harijan parents suffered a sense of neglect at the hands of school teachers who mostly belonged to socially dominant caste groups. Most of the school teachers enjoyed economically superior positions than that of even relatively well-off Harijan families. There was also a tendency in some of the school teachers to keep a conventionally legitimised social distance between themselves and the Harijan parents.

Some Harijan parents criticised the behaviour of teachers towards them. The latter would keep them waiting outside the building, give evasive answers to their anxious queries and comment on the educational backwardness of their community. One Harijan parent described the situation thus:

> "When I went to my child's school once to find out why he was not doing any homework assignments, I was expecting a reasonably hospitable climate in the school. The school teacher who was Ahir by caste replied that Harijan children were better suited to jobs in agriculture than to schooling. They have no brain for ideas and no capacity for school work, the school teacher retorted. He further warned me that he would strike off the name of my child from the school roll if I ever again visited the school for seeking such clarifications. He misunderstood the purpose of the my visit. He thought I was cross-examining him on his duties. I felt very much hurt by his derisive remarks. But what could I do in the circumstances? I left the school quietly consoling that it was better that I never went to school myself for education."[1]

Social distance which the teachers wanted to maintain with

the Harijan parent was verbalised during such encounters. Such incidence as one just reported are capable of scaring away many a sensitive and self-respecting parent. Infrequency of contacts between the parents and teachers may partly be explained by such an unreceptive outlook of the teaching community.

It is, however, erroneous to blame the school teachers alone for lack of parents' affinity with the school system. Some Harijan parents were equally responsible for this. They were totally unaware of their obligations towards their child's educational needs. Mostly illiterate they were apathetic and unconcerned. They thought that after an act of enrolling their child's name in the school, their commitment came to an end.

> "Why should I go and visit the school? I have done my duty of putting my son in the school. It is my son who should go to school and learn something. I myself know nothing of basic alphabets. What can I tell the teacher who is the master of all knowledge. Now it is my son and that teacher who are concerned with each other. I am in no way connected with what goes on in the school. Don't you think I am right in my thinking?"

One Harijan parent concluded his remarks with this question. According to them, school education was a matter strictly between the school teachers and children, and parents had at best a peripheral role in it. Why were these parents clinging on to a traditional and obsolete viewpoint? It is difficult to answer this question offhand. However, our guess is that a number of factors were responsible in making Harijan parents less responsive to the demands of the school system. And these can be enumerated as their illiteracy, culturally-conditioned inhibitions, lack of exposure to changing social responsibilities of the parents, unfriendly outlook of the teaching community etc. Their inferior position in the status system of the village community helped to aggravate the social distance between the school and their family. This may explain why the Harijan parents were mostly unable to establish enduring links with the school system which, after family, was the next important for their child.

It was already explained that whatever knowledge or information the parents had about the child's school, it was gathered by them mostly through secondary sources. His own child, neighbouring children and others in the community shared their experience and views about the school education, facilities and the like. Sometimes Harijan teachers visited their locality and discussed the issues pertaining to the school. By far, the Harijan teachers formed the most important group that offered a link between the Harijan families and the school. Some of them were instrumental in motivating the Harijan parents for enrolling their child in the school, in providing guidance to Harijan children in studies and in meeting the basic educational needs of some poor children. In most of the cases, whatever inspiration or guidance that was available to the Harijan families, came from the Harijan teachers. This also indicates how imperceptibly caste alignments take place in a village setting. By and large, however, the Harijan parents remained deprived of any direct information about his child's classroom behaviour, studies, regularity etc. This is evident from the responsed in Table 6.2.

Table 6.2

Question: Did the School Teacher Make any Specific Comments about the Child; His/Her Class-room Behaviour, Studies, Regularity etc.? (Parent's Version)

Response	*Rasra Block*	*Ranipur Block*	*Total*
Received no comments	112 (74.7%)	116 (77.4%)	228 (76.0%)
Made positive comments	17 (11.3%)	14 (9.3%)	31 (10.3%)
Made negative comments	21 (14.0%)	20 (14.0%)	41 (13.7%)
	150 (100.0%)	150 (100.0%)	300 (100.0%)

Poverty and economic backwardness have many dimensions. It is reasonable to say that a Harijan home stands distinguished in its incapacity to provide sufficient leverage to the youngsters to grow in a natural way, to embibe experiences compatible with their age and interests. Even school teachers have fully recognised this fact. When they were asked to explain the reasons for irregularity in school attendance of Harijan children, most of them have given priority to three factors, domestic duties including child care, minor agricultural jobs or tending the cattle or sheep, and starvation at home. They argued that compared to the above, reasons such as migration of the family, community or caste influences or lack of parental concern are less significant in influencing school attendance. It was their view that children who are initiated into domestic tasks at a much lower age tend to develop tendencies of absenting from school. Some of the physical tasks done through the children in Harijan families were strenuous and unbearable for the child, 8 or 9 years old. It was economically compulsive for the Harijan families to engage the child in these unwelcome tasks, but its direct consequence for the child was his declining interest in school activities. in the last chapter, we had seen that 77 out of 300 parents had spoken of 'lack of interest in studies' as one of the drop-out reasons. The same reasoning was given by 24 drop-out cases. We are now beginning to realise how poverty conditions exercise their sway in different directions. Lack of food or other basic necessities, absence of adequate freedom to participate in school activities due to pressures of domestic chores and physical strain associated with cumbersome manual tasks are responsible for driving a school-going child to a point of total withdrawal from the school system.

Impact of poverty can be seen in another context also. Out of 40 school teachers, 19 had stated that only a few Harijan students were able to pick up/learn easily the lessons in their class-room. When they were further asked to specify the reasons as to why some Harijan students have difficulties, they gave multiple responses in this respect (Table 6.3). It is pointed out by the teachers that paucity of educational material, starvation and hunger and frequent absenteeism of the child are accountable for his poor class-room performance. It is entirely a new finding and perhaps a strategic one that domestic problems and anxieties accompanied by these are responsible for lack of the child's attention in the class-room. Observations recorded in the table go to prove that children with lowest economic background have to encounter a series of obstacles to attain their goals. Poverty may reflect not only in his dress or school wallet but also in his mood, his interactional patterns, his relationship with teachers and school mates. His whole personality may undergo a conditioning process. An attitude of listlessness or withdrawal in the class-room may be treated as only one expression of this conditioning.[2]

Table 6.3
Showing the Difficulties before the Harijan Child in Learning Easily the Class-room Lessons (Teacher's Version)

Difficulties	*No. of Responses (N=19)*
Lack of text books, exercise books, etc.	10
Irregularity in attendance	8
Mental preoccupation with household problems	7
Starvation and hunger	6
Lack of guidance/help at home	3
Any others — Poor innate capacity, lack of interest in studies, etc.	9
	43

Were the Harijan parents aware of the educational backwardness of their children? Yes, some of them were. Out of 300 parents, 49 of them (nearly 17 per cent) stated that their children were much behind other students in class-room studies. They had this knowledge through school visits, observations of the child's goings-on at home and through the reports of school-going children in the neighbourhood. What did they do to rectify the educational backwardness of the child? Nothing tangible as such. Some of them brought the matter to the school and implored the school teachers to 'improve' the child. Others warned their children of waywardness and supervised for sometime that their child does some lessons at home. But being illiterate or apathetic, the parents could hardly improve the situation. Still others kept quiet and allowed the child to drift and waver in his own way.

From earlier observations, we are tempted to regard parental involvement in the educational activities of the child as sporadic and peripheral. It may also be recalled that only 34 children (15.3 per cent) had received proper academic guidance from the family members in their educational efforts. Other children had received marginal attention in this respect or no attention at all. Would it then be correct to say that Harijan parents have no interest in the educational activities of their school-going child? Perhaps this question has a misplaced emphasis on the term 'interest'. Most of the Harijan families were operating in a culture of illiteracy, with no long-standing tradition of learning or scholarship in their ancestry. Schooling of the child was conceived as an important issue and hence the enrolment of the child at the right age. Low social and economic status was the inhibiting factor which compelled many a loving father to send his tender-aged son to the agricultural field rather than to the school. Their financial condition was critical for most of the year and yet they kept on bearing the expenses involved in educational activities. When asked whether the expenses relating to the school education of the child were within their capacity, only 95 parents (nearly 32 per cent) answered in the affirmative. In other words; two out of every three Harijan parents found the expenses beyond their capacity to bear.

Provision of food, books and other miscellaneous items required in the school, supply of kerosene and lamp for night study and relieving the child from much-needed domestic services are acts of parental concern and sense of obligation towards the schooling child. Exceptions apart, most of the parents had the genuine desire of educating the child and had the willingness to make necessary sacrifices to attain that goal. They were hopeful that their child would rise above the conventional level and would make a mark. Academic guidance and support was available to only a few because they had literate and fairly educated family members around. Others were left unattended in this respect because their parents and other family members were illiterate or semi-literate. It is, therefore, idle to conclude that Harijan parents were totally disinterested in the studies of their child.[3] Even school teachers have supported this contention with a forceful logic. When asked to specify whether Harijan parents take interest in the education of their children, 33 out of 40 school teachers replied in the affirmative. According to them, parental concern and responsibility are obvious through their anxious queries with teachers about their child's needs, requirements and class-room performance, meticulous care with which they ensure the regularity in school attendance of the child, some assistance in the child's homework preparations and the like (Table 6.4).

Table 6.4
Indicators of Parental Interest in the School Education of the Harijan Child (Teacher's Version)

Indicators	*Responses*		
	Basra Block	*Ranipur Block*	*Total*
Personal queries about children's needs, requirements and school performance	9	14	23(39.7%)
Help and assistance in child's home-work assignments	7	6	13(22.4%)
Ensuring regularity in school attendance/studies	6	3	9(15.5%)
Personal appeal to the school teachers to pay special attention on the child	1	6	7(12.1%)
Prompt supply of books, slates and other educational aids	3	3	6(10.3%)
	26	32	58(100.0%)

(Report of the Education Commission, 1964-66, Ministry of Education, Government of India, 1966, p. 109).

By now, it is fairly well-established that Harijan parents, barring a minority, were sufficiently responsive to the educational needs of their children. Their financial insecurity as well as other constraints were largely responsible for lack of deeper involvement. From the description in the preceding pages, it can be safely inferred that the social and economic status of the Harijan family was not at all a facilitating factor in most of the cases. The home atmosphere was, in large number of cases, full of deficiencies and hardships. Physical help from the child was more a rule than a exception. It is already known to us that many a child had to leave his school on account of poverty and related contingencies. School and the teaching community were partly responsible for the drop-out of Harijan children and we will discuss their role at length later. For the present, it would suffice to say that most of the Harijan parents have played their role fairly satisfactorily, considering their limitations on different scores. A few of them might have erred seriously and none can pardon them for their inattention or neglect.

Interestingly enough, a large majority of village leaders have spoken in favour of Harijan parents. They admired them as responsible persons and sensitive to the needs of the schooling child. According to leaders, school drop-out among the Harijan children is largely a problem beyond the capacity of their parents to resolve satisfactorily. To a question, "Do you think that the Harijan parents are responsible for the drop-out of their children from the school?" 37 out of 60 village leaders emphatically stated "No, not at all", 15 of them held the parents responsible "to some extent", while the remaining 8 leaders felt that parents were responsible "to a great extent". Further, in support of their arguments, a group of 23 leaders (comprising last two categories) advanced reasons to justify that the onus of drop-out responsibility lies partially or totally on the Harijan parents (Table 6.5). Their contention was that the parents failed to fulfil the educational needs of their children; detained them for domestic work, engaged them in gainful employment or placed them in a wedlock earlier than warranted by the current economic compulsions. The last argument, none can deny, is a valid one and it stands to reason that the parents should not have hurried to get their son or daughter married at an early age. But the earlier three reasons, unless there are cases of brazen selfishness, avarice or cruelty on the part of Harijan parents are conditioned by the economic backwardness of the family. This conclusion has been supported by the evidence obtained earlier.

Table 6.5

Showing How the Harijan Parents are Responsible for the School Drop-out of their Children (Village Leader's Version)

Indications	*Responses (N=23)*
Neglect of educational needs	20
Placement in gainful employment	12
Detention for domestic work	11
Early marriage of children	11
Any others Indebtedness, lack of contacts with school teachers, absence of guidance and encouragement etc.	5
	59

Now we shall turn our attention to other aspects of drop-out situation. It was interesting to notice that the school teachers came to know about the drop-out decision of the child at a much later stage in most of the cases. There were two distinct categories of drop-out cases. Firstly, the Harijan children who passed or failed in a particular class did not continue their schooling in a higher class or same class respectively. The fact that a particular child has preferred to stay out of the school came to the notice of school authorities one or two months after the school's reopening, some time around August or September. Secondly, there were cases who left the school during the academic year. Teachers usually received delayed reports about drop-out of certain Harijan children. Out of 40 school teachers, only 8 stated that the Harijan children communicated their drop-out decision while 32 teachers complained that the children never let them know their drop-out decision. How did the parents act in this respect? Not quite responsibly, it seems. A majority of 22 teachers commented that none of the Harijan parents approached them to communicate the school withdrawal of the child. Teachers were left guessing in most of the cases.

From the view point of preventive action, it is necessary that the school authorities should know about children who are on the verge of withdrawing from the school career. It was clear from our discussion with school teachers that in some cases they found it easy to identify the cases who would stop their education in the middle of the year. Increasingly tendencies of absenteeism, lack of attention in studies and similar traits of disinterestedness on the part of some children provided a basis for the teachers' judgment. But this was a very elementary way of making a judgment. Most of the teachers did not go beyond this exercise to effectively intervene in the very process of dropping out. Reasons and consequences of this shall be discussed later but it is necessary to point out that communication gap did exist between the teachers and the Harijan parents and in some cases, between the teachers and the Harijan children. We cannot, however, absolve the Harijan parents of their responsibility. May be due to lack of awareness, illiteracy or other cultural factors, they did not report to the school authorities about, discontinuation of their child's schooling. And this is a regrettable lapse on the part of Harijan parents. A situation such as this reminds us that a lot more effort needs to be made to bring Harijan parents and school authorities together. Withdrawl of a child from the school at any point of time indicates, in some measure, the tendencies dominant in Harijan parents to view educational activities as outside their comprehension and spheres of influence. Whether their feelings are justified or not is altogether a different matter. It is indeed an unsound practice that drop-out decisions in most of the cases are not timely communicated by the parents or ascertained by the teachers.

Do the Harijan parents make any efforts to re-admit their children later? An affirmative response was given by 35 out of 40 school teachers. They said that the Harijan parents try to send their children to school after a gap of one or two years. In cases where children have left school on their own accord, the parents make persistent efforts to send them back. They further stated that in cases where temporary domestic crisis had resulted into drop-out of a child, the parents put the child back into the school once normalcy was restored. How far were their readmission efforts successful? A rough estimate provided by the teachers in this respect (Table 6.6). A majority view was that out of 10 only one or two drop-out cases are able to make successful re-entry in the school. In other words, nearly 80 per cent of the drop-out cases belong to the category of confirmed school leavers. This is indeed a serious phenomenon. It means that even parental efforts for re-admission remain, to a large extent, infructuous. It also shows the gravity of the situation because once the child is out of school, no matter for what reasons, it is difficult, it seems, to bring him back to school. It looks as if drop-out decisions, once taken, assume a form of finality.

Table 6.6

Question: "Out of Every Ten Drop-out Cases among the Harijan Children, How Many Rejoin their Studies? (Teacher's Version)

Response	*Respondents*
Six or eight	4
Three to five	10
One to two	25
None	1
Total	40

Let us now see the actual position. Our sample consisted of 300 confirmed drop-out cases. When the Harijan parents were asked whether they made any readmission efforts in respect of their children, only 32 (10.7 per cent) replied in the affirmative. This shows that nearly 9 out of 10 parents did not try to readmit the child. In the above cases, drop-out decision was final. This is a somewhat conflicting evidence because the school teachers had stated, as we have seen a little earlier, that Harijan parents try for readmission. It is difficult to resolve this controversy in absence of relevant details. It follows from the above that a small number of Harijan parents genuinely try for the readmission of their child. Still smaller is the number of those Harijan children who restart their educational career with fresh determination and sense of stability. For the majority of drop-outs, it is a total and complete scopestation from the school system.

This brings us to the final summary of contributions of the Harijan family to the educational life of the Harijan child. It may not be out of place to highlight the drawbacks inherent in the Harijan families. Almost all of them live below poverty-line, families living in some comfort can be counted on ones finger-tips.[4] Most of them were incapable of supplying the basic educational requirements of the child on a continuing basis. Quite a significant number among them was unable to provide food to their children. In this context of poverty and deprivation, it is not surprising to witness an exodus of Harijan children from schools. Another dimension of the family life of the Harijan child is a social one, and refers to low literacy level in the family and lack of experience in dealing with the school system. Some of the beliefs and values prevalent in the Harijan community were decidedly counter-productive. These were responsible for shortening the educational career of the child. The social life of the Harijan community was restricted to a small, cloistered groove with caste boundaries. Personal contacts and interactions acquired intimacy and a touch of informality only within the context of caste. Conditions such as these imposed severe limitations on the availability of information, exchange of ideas and experiences within a broader community framework. It is in view of these factors that the Harijan child seems to have received less than adequate attention and support from his parents. There were innumerable difficulties at home that could eventually distract the attention of the schooling child and compel him to relinquish his contacts with school. Observations of teachers in this respect are quite penetrating (Table 6.7).

Table 6.7
"What Do You Think are the Difficulties and Problems Facing the Harijan Child at His Home that Come in the Way of His Educational Pursuits? (Teacher's Version)

Responses Categories	*No. of Responses (N=40)*
1. Lack of physical and other facilities such as space, kerosene, lamp, etc.	28(24.7%)
2. Pressure of domestic work and other onerous responsibilities outside	22(19.3%)
3. Lack of guidance/encouragement from parents or other family members	16(14.0%)
4. Unhealthy community influences; bad habits in children etc.	16(14.0%)
5. Lack of food; starvation and hunger	16(14.0%)
6. Lack of clothes, books, etc.	16(14.0%)
Total	114(100.0%)

School teachers have provided a perceptive outline On the difficulties of the Harijan child at home (Table 6.7). Absence of basic physical necessities at home and pressures of household duties were reported to be two important barriers (50 out of 114 responses). Remaining inhibiting factors include lack of parental guidance, undesirable community influences and absence of food and clothing (64 out of 114 responses). Observations of the teachers aptly illustrate the handicaps of the schooling Harijan child. All these difficulties may not show up in each and every Harijan household, but a combination of two or three of the above-mentioned difficulties is enough to discourage and dissuade a Harijan child from schooling. Difficulties just enumerated may precipitate the drop-out action among the Harijan children and this has happened in a majority of cases. Evidence such as this suggests that the education of the Harijan child should not be viewed as an isolated phenomenon. It is closely linked up with the family set-up, its social and economic status.[5] So far we have seen the performance of the Harijan families and their limitations as well. Now we shall have a closer look at the school administration with a view to examining its role in relation to the education of the Harijan child.

Role of the Village School

By and large the village schools were under the personal supervision of the Head Master who usually had a long teaching experience in different schools in the region. Under him there were three to four teachers on junior grade. Special Harijan schools which received grants from the Department of Social Welfare, had the privilege of Harijan teachers being on their staff roll, while the girls schools were under the complete charge of the Head Mistress and the female teachers. By and large, the school teachers came from the higher castes and from families of agriculturists. Harijan teachers mostly belonged to the families of low income group. Most of them were reported to be landless or marginal holders. Monthly income from teaching varied from Rs.175 to Rs.250 depending on their length of service and designation in a hierarchy. Most of the school teachers lived within a manageable distance from the school, say 4 to 5 kilometres. This helped them to travel easily to and from school daily.

The physical condition of the school buildings, in most cases, was less than desirable.[6] An old rickety structure with broken pillars and cracked walls was the common mark of a village school. In some schools, during the monsoons children of all classes were herded together in one safe room, as there was no dry space around. Paucity of space was a perennial problem before the school teachers and during the summer days, they conducted the classes in the open. Children and the teachers settled themselves under the shade of trees to avoid the problem of overcrowding and suffocation in the class rooms. Senior basic schools had comparatively better buildings. On the whole, the physical conditions of the schools were of deplorably low standards.

There was no separate room for the office of the Head Master or Head Mistress of the school, no common room for the students either. Some schools were provided with basic furniture like tables, chairs, cupboards etc. But these were given a long time ago and the school authorities had not bothered to repair or replace them. As such, most of the furniture and other material remained out and hence mostly out of use. Mats made of coarse jute were provided to schools but were insufficient in number. Lacking replacement, the torn mats were used by the students for sitting purposes. Some students brought mats from their homes. Other paraphernalia like blackboard, bucket, tumbler, chalks, text books, maps etc. were woefully short of the actual requirements. Teachers vehemently complained about the lack of these essential materials. Some of them reportedly brought the matter before the authorities during the time of school inspection, others wrote to the higher authorities at the district level. But nothing spectacular happened and most of the schools we visited, remained neglected as ever.

In spite these odds and inconveniences, some teachers managed the school affairs with skill and resourcefulness. Some of them were residents of the very village in which the school was located. They could fruitfully mobilize the village community resources for specific tasks. The teachers who came from distant places could not command as much influence. It was reported that some teachers were making sincere efforts in enrolling the village children in the schools including those in the Harijan communities. Teachers themselves explained to us the ways in which they increased the enrolment of Harijan children in their schools. By far the most important and effective strategy they adopted was visiting the Harijan *bustees* and individual households. They tried to motivate the parents in personal meetings. Even during casual contacts they tried to impress upon them the advantages of school education. It was also revealed during these discussions that the Harijan teachers were more successful because of their caste affinities and exalted status in their community. In most of the schools, the task of visiting the Harijan localities and contacting the parents was assigned to the Harijan teachers. Another method for popularising enrolment was requesting the school children at the end of the term to bring in fresh cases after summer vacation.

Despite the use of various techniques for increasing the enrolment position among the Harijan children, there was no encouraging response from some Harijan parents. Out of 40 teachers, only 14 stated that they had no difficulties in their enrolment efforts. The remaining 26 teachers described their experience as tough and sometimes unrewarding. What were the reasons behind the unreceptive response from Harijan families? The teachers replied that in some cases, the parents were apathetic and indifferent, in others, conditions of acute poverty and helplessness prevented families to enrol the names, in still others, the families wanted to use the services of the child at home. Anti-literacy environment in the family, unhelpful community influences and lack of proper incentive structure at schools were also the subordinate factors at work which kept the enrolment figure in the Harijan communities at a low level. The teachers, however, stressed that there is slow but perceptible change in the Harijan community and parents are becoming conscious of the importance of enroling the child in the school.

But once the Harijan child enters the school, the school teachers do not seem to make deliberate attempts to involve his parents in the educational activities of the child. Out of 300 Harijan parents, only 121 (40.3 per cent) were specifically invited by the school teachers and this suggests that the initiative to introduce the parents to the school system was not taken by the school teachers in majority of the cases. It is further observed that parental visits to school were mostly related to problematic issues or formal occasions. No stable relationship could possibly be invoked through such sporadic and problem-oriented contacts (Table 6.8). This reinforces our earlier view that Harijan parents were placed at a distance by the school system. It was, therefore, plausible that the Harijan families did not view the school as their own institution which had intimate connection with their values and orientations. In a majority of cases, the Harijan parents displayed inertia and teachers overlooked the need to combat it by establishing fruitful rapport with them on a durable basis. This lacunae remained unattended to in most of the village schools.

Table 6.8
Showing the Nature of Occasions for Parental Visits to the School (Teacher's Version)

	Purpose of visits	*No. of Responses*
(i)	To enquire into irregularities/absenteeism of the child	20
(ii)	Failure in examination/deficiencies in studies	14
(iii)	Special programmes/festivals	14
(iv)	Admission/examination formalities	11
(v)	Behaviour problems/bad habits of the child	8
(vi)	Lack of personal hygiene and cleanliness or absence of educational material.	6
		73

There is a substantial gap between what the Harijan parents and school teachers say on the same issue. As many as 60 per cent of Harijan parents stated that they were not called by the school teachers at all. Teachers on the other hand claim that it is their usual practice to invite parents on a number of occasions, formal as well as informal (37 out of 40 teachers made this claim). It is difficult to judge who is right in this matter. But it appears that all the school teachers did not maintain close contacts with the Harijan parents. Out of 40 teachers, only 25 stated that they know closely most of the Harijan parents. In the remaining group of 15 teachers, seven said that they have close contacts with some of the parents while eight stated that they have contacts with a few or none of them. A result like this indicates that there certainly exists a distance between the teachers and Harijan parents. In a rural setting where schools are located at close distances, it should not have been difficult for the teaching community to maintain closer ties with all Harijan parents.

Some teachers, however, had an inner urge to develop and maintain contacts with the parents of lower social strata. Calling them to school or at their own residence, visiting them at their *bustee* and providing help and guidance in their domestic difficulties were some of the ways through which the school teachers had built up a good image for themselves. Unfortunately, their number was not large enough. Some teachers complained that their attempts to go near the Harijan people were not appreciated by the caste Hindus. In some villages, the caste feelings were so intense that the teacher who displayed sympathy with Harijans was instantly rebuked for his behaviour. Some of them were told not to pamper the members of the Harijan community. In such a climate, it was well-nigh impossible for the teachers to deviate from the traditional image of his calling and brave the criticism of the village elders. Hence, the teachers adopted the safest course of maintaining a customary distance from the Harijan. The hope for building bridges between the school and the Harijan community, therefore, lay in the Harijan teachers. They had caste moorings and a common cultural environment. Their own residence was in a Harijan *bustee* and they were part of the Harijan community. They could, therefore, easily motivate the parents. The teaching community admitted that the Harijan teachers took pains to bring children of their community into the educational system. They played their role with sufficient tact and resourcefulness. Their special efforts for enrolment, accompanying the Harijan children while going to schools, close attention on their studies and extra curricular activities and occasional financial and material help to poor children, unmistakably point towards the Harijan teachers' concern and feelings of identification with their community.

What was the image of the school teacher in the Harijan community? We had asked the Harijan parents to comment on the school teacher who taught their children. Their comments covered a wide range of attributes like character, approach towards studies and Harijan children, regularity and discipline in the class, familiarity with parents etc. These comments were further classified into favourable and unfavourable attitudes depending upon their positive and negative emphasis. After doing this exercise we observed that out of 300 Harijan parents, 203 (67 per cent) were favourably disposed towards the school teachers while the rest *i.e.* 97 (33 per cent) were totally critical about them. In other words, two out of every three Harijan parents had a favourable opinion about the school teachers. It is a somewhat painful observation that over one-third Harijan parents should have a negative estimation of the school teachers. In point of fact, all or at least a very large majority of school teachers should have received a word of praise from the parents.

The leaders' opinion also points toward a similar trend. When asked to describe the attitudes of the teachers towards Harijan children 40 out of 60 leaders stated that the teachers were generally helpful and sympathetic to Harijan children. Another nine leaders characterised the teachers' attitudes as indifferent while the remaining 11 leaders commented that teachers were unhelpful and prejudiced. This minority opinion of the leaders suggests that there are some teachers who are found wanting in sincerity of purpose and evenhandedness. This is, indeed, an undesirable situation and needs immediate attention.

There are many ways through which the image of the teachers gets eroded. His behaviour, attitudes and actual dealings with the Harijan child and his parents provide indications of his role and underlying motivations. As many as 107 Harijan parents (36 per cent of the total sample) stated that their children reported at home the incidence of beating, scolding, harassment, or excessive punishment meted out to them in the school. Sometimes, the incidence of beating or harassment involved the Harijan child and the children of the caste-Hindus as well. The teacher's behaviour received critical comments in some places. His tendency to exploit student labour, giving punishment to the Harijan child through upper caste children, isolating him in a class-room, were some of the themes that were brought before us in general discussion. One Harijan teacher reported that menial jobs like cleaning the mats, arranging school furniture etc. were done through Harijan children by upper caste teachers. Harijan children were reportedly not allowed to draw water from the hand-pumps or wells. One teacher also stated that in some schools in another region, the Harijan children were generally not allowed to take part in dramas, musical concerts etc. which were to be staged as public performances.

School teachers, on the other hand, seem to hold a somewhat different view. They are of the opinion that by and large Harijan children are favourably disposed towards them. When asked to specify the attitudes of Harijan students towards them, 23 out of 40 teachers described these as 'very favourable', 14 as 'favourable' while only three described these attitudes as 'just alright'. It follows that, according to teachers, the Harijan children have no grouse or complaint against them. Rather, the children felt happy and secure in the company of school teachers. In elaborating the feelings of the child, the teachers gave examples of how the child sought their help and assistance in studies, games and other activities, how the child followed them when other children picked up a quarrel with him. Really speaking, very few teachers could correctly analyse the feelings of the Harijan child towards them. In most of the cases, they interpreted the qualities of meek obedience, servility, fear complex and the like as indices of their affection and love towards their teacher. But an analysis of our interviews with the teachers showed that most of the teachers were unable to feel the pulse of the Harijan children in true sense. It appears that, excepting a few teachers, a majority of the teachers could not successfully identify themselves with the Harijan children. This inference is further strengthened by the testimony of drop-out cases. Out of 198 children whom we interviewed only 88 stated that their teacher was helpful and cooperative. As many as 110 children made a firm observation that teachers were not helpful or cooperative to them during their school life.

Harijan parents were articulate enough to describe the feelings of their child towards his school, teachers and classmates. We have already detailed the aspects which the Harijan children liked most in their educational pursuits. Now we shall examine the other side of the coin. To a question: 'What were the things which your child did not like in his/her school?' the Harijan parents gave multiple answers (see

Table 6.9). It is indeed an interesting exercise to compare the figures under 'likes' and 'dislikes' of the Harijan children as conveyed by their parents. Except for a liking for two items *i.e.* curricular and extra-curricular activities, in all other respects, the greater number of Harijan children had developed a dislike and a sense of grievance. In as many as 95 cases, there was positive disapproval of the behaviour of the schoolmates. Similar criticism against teachers was levelled in 75 cases. The largest single group of responses (111 in all) relates to the physical aspects of the school and this denotes the distance, inaccessibility during rainy season, poor sitting arrangements; lack of drinking water facility and the like. Even the drop out cases themselves came out strongly against some of these inadequacies. By and large the evidence that we have is sufficient to reach a conclusion that the school system did not much succeed in forging durable and satisfying relationship with most of the Harijan children. Its staying or holding power was very weak.

Table 6.9
Question: What were the Things which Your Child did not Like in His/Her School? (Parent's Version)

(Figures in bracket indicate the number of responses from Table 6.5 showing positive disposition towards the aspect).

Responses	*Disliked (No. 227)**	*Liked*
Curricular programme	34 12.2%	(133)
Extra-curricular programme	11 3.9%	(168)
Behaviour of schoolmates	95 34.3%	(33)
Behaviour of school teacher	75 27.1%	(22)
Physical aspects and others facilities in the school	111 40.1%	(5)

* Out of 300 parents, 23 did not give any response to this question.

Some of these drawbacks are poignantly illustrated by the

village leaders in our sample (Table 6.10). Most of them were extremely critical of the role of the teaching staff in the village schools. Adjectives such as 'unco-operative' 'vindictive', 'inept' and 'inefficient' were used in describing the performance of the teachers. Some of the leaders went to the extent of branding them as 'caste supremacist' and prejudicial to the interest of Harijan children. Distance, poor approachability, lack of equipments and basic facilities like water, were other aspects which the village leaders considered as responsible for creating a negative image of the school. They also feel that these factors are positively related to the drop out incidence among the Harijan children. It is thus imperative that these limitations are countered to improve the holding powers of the school.

Table 6.10
Drawbacks/Limitations of the School which Directly or Indirectly are Responsible for the Drop-out among Harijan Children (Village Leader's Version)

Drawbacks/limitations	*No. of Responses*
No limitations at all	4
Uncooperative, inefficient teaching staff	42
Distant location, poor approachability	37
Lack of educational equipments, aids etc.	32
Lack of incentives, facilities to Harijan students	18
Poor physical structure	17
Lack of drinking water facilities	12
No proper incentives to teaching community	8

How do the school teachers react to the drop-out situation? What efforts do they make to reduce the number of drop-out cases from the Harijan community? School teachers made it clear that, to the extent possible, they tried to make the school life of the Harijan children bearable and satisfying. Some said that they maintained excellent relationship with these children, gave them help by words or deeds, supplied them books, copies etc. and at times gave them food to eat. Some gave them clothes too. But such humanitarian souls were few in number. A large majority of the teachers answered that they personally approached the parents, conducted group meetings in their locality and tried to convince the parents to readmit their child in the school. They, however, expressed their helpnessess in dealing with the drop-out problem. They said that acute poverty among the Harijan families was primarily responsible for drop out of the child. A large number of these families, they submitted, were compelled to use child labour for economic support. Some of them also agreed that low literacy level among the Harijan parents made their task difficult in convincing them on advantages of higher education. In short, the school teachers were mostly unsure of themselves and felt that they would not succeed in curbing the drop out problem of Harijan children. Part of this defeatist attitude among the school teachers can be safely ascribed to the nature of issues involved. Economic hardships and consequent domestic instability were clearly outside the manoeuvrability of the school teachers.

Besides, there was no organised community support available to the teachers in effectively dealing with this problem. Most of the teachers lamented over the lack of cooperation from any individual or village organisation in motivating Harijan parents to continue their child's education. "It is nobody's concern whether Harijan children go to school or slog in the agricultural field. There is complete inertia and apathy among the villagers, including the community leaders" — said one teacher frankly. When asked whether they contacted the parents of drop out cases to convince them to send their children back to school, three teachers replied 'no, never; 15 stated that in a few cases they made attempt: 12 stated that in some cases they made attempts and only 10 teachers 'in all cases' tried to contact the Harijan households to get back the cases. Out of 37 teachers who made some efforts in this direction, 21 stated that the Harijan parents patiently listened to their arguments and some of them even promised to consider the readmission issue. The remaining 16 teachers explained that the Harijan parents reacted unfavourably and paid no heed to their persuasive efforts. There is some truth in what the school teachers, have claimed to be doing in certain cases. A majority of village leaders (32 out of 60) have testified that the school teachers did approach the parents in Harijan localities to motivate them to send their children back to school. These trends are indicative of involvement of some teachers in the educational activities of the Harijan child. Their efforts might not lead to any spectacular change in the attitudes of the Harijan child or their parents yet we cannot overlook the advantages inherent in the personal approach of the school teachers. This might help in dispelling any doubts or apprehension the Harijan parents carry in respect of weaknesses of the school system and also dispel strains in interpersonal relations of ill-treatment meted out to the Harijan child.

It is needed a matter of satisfaction that almost all teachers whom we interviewed perceived school drop out among Harijan children as a problematic situation. Out of 40 teachers, 27 considered it as a serious issue that needed immediate remedial measures. It is, however, unfortunate that the drop out problem did not receive much attention from the higher administrative machinery. In actual practice, no major steps seemed to have been taken to counter the menace of the dropping out of the Harijan children. Out of 40 teachers, only 14 reported that they discussed the drop out issue with the higher authorities. It was during school inspection, examination or other cultural programmes that the teachers conveyed their anxiety about drop out of Harijan children. Did the higher authorities make any positive attempts to examine the problem? The answer that we get is quite frustrating. Out of 40 teachers, 32 categorically emphasized that the higher authorities, did not at all refer to the drop out problem in personal meetings, inspection visits or through correspondence. These responses fairly illustrate that in the higher echelons the drop-out problem did not arouse much interest and hence it was accorded very low priority in the scheme of things undertaken at the higher level. The picture that ultimately emerges is one of more darkness and less light. At the higher levels of the administrative hierarchy, there is insufficient awareness about the problem. At grassroot level *i.e.* school, feeble efforts are carried out by some crusading school teacher. There are, as we have noted earlier, many substantial drawbacks and limitations under which the village schools are functioning. Improvements are needed on several fronts in order to effectively bring down the rate of drop-out incidence among Harijan children.

Role of the Village Community

The village community can play an important role in promoting educational standards. For any village school to grow and prosper, the support of the rural community is considered an essentiality. However, these articles of faith have mostly remained in the domain of ideals and in practice we see very little demonstration of positive community pressures working for the growth of education in a rural setting. Our experiences in this regard were not at all encouraging because in most of the villages there was a lack of any concerted community action or involvement in the educational sphere. No doubt in two or three places there was a contrasting picture but it was mainly due to personal interest and devotion of village leaders who themselves worked hard to bring up the school. But it was also true that they had failed to rally other people round their missionary enterprise. In this atmosphere of general apathy, it is rather too much to look out for any specific contributions of the village community towards the school system. All the same, it is necessary to examine correctly the attitudes of the village community and reasons for their lack of sustained participation in the school activities.

It may be mentioned that caste system, played a dominant role in every aspect of village life. Caste-Hindus believed in the concept of pollution and as a consequence, they did not generally tolerate the violation of the commensal rules and prescriptions. Caste-Hindus did not accept even water from the Harijans, leave alone sharing food with them. Harijans were not generally allowed to draw water from the wells located in the settlements of caste-Hindus. Harijans were usually not permitted to enter the house of a caste-Hindu and they had to wait in the outer courtyard if they wished to visit someone from the caste-Hindu family. Separate utensils or earthen wares were kept in some high-caste households to serve water or food items to the members of Harijan families who worked as labourers in their farms. These were common disabilities which the Harijans had to put up with. In the economic sphere, the Harijans occupied the lowest rung of the ladder. Most of them were landless or land poor, meaning marginal or sub-marginal land owners. Many Harijan families were traditionally attached to certain caste-Hindu households for undertaking all kinds of manual work. They could not break away from this traditional bondage because they had secured monetary and material help from the caste-Hindu families. Servility and bonded about had affected many a Harijan household.

The Gram Sabha, a village organisation, that came into being for the fulfilment of Panchayati Raj objectives has unwittingly become an instrument of perpetuating the existing caste hierarchy and fissions. In most cases, the leadership position of the Gram Sabha was in the hands of caste-Hindu. The role of the Harijan community in the Gram Sabha deliberations and activities had been at best a symbolic one, with no effective influence to determine its policies and programmes. Their social and economic handicaps have further weakened their position in the Gram Sabha. Leaders of the Harijan community complained of neglect and inattention shown to their basic grievances by the Gram Sabha representatives. It was their view that the Gram Sabha was not an effective agency to promote the interests of the weaker sections in rural areas. Rather, it was used by the caste-Hindu as a source of strengthening their social and economic hegemony at the cost of the poorer sections of the rural community.

In a socio-economic matrix described above, it is difficult to imagine that the village school could preserve its separate identity and ably perform its duties without fear or favour. The caste of school teacher was a matter of great importance to the village community. A teacher belonging to a higher caste was respected and given recognition by the caste-Hindus. If he came from a far away place, he was given accommodation and other basic facilities in the village where the school was located. For Harijan teachers, there were innumerable difficulties. It was essential for him to observe correctly the conventions and cultural prescriptions of the caste hierarchy. It was his caste and not his professional status that generally determined his relationship pattern with the village community.[7] Even his colleagues at school maintained a definite distance from him. At one place, it was reported, that the Head Master of a school who was a Brahmin by caste had asked his Harijan colleague to bring a bucket and tumbler from home despite the fact that these were already provided by the school administration. This Brahmin teacher did not want that the Harijan teacher should defile' the bucket and hurt his values on ritual purity. The Harijan teacher who gave us this piece of information begged of us not to reveal his identity as this would cost him his job in the village. Instances of similar nature may be many and it was common knowledge that discrimination on caste lines was practised, though in a muted form, in other village schools also.

As stated earlier, there was not much enthusiasm in the village community to participate collectively in the school activities. Literate members of caste-Hindu families as well as other influential persons like the lekhpal, land-lords etc. were reported to be maintaining a somewhat closer relationship with the school teachers with a view to guarding the interests of their school-going children. It was also evident that in the families of upper castes, there was encouragement and material support to the schooling children. In some households regular private tuitions were reportedly arranged to help the children to improve their learning capacity. For this work, the school teachers were paid in cash or kind or both. Besides, some teachers were keeping intimate relationships with the emerging power structure which was predominantly in favour of upper castes. Partly out of fear or insecurity and partly due to their own caste biases and predilections, some caste-Hindus teachers had no desire to act independently or to safeguard the interests of the Harijan children. Tendency to maintain physical distance from the children in the school, failure to provide them even drinking water from a well—owned by a caste Hindu; insistence on getting all sorts of manual work done through them; negligence in establishing rapport with the Harijan community and endearing them to the cause of education, the practice of punishing their own colleagues because of caste appellation; all these are clear illustrations of how some members of the teaching community failed to use a school system as an agency of social equality. Instead of the school bringing in new ideas and social experiences in a village community, it was itself moulded and conditioned to respond to the existing caste-based conventions, values and practices.[8] A silver lining to as otherwise dark picture was provided by the conscientious efforts of some Harijan teachers, and a few others belonging to upper castes but imbued with the genuine desire to help the poor and vulnerable families.

It is necessary to emphasize the contributions of Harijan teachers in the field of education of the backward classes. Possibly due to their own past experiences of living in poverty they were reported to be helping the other Harijan children in more than one way. Books, copies, slates and pencils, uniform and even food articles were provided by the Harijan teachers to those coming from poverty-stricken families. Besides free tuitions and guidance, some of them even gave monetary help to deserving Harijan students to take up higher education at district place. A word of assurance and help was certainly an incentive for parents to take more interest in the education of their child. Leaders in the Harijan community also took positive interest and helped the Harijan teachers in their mission. Though most of them were illiterate or semi-literate they realised the value of education to the Harijan children and to their community. Most of them felt that an educated Harijan can render far more effective service to the cause of the downtrodden community. Harijan leaders were mostly from poor families and hence could not offer financial help to others. Yet their indirect contributions in the form of encouraging and stimulating individual cases to continue schooling; arranging meetings between school teachers and Harijan parents, motivating parents, to send their children to school regularly; contacting teachers at school to enquire about the general progress of the Harijan children and pleading the case of more material and financial help to poor and deserving students, cannot be under-rated.

Village leaders who belonged generally to upper socio-economic strata were somewhat reticent and less active in this direction. Teachers maintained that village leaders' contributions related at best to specific issues like maintenance and repair of the school buildings, organisation of cultural programmes or sports meet, financial help in purchasing prizes or other minor items of educational importance etc. It was reported that as per the directive of the Basic Education office, a local Advisory Committee was required to be set up in every school to help the teachers to build bridges between the school administration and the community. Another objective behind the formation of this Committee was to develop the school as a socially viable institution, responsive to the needs and demands of all sections of the village community. But we were informed by the school teachers that the committee experiment had not yet taken the roots. In some villages the Committee die not conduct even its first meeting during the 10 to 12 months. In others, the committee had not conducted serious deliberations worth mentioning. It was argued that experiment such as this requires long-term planning and organisational resources which at present are missing. Whatever may be the strength of this argument, it was our experience that the village elders did not display requisite spirit and involvement in educational matters. Enrolment or drop-out issues were considered by most of them as outside their initiative and leadership functions.

In respect of rural education, even Gram Sabha's role has been minimal and largely related to material and not human aspects. To illustrate, the Gram Sabha helped the school to carry out repairs and provided free manpower and material towards that end. In some places, expansion of school buildings by constructing additional rooms was carried out with the financial help of the Gram Sabha. In some villages, money was made available to the school authorities by the Gram Sabha for purchasing educational material, prizes or refreshment items. In two villages the Gram Sabha constructed pucca roads and provided water facilities. By and large, however, most of the Gram Sabha units demonstrated limited involvement in the affairs of the village school. According to school teachers, it required continuous prodding to stir the Gram Sabha members for bringing about some improvement in the schools. The Harijan school at Rasra functioned within the jurisdiction of the notified area and yet it did not receive substantial help or assistance from the councillors. Out of 40 school teachers belonging to different village schools, 28 stated that their school received no help from the Gram Sabha.

It is necessary to mention that although village leaders did not take a very active part in the promotion of educational standards in the Harijan community, they were conscious of the importance of education to the community. Village leaders categorically stated that education constitutes a very valuable experience to those who belong to weaker sections. Responses received from 60 village leaders underscore the significance thus; importance of school education to Harijan children in terms of rise in social and economic status (41 responses); personal growth, good habits and manners (40 responses); better job opportunities (36 responses); getting rid of inferiority complex and low status (27 responses); accumulation of fixed assets like housing, land, tube-well etc. (13 responses), and smooth and early social assimilation (11 responses). There are, according to leaders, direct and indirect advantages to the Harijan family which educates the child up to a certain level. These were listed as; rise in the economic level (47 responses); improvement in the social status of the family (38 responses); a better future outlook towards education (27 responses); expansion of family resources (26 responses); freedom from unhealthy family tradition and wasteful community practices (11 responses); and relief from indebtedness (6 responses). If we scan through these perceptive answers we feel that the village leaders fully recognised the utility and beneficial impact of school education for Harijan children.

It is somewhat perplexing that despite this clear awareness, the village leaders had failed to exercise their influence in the education field and to help Harijan children to take benefits from the school system. We may identify two main reasons for the lack of involvement of village leadership in promoting the cause of education among the Harijan community. Firstly, those leaders (and they are the majority in any village) who have landed property feel that the schooling of more and more. Harijan children would ultimately result in reduction of manpower for agricultural labour. It is against their economic interest that the low caste children should receive education and later enter into occupations of different kinds. This would also constitute a break from traditional bonded relationship that existed in villages. Many leaders gave expression to these doubts and fears. Secondly, the present leadership which is predominantly in the hands of higher caste is likely to face rough weather if the younger generations of the Harijan community secure higher education and thereby strengthen its economic position. Such a direct threat has been experienced by the leaders in some villages. A respectable government position, regular income and expansion of agricultural holdings have been possible in some cases because the Harijan youth had acquired sufficient education. Such successful Harijans though they are few are now in the forefront of their community leadership. Village leaders may be aware that it is difficult to rule the literate and educated Harijans.

Against this background of very limited involvement of village leadership in the educational sphere, it is not surprising that out of 300 drop-out cases, only 36 (12 per cent) received some kind of attention from the neighbourhood. Harijan parents of these cases revealed that neighbours, friends, relative and school teachers had approached them for readmission, discussed with them their problems and difficulties coming in their way of readmitting children in schools. In the remaining 88 per cent of the cases there was not the slightest evidence of concern shown by the village community towards a drop-out child. This finding further reinforces our view point that by and large, other village institutions, organisations or influential persons had not taken up a positive role in respect of the educational activities of the Harijan children.

It is also important to note that there are very few formal, organised groups within the Harijan community and these exist in large villages only. Besides their functions are largely related to the cultural religious or political aspects and they hardly address to the educational needs of the Harijan community. Whatever involvement or participation in the educational activities of the Harijan children that we saw in the villages, came from a few individuals like influential persons from the Harijan community and some village leaders. Similarly, some Harijan and caste-Hindu teachers were seen striving towards bringing more and more Harijan children into the schools and helping them keep up their studies. But these efforts betray lack of consistent and determined involvement to promote educational goals among the lowest social group *i.e.* Harijans.

The whole question of school drop-out needs to be seen in a wider perspective of social and economic framework that exists in the villages. Caste variable assumes importance because of its social as well as economic current and under-currents. Hence the prevention of drop-out or other remedial measure should take into account the broader dimensions of the problem. In this respect, the Harijan family, the school system and the village community can help reduce the magnitude of the problem through their specific contributions. It is necessary to study the approaches with regard to drop out prevention as suggested by the Harijan parents, school teachers and the village leaders. These may provide some important hints in the direction of mitigating this problem.

REFERENCES

1. Among the Jatavs of Agra, Lynch has observed similar resentment. "There are some Jatavs also who, being crushed by them (by upper castes), think it to be a great sin to educate their children." See Owen M. Lynch, *The Politics of Untouchability*, Columbia University Press, 1969, p. 69.
2. Khandekar writes: "Non-economic reasons are more important at the primary and the secondary stages than at the middle stage of education". She, however, makes a forceful argument that, "Although a very large number of the respondents gave non-economic reasons for dropping out, it should be noted that lack of money was the single most important answer." (see her: A study of Drop-outs, the Indian Journal

of Social Work, Vol. xxxiv, No. 4, Jan. 1974, p. 377).

3. The Education Commission Comments: "A child from a rural household or an urban slum having illiterate parents does not have the same opportunity which a child from an upper class home with highly educated parents has."

4. Andre Beteille writes in his essay on *Pollution and Poverty*. Not only are Harijans at the bottom of Indian society, but in purely material terms their levels of living are far below those of comparable strata elsewhere. Although not all 60 million Harijans are destitute, the lives of a vast majority are characterized by uniform conditions of poverty." (See J. Michael Mahar (Ed.). The Untouchables in Contemporary India, the University of Arizona Press, Tueson, Arizona, 1972, p. 412).

5. "Economic privation of parents is the main reason for poor attendance of children in school; the position is getting worse with mounting inflation." (The Hindu, Madras, July 8, 1974).

6. Report of the National Seminar on Public Cooperation in the Field of Elementary and Social Education, Government of India, Planning Commission, 1963, p. 7. In this report, condition of primary schools in Tamil Nadu is graphically described.

7. A Khalapur study provides a graphic description of the social status of Harijan teachers. It says: "This untouchable teacher avoided situations involving interaction with upper caste villagers outside the classroom. On the few occasions where interaction of this kind was observed, both parties were embarrassed by problem of seating which was resolved by placing the untouchable teacher on a separate cot. After one situation of this kind the Rajput housewife insisted that the men of her family who had sat with the chamar bathe before she would serve them food. (See *the Agents of Dharma* in the Untouchables in Contemporary India, *op cit.*, p. 23).

8. Even Harijan students were required to obey the prevailing code of conduct demanding isolation from the community on selective occasions. J. Michael Mahar writes: "These untouchables sat in the classrooms with uppercaste students and participated in the full curriculum, but they kept to themselves in most situations and they were not allowed to use the school dining facility. Untouchables from other villages resided in the untouchable quarters of Khalapur rather than in the school hostel." See his Agents of Dharma in the Untouchable in Contemporary India, *op cit.*, p. 27.

7

Education and Social Mobility Disparities among Dalit and Non-Dalit Student Communities

Introduction

Formal education, especially higher education, has been considered the main instrument of modernisation. That is, education is supposed to be a means of occupational mobility and as such has been considered to provide equality of opportunity for the Scheduled Castes and Tribes. (Government of India: Commissioner for Scheduled Castes and Tribes, 1965: 15). Accordingly, the Government of India has been taking radical measures to raise their socio-economic status, mainly by providing greater concessions in higher education and reserving 15 per cent of the vaccancies for recruitment and a certain percentage for promotion in Government services for them. However, the policy makers seem to have seldom thought about the relationship between education and social background — Caste and Class. For example, it may be asked whether the present system of elitist education, a colonial heritage, can bring about occupational mobility among the Scheduled castes and Tribes students who come from a low social background — (ritual and class status) and who suffer from a number of social disabilities. The available data and studies carried out to date show that only a small proportion of Scheduled Castes and Tribes students have been able to reap the major benefits of higher education and modern (white-collar) occupations. Instead of providing equality if opportunity to all as envisage by the Constitution framers and national policy-makers, the present system of education is creating new inequalities (Chitnis, 1972; Premi, 1974). Evidence also shows that the incidence of stagnation and drop-out is higher among the Scheduled Castes and Tribes than among the Non-Scheduled Castes students (Aikara, 1980). Thus the lofty idealism of building an egalitarian society cannot be achieved merely by providing economic facilities or extending concessions. It is more important to take note of the model of modernisation, namely, the system of education which we adopt as the main means of upward mobility. The whole question of modernisation-mobility through education among the Scheduled Caste and Tribe students should be viewed in the broader—context of their social background which acts as an ancillary agency of socialisation and through which they perceive the opportunity structure.

Caste System: Sociological Parameters

Caste, as a social institution, has both ritual and non-ritual or secular dimensions. On the one hand, it refers to ritual status, and on the other hand, it means class status. Thus, the institution of caste includes both sacred and secular or ascribed and achieved dimensions. (Sharma, 1980). Caste may be further viewed in terms of one's social background consisting of ritual and/or secular status of family, kin, peers and neighbours and rural/urban background. An individual has by virtue of his membership of a given caste/class, a corresponding broader or narrower social background in which he participates. To be specific, an individual may have a ritual background on the one hand, and a differing class background on the other: say his ritual background consists of his family's, kins', peers' and neighbours' caste status and rural background. On the other hand, his class background, consists of his family's kins' peers' and neighbour's class status and urban background. We shall call the former as, "ritual social background" and the latter as "social class background." However, it should be borne in mind that these two types of social background are not watertight compartments; they are interdependent. In actual practice, an individual's social background is a combination of ritual and social class background in varying degrees. By and large, there is a close correspondence between caste and class status; a low caste status means a low social class background, and a low class status means a low ritual social background. Available evidence shows that it is only a small proportion of lower-caste members who have a higher class status (Singh, 1978).

The occupations one chooses or aspires for reflect one's self-identification in the status hierarchy. According to Super and Bohn (1970;108): "A person's self-concept, his picture of himself, influences his actions and helps determine the occupations he prefers, the kind of training he undertakes, and the degree of satisfaction he experiences on his jobs." Bordin (1943) postulated that in answering an "interest inventory," a person indicates his concept of himself in terms of his acceptance of occupational stereotypes. The matter of self-concept is thus translated directly into attitudes and behavioural patterns related to occupations.

The individual member acquires his self-concept or self-image through the process of socialisation. In short, self-concepts are formed in early experiences with other people and with life situations; they are translated into occupational preferences through goal-identification, early experiences and observation. They are reflected in educational and occupational choices and refracted by the resulting experiences. Situational determinants particulars relevant to the self are the role expectations of others, which are incorporated into the self-concept, which an individual forms of himself tentatively after he has perceived the role on his own.

According to Erikson (1950), the social self, in terms of social perception, crystallises through the process of identity formation, which mainly refers to a psycho-social self-definition, the choice of an occupation and marriage partner, when the youth passes from childhood roles to adult ones. Social background, in terms of social stratification, plays an important role in moulding self-concepts of the individual members. Social Action theorists (Parsons *et. al.*, 1951) argue that actors tend to develop differential motivation which, in turn, is the result of the position occupied by them during their pre-adult socialisation period. That means that the very perception of roles in terms of higher/lower aspirations is determined by the type, favourable/unfavourable, of social background of which the individual is a part. For instance, an upper-caste member is, because of his high ritual status, more likely to aspire for a high and clean occupation, while a backward and a scheduled caste student, because of his socialisation into low ritual values is more likely to aspire for lower and unclean occupations. A high ritual status also enables the upper-caste members to have more contacts with upper-caste-and-class members who act as agents of anticipatory socialisation. Similarly, social class background plays an important role in socialisation. For instance, family class status determines one's material life-chances such as standard of living, housing, clothing and food. Children coming from the upper-classes have better material facilities than do the lower-class families. Better material facilities, thus, provide an initial advantage to the children of the upper classes and enhance their self-concept. Parents with low class status may not only fail to encourage their children to achieve, they may not even recognise the achievement of their children unless their attention is drawn to it. Upper-class children are also likely to perceive higher occupational goals because of early counselling and guidance. Their self-concept is further enhanced and reinforced by their upper class kins, peers and neighbours and urban background.

The main objective of the study was to analyse the part played by social background (caste and class) in influencing the occupational aspirations of SC students *vis-a-vis* non-SC students.

It was hypothesized that *(a)* the occupational aspirations of the SC students were likely to be lower than those of the non-SC students when the effect of social class background was controlled and *(b)* the occupational aspirations of the SC students with a low social class background were likely to be lower than those of the non-SC students with a middle and high social class background.

The universe of the present study consisted of all the pre-university second-year students (1002, Hindus) studying in all the colleges of Gulbarga city (Karnataka) during the year 1979-80. The data for the study were collected by administering a semi-structured questionnaire in English and in Kanada. The social class background of the respondents was measured by constructing a Composite Index for Class Background (CICB). The index consisted the respondents' family class status — fathers' education, occupation, and income (FCS), kins' class status — educational and occupational status of kin-members such as grand parents, uncles and siblings (KCS), peers' class status — intimate peers' fathers' occupational and status (PCS), neighbours' class status — educational and occupational status of the neighbours with whom the respondent interacted frequently (NCS), and Rural-urban background — village, town and city.

Salients of Sample

A large proportion of the respondents were in the age group of 16-20. The mean age for the population was 18.98. The SC students were older than the non-SC students. While 74 per cent of students were from such castes as Brahmins, Lingayats, Marathas, Reddys and Kurubas, 25 per cent were from the Scheduled Castes and Tribes. The analysis further revealed that a majority (75 per cent) of the non-SC castes students came from a higher social class background. The fact that higher education continues to be the privilege of the upper castes and classes, shows that the present system of higher education is not suited to a large number of Scheduled Castes and Tribes who came from a lower class status and rural background.

Caste and Family Class Status: It be can seen from Table 7.1 that caste as a ritual status plays an important role in influencing the occupational aspirations of the SC and non-SC students among the low and middle-class families. Among the low class families, 74 per cent of SC students, as against 57 per cent non-SC students had low occupational aspirations. The data further show that 20 per cent of the SC students, as against 28 per cent of the non-SC, and six per cent of the SC students, as against 15 per cent of the non-SC, had middle and high occupational aspirations, respectively. It is clear that the occupational aspirations of the SC students were significantly lower than those of the non-SC students among the low class families.

An examination of the middle-class families shows that the occupational aspirations of the SC students were, to some extent, higher than those of the non-SC students. For instance, only 11 per cent of the SC students, as against 30 per cent of the non-SC students, had low occupational aspirations. It is further important to note that 64 per cent of the Scheduled Castes students, as against 33 per cent of the non-SC students had middle level occupational aspirations. However, the proportion of the SC students with higher occupational aspirations was lower (25 per cent) than that of the non-SC students (37 per cent). These analysis indicates that by and large, the occupational aspirations of the middle class SC student were higher than those of the non-SC students. Possibly, the reason may be that the socio-economic facilities provided by the Government have boosted the self-image of the SC students in higher education. A further analysis shows that the occupational aspirations of the SC students were higher than those of non-SC

Table 7.1
Percentages Showing Occupational Aspirations of Scheduled Caste and Non-Scheduled Caste Students by FCS

Occupational Aspirations	FCS								
	*Low**			*Middle**			*High*		
	S.C.	*Non-SC*	*Total*	*S.C.*	*Non-SC*	*Total*	*S.C.*	*Non-SC*	*Total*
1	2	3	4	5	6	7	8	9	10
Low	74	57	65	11	30	27	4	14	14
Middle	20	28	24	64	33	38	33	22	22
High	6	15	11	25	37	35	63	64	64
Total	100	100	100	100	100	100	100	100	100
	(200)	(274)	(474)	(61)	(279)	(340)	(27)	(261)	(288)

* The differences between S.C. and Non-SC in this columns are significant at .001 level of statistical significance. Also, the differences for S.C. in *(a)* Low and Middle FCS and *(b)* Low and High FCS are significant at .01 level of statistical significance.

students in higher FCS. However, the differences were not statistically significant. The main finding is that while a majority of SC students with low FCS had low occupational aspirations, those with middle and high FCS tended to have higher occupational aspirations that those of the non-SC students in the middle and high status families. One should not, however, rush to the conclusion that in the middle and high class families caste status has ceased to influence one's exception. This is because, the majority of SC students were drawn from a low FCS, while the majority of non-SC students were from middle and high status families. Therefore, a true picture would emerge when the occupational aspirations of the SC students with low FCS are compared with those of the non-SC students with middle and high FCS.

Caste and Kins' Class Status (KCS): Data in Table 7.2 reveal that the occupational aspirations of the SC students were significantly lower than those of the non-SC students with low KCS. It was also found that the occupational aspirations of the SC students with low KCS were lower than those of the non-SC students with middle and high KCS. For instance, 55 per cent of SC students with low KCS, as against 22 per cent and seven per cent of non-SC students with middle and high KCS, respectively had low occupational aspirations. Similarly, only 14 per cent of SC students, as against 51 per cent and 75 per cent of the middle and high KCS non-SC students, respectively, had high occupational aspirations (see columns 2 and 6, 2 and 9). It is clear that a low caste and low KCS and a high Caste and high KCS reinforce each other and influence the occupational aspirations of college students.

Caste and Peers' Class Status (PCS): Table 7.3 shows that there were significant differences in the occupational aspirations of the SC and non-SC students in the low PCS category, while in the middle and high PCS categories the differences were not statistically significant, because the proportion of the SC students in both the categories was low. The occupational aspirations of the SC students were significantly lower than those of the non-SC students with low PCS (see columns 2 and 3). This indicates that the low ritual status of the Scheduled Castes does not motivate for higher occupations. A comparison of SC students with low PCS with those of non-SC students with middle and high PCS shows that the occupational aspirations of the former were significantly lower than those of the latter (see columns 2 and 6, 2 and 9).

Table 7.2
Percentages Showing Occupational Aspirations of Scheduled Caste and Non-Scheduled Caste Students by KCS

Occupational Aspirations	*KCS*								
	*Low**			*Middle**			*High*		
	S.C.	*Non-SC*	*Total*	*S.C.*	*Non-SC*	*Total*	*S.C.*	*Non-SC*	*Total*
1	2	3	4	5	6	7	8	9	10
Low	55	41	46	13	22	20	33	7	9
Middle	31	29	29	37	27	28	—	18	17
High	14	30	25	50	51	52	67	75	74
Total	100	100	100	100	100	100	100	100	100
	(277)	(588)	(865)	(8)	(154)	(162)	(3)	(72)	(75)

* The differences between S.C. and Non-SC in this column are significant at .001 level of statistical significance. Also, the differences for S.C. in *(a)* Low and Middle FCS and *(b)* Low and High FCS are significant at .01 level of statistical significance.

Table 7.3
Percentages Showing Occupational Aspirations of Scheduled Caste and Non-Scheduled Caste Students by PCS

Occupational Aspirations	PCS								
	Low*			Middle*			High		
	S.C.	Non-SC	Total	S.C.	Non-SC	Total	S.C.	Non-SC	Total
1	2	3	4	5	6	7	8	9	10
Low	60	44	50	18	19	19	17	21	20
Middle	30	30	30	38	27	29	—	18	20
High	10	26	20	44	54	52	83	61	60
Total	100	100	100	100	100	100	100	100	100
	(248)	(494)	(742)	(34)	(190)	(224)	(6)	(130)	(136)

* The differences between S.C. and Non-SC in this column are significant at .001 level of statistical significance. Also, the differences for S.C. in *(a)* Low and Middle FCS and *(b)* Low and High FCS are significant at .01 level of statistical significance.

Table 7.4
Percentages Showing Occupational Aspirations of Scheduled Caste and Non-Scheduled Caste Students by NCS

Occupational Aspirations	NCS								
	*Low**			*Middle**			*High*		
	S.C.	Non-SC	Total	S.C.	Non-SC	Total	S.C.	Non-SC	Total
1	2	3	4	5	6	7	8	9	10
Low	62	52.29	56	14	27.00	26	40	19.10	20
Middle	29	29.29	30	38	29.94	30	20	18.47	18
High	9	18.32	14	48	43.04	44	40	62.42	62
Total	100	100	100	100	100	100	100	100	100
	(241)	(283)	(524)	(42)	(374)	(416)	(5)	(157)	(162)

* The differences between S.C. and Non-SC in this column are significant at .001 level of statistical significance. Also, the differences for S.C. in *(a)* Low and Middle FCS and *(b)* Low and High FCS are significant at .01 level of statistical significance.

Caste and Neighbours' Class Status (NCS): An examination of the part (Table 7.4) played by caste in influencing the occupational aspirations of the respondents, after controlling for the effect of NCS, shows that caste status did not make a difference for the occupational aspirations of the SC and non-SC students except, to some extent for the low NCS category. That is, the occupational aspirations of the former to some extent were significantly lower than those of the latter in the low NCS category. In the middle and high NCS categories, because of the low proportions of SC students, there were no significant differences in the occupational aspirations of the two groups.

A comparison of the occupational aspirations of the low NCS SC students with those of the middle and high NCS non-SC students (see columns 2 and 6 and 2 and 9) revealed that the former had lower occupational aspirations than the latter. It clearly shows that the SC students who mostly stayed in the low status neighbourhoods, had lower occupational aspirations than those non-SC students who, by and large, resided in middle and high status neighbourhoods.

Caste and Rural-urban Background: It will be seen from Table 7.5 that the occupational aspirations of the SC students were lower than those of the non-SC students from the village, town and city. However, the differences in the occupational aspirations of the two groups were significant in the village and city categories but not in the town category. This may be due to the fact that the distribution was due to chance. The data with regard to the rural respondents show that a majority of the SC students (81 per cent), as against a small per cent (45) of the non-SC students, had low occupational aspirations. Similarly, it was only 10 per cent of SC students, as against 31 per cent of non-SC students, and it was only nine per cent of SC students, as against 25 per cent of non-SC students had middle and high occupational aspirations, respectively. Despite a majority of the SC students having come from the city back-ground, their (SCs) occupational aspirations, were significantly lower than those of the non-SC students. For instance, while 41 per cent of SC students as against 28 per cent of the non-SC students had low occupational aspirations, it was only 22 per cent of the former, as against 47 per cent of the latter had high occupational aspirations, respectively. This clearly indicates the differential part played by caste status in motivating the aspirations of the respondents.

Table 7.5
Percentages Showing Occupational Aspirations of Scheduled Caste and Non-Scheduled Caste Students by Rural-urban Background

Occupational Aspirations	*Rural-urban Background*								
	*Village**			*Town**			*City*		
	S.C.	*Non-SC*	*Total*	*S.C.*	*Non-SC*	*Total*	*S.C.*	*Non-SC*	*Total*
1	*2*	*3*	*4*	*5*	*6*	*7*	*8*	*9*	*10*
Low	81	45	56	49	45	46	41	28	30
Middle	10	31	25	40	31	34	37	25	28
High	9	24	19	11	24	20	22	47	42
Total	100	100	100	100	100	100	100	100	100
	(80)	(186)	(266)	(67)	(136)	(203)	(141)	(492)	(633)

* The differences between S.C. and Non-SC in this column are significant at .001 level of statistical significance. Also, the differences for S.C. in *(a)* Low and Middle FCS and *(b)* Low and High FCS are significant at .01 level of statistical significance.

Table 7.6
Percentages Showing Occupational Aspirations of Scheduled Caste and Non-Scheduled Caste Students by SCB

Occupational Aspirations	*SCB*								
	Low			*Middle**			*High*		
	S.C.	*Non-SC*	*Total*	*S.C.*	*Non-SC*	*Total*	*S.C.*	*Non-SC*	*Total*
1	*2*	*3*	*4*	*5*	*6*	*7*	*8*	*9*	*10*
Low	69	68	68	8	35	31	9	16	15
Middle	27	25	25	51	36	39	22	21	22
High	4	7	7	41	29	30	69	63	63
Total	100	100	100	100	100	100	100	100	100
	(216)	(205)	(421)	(49)	(281)	(330)	(23)	(388)	(361)

* The differences between S.C. and Non-SC in this column are significant at .001 level of statistical significance. Also, the differences for S.C. in *(a)* Low and Middle FCS and *(b)* Low and High FCS are significant at .01 level of statistical significance.

Caste and Social Class Background (SCB): From table 7.6 it will be observed that the occupational aspirations of the SC students were significantly higher than those of the non-SC students in the middle and high SCB categories. In the low SCB category, however, the differences were neither statistically significant nor wide in terms of percentages. This was because, of the SC students, 75 per cent had come from a low SCB, while it was only 25 per cent of the non-SC students who had come from a low SCB. Obviously, the distribution of the data might have been due to chance.

An examination of the middle SCB category shows that eight per cent of SC students as against 35 per cent of the non-SC students, 51 per cent of SC students as against 36 per cent of the non-SC students and 41 per cent of the SC students as against 29 per cent of the non-SC students had low, middle and high occupational aspirations, respectively. A similar trend was observed between SC and non-SC students in the high CICB category.

It becomes evident that a small proportion of SC students with a high social class background tended to have higher occupational aspirations. That is, it was only the elite scheduled castes students who are making use of the facilities of modern education as an avenue of occupational mobility. However, it should not mean that the differences in the SC and non-SC students have eroded. For instance, a comparison of the occupational aspirations of the SC students with a low SCB and those of the non-SC with a middle and high SCB shows that the occupational aspirations of the former were significantly lower than those of the latter (see columns 2 and 6 and 2 and 9). This shows that the SC students continue to lag behind the non-SC students in their drive for mobility.

Conclusion

In summary, the lower traditions do not adapt themselves, as Singer (1972) and the Radolphs (1967) have demonstrated, to the demands of elite models of modernisation (education and occupation). On the contrary, modernisation (education) has to come to terms with the demands of tradition (low caste and class). This means a call for a two-pronged action on the part of the Government: *(i)* a change in the manner in which the socio-economic facilities to the Scheduled Caste and Tribes are being distributed now and *(ii)* a restructuring of the education system so as to suit the needs of low castes and classes. Indeed, there is a great need for research in the sphere of the sociology of education as an instrument of modernisation in India.

Notes

Aberlc, D.F., "Culture and Socialisation" in *Psychological Anthropology*, (Ed.) F.K. Hsu, Homewood, Illinois, Dossey Press, 1961.

Aikara, J., *Scheduled Castes and Higher Education: A Study of College Students in Bombay*, Poona, Dastane Ramachandra and Co., 1980.

Ambarao, U., "Higher Education and Occupational Mobility Among the Scheduled Caste Youth," *Journal of Higher Education*, Vol. 3, Spring, 1976.

Bordin, E.S., "A Theory of Vocational Interests as Dynamic Phenomena," *Educational Psychological Measurement*, 1943, pp. 314-317.

Brookover, W.B. and Gottlieb, D.A., *Sociology of Education*, New York, American Book Co., 2nd Edn., 1964.

Chitnis, S., "Education for Equality", *Economic and Political Weekly*, 7 (31-3), 1972, pp. 1675-81.

Edwards, A.L., *Techniques of Attitude Scale Construction*, Bombay, Vakils, Feffer and Simons Pvt. Ltd., 1969.

Erikson, E.H., *Childhood and Society*, New York, W.W. Norton, 1950.

Government of India 1965, Report of the Commissioner for Scheduled Castes and Tribes.

Premi, K.K., "Educational Opportunities for the Scheduled Castes: Role of Protective Discrimination in Equalisation," *Economic and Political Weekly*, Vol. IX, Nos. 45 and 46, No. 9, 1974, pp. 1902-10.

Parsons, T., *et al.*, *Towards a General Theory of Action*, Cambridge, Mass, Harvard University Press, 1951.

Rudolph, L.I. and Rudolph, S.H., *The Modernity of Tradition: Political Development in India*, Chicago and London, The University of Chicago Press, 1967.

Sharma, K.L., *Essays on Social Stratification*, Jaipur, Rawat Publishers, Jaipur, 1980.

Singer, M., *When A Great Tradition Modernizes*, Praeger Publications, New York, 1972.

Singh, Y., 'The Changing Pattern of Social Stratification in India' in Srinivas, *et al.*, (eds.) *Dimensions of Social Change in India*, New Delhi, Allied Publishers Private Limited, 1978.

Super, D.E., and Bohn, M.J., *Occupational Psychology*, Tavistock Publications, 1970.

8

Dalit Children and School System

The school system is supposed to offer the Harijan children an opportunity, on equal terms with others, to gain knowledge and enable them to rise in social and economic status. It allows them to learn and develop together with other caste children, to see and imbibe values of higher communities, the experience of and exposure to which was possible not available to their parents and grand-parents. Briefly, therefore, education can be conceived as a great human experiment in community interaction, a process of continuing learning. An act of dropping out, therefore, signifies an end of a potentially fruitful adventure, School drop-out stands for a withdrawal from a system which could eventually render a most valuable support to one's development. Then why do Harijan children drop-out from the school if the latter has the potency to deliver them goods? In this paper we will attempt to answer this question. It is observed that generally the explanations offered in reply to this question are too simplistic or evasive in nature with an implicit assumption that the actual situation does not admit of any complexities. This is really not the case, as we shall soon see. Being aware of these explanations and their implicit inadequacies, we have attempted here a more detailed analysis of the factors that are responsible for the drop-out of Harijan children.

Let us find out the reasons underlying the school drop-out of Harijan children. For this, a direct question was asked to the parents. "Why did your child stop going to school?" Investigators, who were asked to record detailed answers, did an excellent probing and came out with manifold dimensions of the problem.

Table 8.1 gives thirteen broad categories of responses in which the answer from Harijan parents are classified. It may be seen that the question on drop-out reasons elicited over two responses of discrete categories per case (623 responses from 300 respondents) and in this there was no significant gap between Rasra and Ranipur Blocks (293 and 330 responses respectively).

The most significant variable relating to drop-out is the incapacity of parents to meet the educational needs of the child (86 out of 300 cases). These include expenses for books, exercise note books, slates, pencils, etc. On enquiry it was reported that the Harijan Welfare Office in the region or the offices of Basic education were supplying, at irregular intervals, such items as text books, copies (exercise books) etc. But these supplies, extremely inadequate, were limited to a few schools. Harijans parents were, therefore, justified in claiming that no assistance or help was rendered to their children in this respect (all the 300 parents replied that they received no help whatsoever from educational authorities). Further, because of their poor financial conditions, the parents were unable to spend money towards these items. As long as they could, they helped the child as per their capacity. Continued lack of books and other material was stated to be the cause of child's declining involvement in school studies. Some school teachers, as part of their duty, requested the child to bring this material. Some reproached him for lack of such basic equipment. The child was, in most cases, helpless, and so were his parents. This resulted in school drop-out of some Harijan children.

Another variable (see again item ix of Table 8.1 contributing to school drop-out was the direct monetary liability on the part of Harijan parents. As over 80 per cent of Harijan parents were required to pay between Rs. 2 and Rs. 15 per annum towards fees. Though game fees charged to the students were reportedly nominal *i.e.* 10 N.P. per month per student, there were, in some quarters, other channels through which the school teachers reportedly used to collect money from students, both Harijans and Non Harijans. These practices were popularly known as 'Pass Karahi'; Centre Kharcha' and 'TC Expenses'. It was reported by some parents that the school children had to pay 'pass Karahi' meaning thereby payments for promoting the child to higher class. This payment, ranging between Rs. 2 and Rs. 10 collected as a matter of right by some teachers. Some parents even alleged that when this payment

Table 8.1
Drop-out Causes Indicated by Harijan/Parents

	Reasons	*Rasra Block (N=150)*	*Ranipur Block (N=150)*	*Total (N=300)%*
(i)	Domestic work including the care of infants	25	45	70 (11.1)
(ii)	For placing the child in gainful employment	26	21	47 (7.5)
(iii)	Sickness/death in the family	25	36	61 (9.8)
(iv)	Prolonged illness of the child	8	8	16 (2.6)
(v)	Distance, location and other incongenial aspects of the school	11	18	29 (4.7)
(vi)	Ill-treatment/Unhelpful attitude of school teachers	40	31	71 (11.4)
(vii)	Ill-treatment/dominance by schoolmates	12	12	24 (3.9)
(viii)	Unproductive school expe-riences, bad habits and traits in the child	14	22	36 (5.8)
(ix)	Lack of monetary support books, copies and other educational aids	48	38	86 (13.8)
(x)	Lack of interest in studies	37	40	77 (12.4)
(xi)	Inability to meet physical needs of the child	30	30	60 (9.6)
(xii)	Cultural factors: beliefs and values	14	27	41 (6.6.)
(xiii)	Any others	3	2	5 (0.8)
	Total No. of responses	293	330	623 (100.0)

was not made their children were detained in the same class by declaring them as failure cases. The second practice relates to the contribution realized from children of Class V appearing for the Zilla Parishad Examination. This examination was usually conducted at the Junior High School premises. It was reported that payments ranging between Re. 1 and Rs. 3 were collected from children to defray hospitality expenses on the examiners. Sometimes even tea and other hospitality arrangements during the inspection of a school were made reportedly at the cost of the school children. The last practice known as 'TC Expenses' relates to the payment demanded from the parents by the teaching staff to issue transfer certificate (TC) to the outgoing child. As the inter-school mobility was not very high in the villages, this demand affected primarily those students who desired to join the Senior Basic School after passing the examination in Class V.

When asked to opine, on the above mentioned practices many a school teachers tried hard to defend their school against such charges and in the same breath pointed an accusing finger at other schools. A few teachers, however, confessed that their meagre salary did not permit them to spend lavishly on those conducting school inspection or examination. Whatever, the facts the poor parents being coerced to make gratifications is in itself a most disturbing phenomenon. Children of other castes were equally affected by such unofficial demands, but many of their parents were probably in a better position to comply with these. Harijan parents, poor as they were, continued to pay to the school teachers and make sacrifices. But as their financial helplessness grew, they were constrained to drop the child from the school. Nearly one out of every three Harijan children was out of school due to lack of financial support and educational material (86 responses against Item-ix.

Another crucial reason for drop-out seems to be the lack of child's interest in studies (77 out of 300 cases). This particular drawback among children was highlighted by some Harijan parents in a state of emotional disturbance. The child became less and less punctual in his school attendance and home assignments, grew careless about examination and felt more secure at home than in school. Together with this attitude of indifference towards school, he showed signs of mental irritation whenever asked about school activities. Some parents bemoaned that their child reached aggressively and stubbornly refused to study at home. Quite a few parents were at a loss to understand the reasons behind such a sweeping change in the child from a peaceful and well-adjusted to a disturbed and aggressive behaviour. In some cases, the teachers reported the undesirable developments in the child to the parents and advised them to pay closer attention. In a few cases, the parents went to the school to request the teacher to help the child in studies. But efforts such as these proved infructuous.

That the unhelpful attitude of the teachers and illtreatment meted out by them to the Harijan students that forced as many as 71 of them (23 per cent of the total sample) to leave the school was another disturbing factor. Articulate parents gave a brief account of how their children were ili-treated, harassed and discriminated against. We may cite a few instances as reported by them. A major complaint of the parents in this group referred to the incidence of beating. A Harijan child was beaten up by the teachers for various reasons. It was, however, alleged by the parents that the teachers ill-treated the child simply because the latter could not fulfil their demands of 'Fee; 'Pass Karahi; Donations '(Chanda)' etc. In some cases, the Harijan child got scared of his teacher after witnessing the way the other children were handled in the class-room. Scolding, use of indecent language and wilful neglect of the child's interest were other dimensions of the teacher's unhelpful attitudes. It was also reported that the Harijan child was asked to sit away from other students. More humiliating were the assignments given by like teachers carrying their personal luggage, doing their domestic work and even rendering free help in agricultural operations. These are indeed very objectionable practices. At some places, it was reported, that Harijan children were not permitted to touch the blackboard, chalk or a book handled by the teacher. It is an irony that teachers whose hands should shape the personality of the child in a constructive manner, should practice such subtle forms of exploitation and harassment.

"But this happened and happens every day," said one Harijan parent agitatedly waving his hands in the air. He added:

> "When my child casually reported these happenings in the school. I hardly believed them to be true. I went to school and saw with my own eyes that Harijan children were accommodated in the rearmost part of the class, huddled together on a shabby may (which later I came to know was brought by one of the Harijan boys from home). All of these children (they were nine in total), were looking alike in dress and in everything. Why this separation? Why this isolation on caste lines? How my child and other children can learn better human values in this atmosphere? He will grow and die in this world in the same degraded manner as I would and as my

parents and grand-parents did. Education is force and nothing less than a force in the hands of these fanatic teachers".

He was fuming with anger when he ended his arguments. Could we say that he was projecting his prejudice and bias? No, probably he was moderate in his expressions, we felt. We ourselves saw and heard about many such instances. It would suffice to say here that practices, as outlined above, hurt many a sensitive child. The parents saw no justification in coercing the child to remain in the school.

Added to this discriminatory, debasing treatment meted out by the teachers was the highhanded, arrogant and aggressive attitudes of school mates mostly belonging to the upper castes. Though this was less prevalent, it is not an ignorable matter. Most of the Harijan parents spoke very mighty of the cooperative and helping attitudes of the caste-Hindu children. But those whose children were directly affected by the unseemly deeds of these uppercaste children were severely critical about them. How exactly were the Harijan children treated in such cases? A probing on this score revealed that in some schools, the most pampered and arrogant caste-Hindu children harassed the Harijan child, particularly the new entrants, by pinching, hitting or pulling his hair. They used to hide his slate, book and pencil. At the height of mischief, they used to break the slate or tear the book to pieces. In a few cases, they used to form a group (should we call it a gang) of their own and beat the Harijan child, bruise his arm or leg. Such incidents were a few in number but enough to alarm the whole community against the schooling prospect of a child. Nearly one out of every 10 Harijan children was a victim of such boyish banditry. Could we, then, simply dismiss this as an insignificant feature of school system or consider it seriously as a breeding ground for caste-hatred and rivalries among children? It is difficult to make a categorical statement for want of sufficient evidence.

We have already observed that Harijan children took an active part in the household activities. But the fact that pressure of domestic work should cause the drop-out of 70 children (23 per cent of the total) is at once surprising the discouraging. On their own showing, the Harijan children seemed to be handling very many aspects of household routine. The job of taking care of infants and younger siblings might have presented a barrier in his way of schooling. Since both the parents went out for work and remained out for uncertain hours, it fell to the lot of the unfortunate schooling child to wind up his studies in order to take care of the young ones. The case of the Harijan girls was more indefensible than that of the boys because they were the first to be asked to leave the school should there arise any need or eventuality at home.[1]

It is not out of place to mention that some parents, albeit a minority, were selfish and short-sighted. They used the services of the child for domestic work without showing any consideration for their age, interest and aptitudes. They were guided by the immediate, short range benefits. Cattle-grazing, sheep care, grass cutting and collection of firewood were the jobs some parents trusted on their children at the expense of their school education. Of course, this was not the case with the majority. Most of them were living from hand-to-mouth and yet striving hard to educate their children. Being agricultural labourers, they were unable to take the little child along with them. Nor could they leave him alone, unprotected. Similarly poverty taught them to be cautions of their little possessions like a pair of bullocks, sheep or goat which needed shepherding. When no alternative arrangements could be made, they were constrained to use the services of the school-going child. The net result of such engagements was the drop-out. We met many such families during the course of this enquiry and they confided their helplessness to us.

A far more pitiable fate than this was of those 47 families who discontinued the education of their child in order to employ him in some gainful activity. In what occupations could such young, tender-aged, semi-literate children be absorbed? As a full-time agricultural labourer? No, he was too young and ill-equipped to do that. He was placed into such minor occupations as assistance to farm labourers in sowing, weeding operations, selling firewood or basketware in the market, shepherding for others, domestic work for land-owning castes, casual work at brick kilns etc. Economic hardships gnawed at the vitals of their living and parents were compelled to employ gainfully their younger sons and even daughters. Such was the helplessness and plight of these Harijan families. At least one out of every 10 Harijan children in our study was condemned to adulthood tasks before his teens. (see Item ii).

It is difficult to establish a direct relationship between living conditions and the status of health. Yet we can make a reasonable guess that the Harijan families were not better placed in the matter of health. Poor working and living conditions, financial worries including heavy indebtedness, recurring drought situation entailing hunger and starvation; all contributed negatively to their physical well-being. Added to these were, in some cases atleast, the practice of liquor consumption, narcotic addiction etc. Illness in the family was, there, a recurring phenomenon. Lack of money prevented many of them from availing proper medical help and they tried indigenous herbal medicines which often failed to bring early relief. Prolonged illness of the bread-winner put out of gear the entire household economy. It further aggravated their plight. Schooling of the boys as well as girls, came to a halt as soon as the head of the family was bedridden. They were required to attend to the ailing and, luck and age permitting, compensate for the loss of earnings through engagements in gainful activity. Death of the householder was a devastating mishap which directly affected the schooling of the child. Every two out of 10 Harijan children were forced to leave their studies on the grounds of illness or death in the family. In 16 cases, prolonged illness of the school-going child led to his drop-out.

Another significant reason responsible for drop-out relates to the inability of Harijan parents to comply with the physical needs and requirements of the child. What could be the physical needs of the child attending a primary school? Regular breakfast or meals depending upon the school timings, a pair of clothes and possibly a pair of shoes. The last item, *i.e.* footwear was often dispensed with and the Harijan children were accustomed to attend school bare-footed. Clothing was however a problem to most of the Harijan families.[2] When at home, the children could carry on in rags. But in school, when other children came dressed in better clothes, it was indeed humiliating for the poor Harijan child to sit alongwith them. At some places, particularly in the Harijan special schools, even the rags could scrape through; but some families could not afford their children of even higher age remained half-naked, usually the upper garment totally torn or missing. Added to this were the subtle reactions of some sensitivity. Some purists among the teachers scolded the child for inadequate clothing and sent them back home for proper dress. Besides, some poor families could not keep a certain level of cleanliness and hygiene in respect of their children.

Absence of cleanliness and personal hygiene may be the result of many cultural factors including poverty, but this, accompanied by the untidy appearance of the child in the school, was a source of great mental conflict within the child. Parents did realise these problems but were either too helpless or insensitive to resolve these. How can they meet these expenses when many of them were acutely concerned about providing some minimum food to the school-going child? This question may appear superfluous but was in reality a valid one. There was such a horrifying level of poverty in some cases that families lived on borrowed food or cooked herbs and plants to survive. Sending a child to school in the morning was often-times a nightmare because the child had nothing to eat at home. Being hungry or half-starved he was hardly able to concentrate on his studies in the class-room. Many school teachers referred to this pitiable state as they observed it day in and day out. Sometimes, they did extend a helping hand but they could not afford to feed them regularly. Some Harijan parents, on the other hand, felt compelled to ignore the physical needs of their child on account of severe poverty conditions. The end result was the discontinuation of the child's studies which could not claim a priority in a situation where hunger and starvation reigned supreme.

Cultural values and beliefs among the Harijan community sometimes came in the way of the proper growth of children. Significantly enough there was a near-unanimity among them on one issue that higher education to girls of their community was totally undesirable. There was strong feeling that the girls should not be educated beyond junior basic level.

> "What she must know in the school is how to read and write. After all she is somebody else's property. She will be married and sent away from this house. If she knows by way of schooling enough to write a letter to us from her new home, that will be the sufficient achievement on her part."

Remarked one Harijan parent about his expectations of his daughter's education. This was the prevailing mood among most of the parents. There was some amount of diffidence and anxiety among them too. For instance, they thought that higher education would lead their daughter astray, expose them to upper-caste fads and fashions, enthuse them to mix freely with children of the opposite sex and would ultimately bring a bad name to their family and community. Some of these fears were poignantly articulated by the parents who stopped the education of their daughters with these convictions.

In some families, superstitions and beliefs of the elders were responsible for the stoppage of the boys' education. Recurring fever of the school-going child, any major accident inflicting physical injuries and such other events were interpreted as bad omens resulting from his schooling. They put it thus: "Education is harmful to him. It will not do him any good. Even his father had suffered a similar accident in his school days and had left his studies." Such credulous, superstitious ideas haunted many a Harijan father and when they were overwhelmingly supported by their other family members or community people, the natural consequence was to 'save the child' from potential deleterious influences of school. How incredible! yet these beliefs and values disrupted the educational career of 41 cases in our sample. (see Item xii)

In the case of 12 per cent of our sample (36 cases), unproductive school experiences were accountable for their drop-out. The Harijan parents explained that the child was learning bad habits, acquiring undesirable behaviour patterns. Telling balatant lies, absconding from school and playing truants, gambling and smoking were the major lapses which they personally noticed or had a report about. Infuriated as they were, they thought it wise to control his movement and hence stopped his schooling altogether. In a few cases, there were complaints from the school teachers about the Harijan child being violent in the class-room quarrelling with others and coming to blows with them.

Though relatively unimportant, factors such as distance and location of school also contributed to drop-out incidence in a few cases. Physical distance between the school and residence of a Harijan child was sometimes as much as two to three kilometres. Apart from distance, there were other obstacles like absence of walkable pathways, existence of nullah or drain-pits or similar obstacles which made the schoolward movement of a very young child extremely difficult and sometimes insecure. During rainy days the approach road to school was invariably inundated and it was a feat to reach school. Added to this was the appalling physical condition of school buildings, their roots leaking from all sides. Drenched and shivering, the children used to face all these odds. Some school buildings had developed deep cracks in the walls and the supporting pillars and were thoroughly unsafe. Lashing rains or storm could easily bring down the entire edifice within moments. School teachers showed us these cracks and the artificial props they had raised. Some parents were very much worried about their children's schooling in such ramshackle buildings. Briefly, therefore, nearly one out of every 10 Harijan children dropped out of the school because of its distance and location which made its accessibility less easy and also because of its dilapidated physical structure.

The forgoing analysis makes it more than clear that the problem of school drop-out among Harijan children is a complex one, having multiple reasons behind it. We may, however, integrate the items which have some proximate relationship among themselves and attempt to draw a coherent picture. There are 13 items in Table 8.1 detailing drop-out reasons. If we exclude the last category of a miscellaneous nature, we get 618 responses against 12 items by 295 respondents *i.e.* Harijan parents. We may classify these responses into five broad categories as shown in Table 8.2.

The picture that emanates from the above statement clearly reflects that poverty and associated handicaps are chiefly responsible for the drop-out incidence among the Harijan children.[3] The next contributory force to reckon with is the existing inadequacies of the school system. Punitive, unhelpful and impersonal attitudes of the school teachers as well as the aggressive and unfriendly acts of the school inmates seem to have created a credibility gap between the Harijan students and the school system. The last three categories are independent in themselves and relate to family or personal issues like sickness and death, declining interest of the child in studies and superstitious beliefs and values against the continuity of school education. By and large, the economic backwardness of the Harijan families and unreceptive and discourteous atmosphere in the school constitute two major barriers that lie at the root of the drop-out problem among Harijan children.

Information available in peer literature relates to the drop-out reasons as indicated by the children themselves. It appears that there is a great deal of similarity in the responses obtained from the children and their parents. Lack of educational equipments such as books, copies etc., is a most dominating reason. Curiously enough, over one-fourth of the children (45 out of 198) have stated that they left studies due to lack of interest. Among parents too, over 25 per

Table 8.2
Major Categories of Drop-out Causes
(based on the responses of Harijan Parents)

Major Category	*Inclusive Sub-categories and Responses*	*Total No. of Responses*	*%*
I. Poverty and Economic Hardships	*(a)* Child's gainful employment (47) *(b)* Lack of basic educational equipments (86) *(c)* Non-provision of physical needs (60) *(d)* Engagement in domestic work (70)	263	42.6
II. School and School-related Factors	*(e)* Distance, location etc. (29) *(f)* Behaviour of the school teachers (71) *(g)* Behaviour of school-mates (24) *(h)* Unproductive school impact (36)	160	25.9
III. Domestic Existencies	*(i)* Sickness/death in family (61) *(j)* Prolonged illness of the child (16)	77	12.5
IV. Individual Deficiency	*(k)* Lack of interest in studies (77)	77	12.5
V. Cultural Factors	*(l)* Beliefs, values, community reactions (41)	41	6.5
	Grand total of Responses	618	100.0

cent had attributed school drop-out to this factor (77 out of 300, see Table 8.1. If we group these items (excluding Item x) into broad categories as attempted previously (see Table 8.2) we would find identical gradations in emphasis. For instance, the category of

Table 8.3
Drop-out Causes Indicated by Children

	Reasons	*Rasra Block (N=108)*	*Ranipur Block (N=90)*	*Total* (N=198)%*
1.	Domestic work including infant care	10	18	28 (9.9)
2.	For placement in some gainful employment	9	6	15 (5.3)
3.	Sickness/death in the family	21	22	43 (15.3)
4.	Prolonged illness of the child	1	3	4 (1.4)
5.	Distance, location and other incongenial aspects of the school	6	4	10 (3.6)
6.	Ill-treatment/unhelpful attitude of school teachers or school mates	26	18	44 (15.7)
7.	Lack of books, copies and uniform	49	22	71 (25.3)
8.	Lack of interest in studies	21	24	45 (16.0)
9.	Physical needs not met	7	4	11 (3.9)
10.	Any others	3	7	10 (3.6)
	Total No. of responses	153	128	281 (100.0)

Note: * Out of 300 drop-out children, 102 children (42 from Rasra and 60 from Ranipur Block) were not available/suitable, for interviews. Responses shown in this table are from 198 cases only.

poverty and economic hardships (Items i, ii, vii, ix) would get 125 out of 271 responses, and would score a first position in the list. A less than half its total *i.e.* 54 responses are against the second category, namely school and school-related factors (Items v and vi). Domestic exigencies or crises constitute a third major category with a total of 47 responses. (Items iii and iv). A category underlining individual deficiencies has 45 responses and stands last in the numerical order. It is worth noting that the children, unlike their parents, made no reference to cultural factors. On the whole, there is substantial agreement between children, *i.e.* drop-out cases and their parents, regarding the causes that underlie the drop-out incidence.

A supportive evidence is available from other quarters also. A question asked to village leaders and school teachers regarding the factors responsible for drop-out among Harijan children elicited very interesting information. Similarly, Harijan parents who had earlier listed specific reasons for drop-out of their children were further asked to point out the factors contributing to school drop-out in the Harijan community. Views of the parents, leaders and teachers are summarised into broad categories as shown in Table 8.4. Analysis of response categories reveals boldly that economic hardships seem to play a major role in augmenting drop-out situation.

Next in importance is the factor that relates to the apathy and indifference of Harijan parents and child's lack of interest in studies. Significantly enough, even the parents have come out strongly against the prevailing negative attitudes of the Harijan family towards education of their children, though earlier they did not apportion any blame to themselves in respect of school drop-out of their own children. It is important to remember that the school teachers maintained a discreet silence over the inadequacies and deficiencies of the school system (only 0.7 per cent response). This is quite understandable because they probably felt it a risky exercise in self-evaluation. But village leaders and parents spared no words in criticising the inhibitive and discriminatory aspects of the school system. Almost with similar intensity, both these groups have condemned the unhealthy, crippling and regressive caste and community practices. This had reference to a practice of early marriage, liquor addiction, family feuds over petty issues, indebtedness on account of avoidable expenditure on

Table 8.4
A Composite Data in Respect of Major Categories of Drop-out Causes Indicated by Harijan Parents*, Village Leaders and School Teachers

*Major Categories***	*Response Percentage*		
	Parents (N=300)	*Village Leaders* (N=60)	*School Teachers* (N=40)
(i) Poverty and Economic hardships	47.8	51.6	53.6
(ii) School and School related factors	13.7	12.0	0.7
(iii) Domestic Exigencies	0.9	0.5	8.4
(iv) Individual Deficiencies	24.0	24.4	16.1
(v) Cultural Community Factors	13.6	11.5	11.2
Total No. of Responses	(766) 100%	(209) 100%	(143) 100%

* Responses recorded in this table refer to a different question relating to general causes contributing to drop-out problem in a Harijan Community.

** Categories listed here include, in addition to sub-categories (See Table 8.2) mentioned earlier, the following:
Item I: Lack of facilities at home.
Item IV: Parental apathy and indifference.
Item V: Unhealthy caste and community influences.

rituals and ceremonies and blind faith in superstitions. It was their contention that all these forces ran counter to the educational interests of the Harijan child. Domestic exigencies, which accounted for the drop-out of at least one-fourth of our sample (77 cases), find the rear-most place in the general assessment of the parents, teachers and village leaders.

If we consider the various reasons and factors responsible for drop-out among the Harijan children covered in our study, we may reach a conclusion that economic backwardness of Harijans is a dominant factor underlying drop-out, incidence. Other factors of varying significance can be listed as incongenial school atmosphere, domestic exigencies, lack of involvement on the part of parents as well as children in the school activities, and unfavourable influences of caste and community. Each of these factors, singly or in combination, seems to generate an atmosphere in which the schooling of the Harijan child becomes an impossibility. These factors may be analytically distinguished but cannot be separated in reality because of their interlinkage. Apathy of parents or vagrancy of the child may be the result of poverty conditions. In view of this, it was considered necessary to perceive the situation in its totality. Dropping out of the school is a complex event encompassing various trends. Evidence that we have here amply proves the point.

Information on the age at which the Harijan child drops-out from the school system is vital because it can enable us to formulate suitable preventive programmes for such cases. Data obtained in this respect (Table 8.5) suggests that over 72 per cent of drop-out cases (217 out of 300) were below 10 years of age. Of these 217 cases, 100 belonged to the age-group 9-10 years. In other words, one out of every three drop-outs (100 out of 300) belonged to the age group 9-10 years. The mean age for the total sample stood at 9.3 years (9.4 years for Rasra block and 9.2 years for Ranipur block). These are the indicators which prove that the moment the children from the Harijan community reach a critical age of 8-9, or 10 years they withdraw from the school system. At this stage and onwards the usefulness of children for domestic help and outside activities becomes intensive. The Harijan families begin to view their children as working assets.

Table 8.5
Age Factor in Harijan Children Drop-out Rate School System

Drop- out Age	*Rasra Block*	*Ranipur Block*	*Total (%)*
Below 7 years	15	9	24 (8.0)
7 years	27	12	39 (13.0)
8 years	21	33	54 (18.0)
9 years	22	29	51 (17.0)
10 years	18	31	49 (16.3)
11 years	15	19	34 (11.3)
12 years	14	9	23 (7.6)
13 years and above	18	8	26 (8.8)
Total	150	150	300 (100.0)

Now we can turn our attention to other crucial aspects of the drop-out situation. Who in the family generally takes the decision about dropping the child from the school? The answer that we obtain in our study (Table 8.6) is somewhat unexpected. Though, in nearly seven out of ten cases (69.3 per cent) the decision is reported to have been taken by the father, mother or other elderly person from the child's family, it is really strange that in 30 per cent of cases, the drop-out child himself was the sole arbiter. In other words, three out of every 10 children who dropped out of the school, were doing so on their own initiative.

Table 8.6
Question: Who in Your Family Took the Decision of Not Sending Your Child to School? (Parent's Version)

Response	*Rasra Block*	*Ranipur Block*	*Total (%)*
Father	60	69	129 (43.0)
Mother	35	32	67 (22.3)
Child himself	45	47	92 (30.7)
Other Relatives	10	2	12 (4.0)
Total	150	150	300 (100.0)

There can possibly be two explanations for this trend. First, the parents who were asked this question, might have felt little unnerved and hence might have shifted the onus of drop-out decision to their child to conveniently escape from the moral responsibility. Perhaps they did not like to project themselves as irresponsible, careless guardians forcing their child to leave school education halfway. A second explanation could be that the answers are representative of a true position: parents were unwilling or indecided but the child was bent upon withdrawing from the school system. It appears likely that in view of the drop-out reasons mentioned earlier, the latter may be the case. The Harijan child did not find school education a very rewarding experience due to ill-treatment of teachers, unsociability of schoolmates and some incongenial aspects of school itself. He was also suffering from want of books, copies and other educational aids which could help him sustain his interest in school activities. In some cases, neglect of his physical needs was the most dominant disincentive in schooling efforts.

Lack of interest in studies (affecting 77 cases) could be a consequence of the above-mentioned deprivations. These are sharp indications of child's disenchantment with school education. It may, therefore, be possible that the child himself opted against the continuity of school studies. Broadly speaking, however, the child's parents have taken decision in dropping him out of the school.

Table 8.7
Main Consideration Behind the Drop-out Decision

	Main Consideration	*No. of Respondents*
(i)	Relief from school expenses	80 (38.5)
(ii)	Physical help from the child	39 (18.7)
(iii)	Cultural factors, beliefs and attitudes	32 (15.4)
(iv)	Unhealthy school experiences	30 (14.4)
(v)	Economic help from the child	27 (13.0)
	Total	208* (100.0)

* This figure excludes 92 cases wherein the respondents have treated the child as a decision-maker in drop-out situation.

Why did the Harijan parents decide to drop their child from school? What was the main consideration behind their decision? Answers to this question are recorded in Table 8.7. Earlier we had obtained from parents various reasons which contributed to the drop-out of the child from school. Here we shall deal with those factors which are of primary significance in the decision-making process. In other words, the statements or reasons advanced by the parents can be construed as major causes leading to drop-out decision. Understandably, only 208 respondents have replied to the question as they were directly responsible for taking a decision in the matter. The data is quite instructive and once again highlights the economic incapacity of Harijan families. If we combine the figures against Items (i), (ii) and (v), we notice that in nearly 50 per cent of cases (146 out of 300), the Harijan parents decided to keep the child at home due to their financial inability, pressure of domestic work (which frequently emanates from economic hardships) and urgency of some economic support through the employment of the child. This finding squarely supports our earlier contention. It is interesting to note that 62 out of 208 respondents (over 20 per cent in a total sample of 300 decided to stop school education of their child on account of their beliefs and attitudes (which favoured less education) and unpleasant school experiences of the child. The former reason refers to their culturally-conditioned, tradition-bound way of thinking while the latter throws light on the unhealthy, discriminatory practices prevalent in the school. By and large, the economic helplessness, traditional thinking and unproductive school experiences were the three main considerations which acted as a driving force in drop-out situations.

It would be interesting to find out whether the issue of school drop-out of a Harijan child was treated as an insignificant, trivial matter in his family or whether it created some flutter, some argumentative situation with exchange of views between father and mother or between parents and other elderly persons in the family. It was indeed heartening to note that drop-out became a serious subject to discussion in 135 families (45 per cent of the total sample). Whether it was father, mother or the child who ultimately decided to remain out of school, the very decision was discussed and debated in these families, some members supporting and some opposing the decision on various considerations. It is indicative of awareness and involvement of family members in the child's educational prospects. It is, however, unfortunate that in 55 per cent of cases, there was no such anxiety or curiosity and the matter was allowed to be settled unilaterally by the father, mother or a child. In these cases evidently no concern was shown about the future of the child's education.

It is quite apparent that parents who had enrolled their child in the school, should feel unhappy and dejected in the event of their child's dropping out of the school; this has indeed been the case in our study (Table 8.8). To a question: "What did you/your wife feel when your child stopped going to school?" 196 fathers, and 204 mothers were reported to have felt unhappy. Surprisingly, a somewhat different position obtains in regard to a drop-out child.

According to the parents' estimate, nearly 40 per cent of children felt 'happy', over 10 per cent 'indifferent' and around 50 per cent 'unhappy' immediately after drop-out. A fact that quite a large number of drop-out cases had no sense of grief over the loss of school education is very disconcerting. Were they too young and immature to evaluate their prospects? Did they consider a drop-out an opportunity to escape from frustrating and humiliating experiences in school and at home? We have no answers to these questions. But it would be sufficient to conclude that a majority of parents and a fairly large number of drop-outs themselves felt anguished and disheartened for the loss following the discontinuation of school studies.

Table 8.8
Feelings of the Father, Mother and the Child (Drop-out Cause) Immediately After Drop-out: (Parent's Version)

What did they feel?	*Father (%)*	*Mother (%)*	*Drop-out Child (%)*
Happy	51 (18.9)	66 (22.8)	116 (38.7)
Indifferent	22 (8.2)	19 (6.6)	37 (12.3)
Unhappy	196 (72.9)	204 (70.6)	147 (49.0)
Total	269 (100.0)	289 (100.0)	300 (100.0)

If we consider feelings of happiness, indifference and unhappiness as equivalent to positive, neutral and negative reactions to drop-out incidence, we obtain the following position (Table 8.9). In all, 266 families in whose cases the reactions of all the three persons were available, are distributed within two polar limits of extremely positive and extremely negative reactions towards drop-out situation. The result is clear enough to suggest that 62 families had a positive or favourable reaction; only 9 families seemed to be neutral while a large majority of 195 families (nearly two-third of the total sample) were negatively disposed towards drop-out. This further demonstrates that a large number of families have acted under compulsions of social and economic reality, disregarding their personal preferences and volitions.

Table 8.9
Family Reactions to Drop-out Incidence*

Reaction Range	*No. of Families (%)*
Extremely positive	34 (12.8)
Moderately	28 (10.5)
Average/Neutral	9 (3.4)
Moderately Negative	104 (39.1)
Extremely Negative	91 (34.2)
Total	266 (100.0)

* *Note:* It is a composite table based on the addition of scores assigned to each scale. Family includes father, mother and a drop-out case and the reaction evaluation is made by the respondent. For father and mother, a three point scale was given assigning scores as follows:
Happy-1; Indifferent-2; Unhappy-3.
For the child, a five-point scale was designed with the following values:
Very Happy-1; Happy-2; Indifferent-3; Unhappy-4; Very Unhappy-5.
The computation was done in two stages. First, the child's score was recorded by assigning values as under:
1 to 1 or 2; 2 to 3; and 3 to 4 or 5.
Secondly, individual scores of father, mother and child were combined with a result that the total score range varied between 3 and 9.

Though we have the evidence that a large number of children did not show unhappiness or grief over loss of education, parents themselves have given us an inkling of the child's mind when a question in another direction was posed to them. When asked whether the child (drop-out case) had expressed his or her desire to rejoin the studies, 115 have answered the question in the affirmative. In other words, as per parents reports, at least one out of every three drop-out children, had openly expressed their willingness to restart their chequered career. Of these cases, 62 belonged to Rasra while 53 came from Ranipur Block. When a somewhat similar question was asked to children themselves, 72 out of 198 cases (36 per cent) gave positive replies stating that they strongly felt like continuing their studies. These are indeed significant results pointing towards the child's positive frame of mind in respect of school education. A further proof in this respect can be had from the school teachers. When asked, "Do you think that the Harijan children who dropped out were unwilling to discontinue their studies?", 23 out of 40 school teachers replied 'most of them', four 'some of them' and 13 'a few of them'. A majority opinion among the school teachers was that most of the drop-out cases were in fact favourably disposed towards school education and had shown willingness for its continuation.

It was assumed that withdrawal of a child from the school on a permanent basis might lead, at least in some cases, to some behavioural changes among them. This assumption proved to be correct in 86 cases (nearly 29 per cent). These children showed specific changes in their behaviour and dealings with their parents and other family members, friends and neighbours. Their behaviour immediately after drop-out alternated between over aggressiveness and passive, negative withdrawal. As one sensitive mother put it thus:

> "The day after his schooling was discontinued; he started cold-shouldering every one in the family, including his youngest sister. He roamed about in the neighbourhood listlessly and ignored even our slightest demand. He used to come home twice in the day, to take afternoon meals and spent the night. If I tried to penetrate into his thoughts, he would burst out saying all were keen to tie him to the job on land and waste his life toiling. This temperament of his lasted for over six months".

Similar instances were quoted by countless others. Weeping and crying; shirking work; spoiling food and breaking dishes; abusing parents; avoiding friends and relatives; these and many other behavioural postures were adopted by those children who felt seriously jolted by their separation from school.

Dropping-out of a child is not an isolated instance and it may have repercussions on a wider front. For instance, the drop-out of an elder brother might affect the studies of the younger one. It might set an unhealthy precedent in the neighbourhood. If a drop-out child is sociable and has leadership qualities, other neighbouring children who felt secure and happy under his stewardship might soon follow his example. It is, therefore, necessary to view the drop-out problem as consequential, oftentimes capable of introducing many undesirable trends in the family or locality. This argument receives some support from our data (Table 8.10). In 15 per cent of cases, the parents have reported that the other school-going children in the family were affected by the drop-out of a single case. Either they stepped into his shoes or started comparing their own performance with that of a drop-out case. This led to quarrels and unpleasant feelings within the family. Another 17 per cent of cases were those where the impact spilled over to the locality. Children in the neighbourhood started neglecting their studies. Some even stopped going to school. Out of every 10 drop-out cases, three were reported to be positively responsible for adverse effects on school going children in the family or locality. These facts got to prove that impact of drop-outs registers itself not only in the family but it also extends to the neighbourhood.

Table 8.10

Question: Did the School Drop-out of Your Child Adversely Affect the Education of Other Child/Children of Your Family in the Locality?

Reply	*No. of Respondents(%)*
Yes, family children affected	45 (15.0)
Yes, locality children affected	51 (17.0)
No. none was affected	204 (68.0)
Total	300 (100.0)

The drop-out child himself suffered a great deal in terms of learning on account of the absence of any opportunity to practise things at home. While at school, he could read and write, try his hand in drawing and painting, take part in cultural activities and above all play and make friends. Dropping out meant reduced chances to develop his faculties in any of these spheres. The data in this respect gives clear indications of how the drop-out affected the Harijan children (Table 8.11). It was observed that out of 300 drop-out cases, over 57 per cent (172 cases) of them totally abandoned the practice of any of the school subjects or activities. In other words, only four out of ten drop-out children practised at home what they earlier learnt at school. The data clearly show that in each of these areas of learning, there was a steep fall in the number of children showing engagement in activities after drop-out. Surprisingly, even under the category of 'games and sports' there were only 16 children reported to be actively associated with it. In the pre-drop-out situation, the corresponding figure was as high as 159. A comparatively higher number of children seemed to be retaining their knowledge of reading and writing. By and large, the children who dropped out seemed to show little concern or involvement in the subjects or activities they learnt at school and which stimulated them most during the school career. In plain terms, this can be considered as a substantial loss both to drop-out cases as well as to the school administration which invested so much resources for imparting education.

Table 8.11
Showing Drop-out Impact on Learning Areas/Subjects

Subjects/Areas	*No. of children practising subjects at home after drop-out*	*Percentage of children practising the subjects after drop-out (%)*
Reading and writing	77 (199)	38.7
Games and Sports	16 (159)	10.1
Arithmetic/Minor calculations	28 (110)	25.5
Singing/dancing etc.	12 (49)	24.5
Drawing/Painting	4 (45)	8.9
Clay modelling/Craft/Needle work	12 (42)	28.6

(Figures in bracket refer to No. of children reported to have learnt the subjects/activities during the course of schooling)

What was the daily routing of a drop-out child? In which

activities, did the drop-out child engage himself/herself? Data in this matter is recorded in Table 8.12. For purposes of comparison, we have also recorded the routine activities performed by the Harijan child during his school career. Results that we obtain from the table are quite starting. In the first place, it demonstrates (see the foot-note to the table) that the number of children who extended their help in household and other activities has increased from 256 to 289 after their drop-out. Secondly, the number of children in some activities has remained more or less stationary and these activities are: cattle or sheep grazing, household work, looking after younger children etc. After drop-out, more children have taken to farm labour, grass cutting, help in the studies of younger children and independent jobs for earning a livelihood and income supplementation.

Table 8.12

Type of Work in Which the Harijan Child was Engaged Before and After Drop-out

Type of work activity	*After drop-out* (1) (N=289)	*Before drop-out* (2) (N=256)	*Proportionate difference of* (1) over (2) (%)
Farm labour	55	34	+ 61.8
Grass cutting	137	108	+ 26.9
Household work	141	144	— 2.1
Cattle/sheep grazing	124	126	— 1.6
Looking after younger children	65	67	— 3.0
Help in the studies of younger children	22	16	+ 37.5
Independent employment	83	16	+ 418.8
Any others	29	14	+ 107.7

(Out of 300 children, eight in Rasra and three in Ranipur block did not offer any help in domestic or other duties after drop-out. Corresponding figure in pre-drop-out situation was 44).

In fact, there has been a five-fold increase in the number of children doing independent jobs after drop-out. It was learnt from parents that these jobs covered domestic work in the families of higher castes, work at construction sites, casual jobs like house repairing or processing at brick kilns, pulling of cycle-rickshaw etc. Considering that physical strength and age were the limiting factors, it is still amazing that over one-third of the drop-out cases were engaged in independent employment. This finding testifies to the earlier evidence that the economic backwardness of Harijan families contributed a major hurdle in the advancement of their younger generation.

If we recall at this juncture the parent's statement on drop-out reasons (Table 8.1) we would notice that only in 47 cases, did gainful employment constitute one of the factors in drop-out incidence. Later, we were told that only in 27 cases, the employment of the child remained a primary consideration (Table 8.6). In practice, however, this number rose to 83 and this signifies the shaky status of the Harijan's household economy. This data also explains why a large number of children have lost touch with what they had acquired in the school. Once loosened from the school context, the children tended to drift away. Domestic work which claimed only a part of their time during school career, could now absorb most of their time. Whether willing or not, the Harijan child had to support the household in its daily chores, inside or outside. It was, as it were, their inescapable destiny.

Differences in time devoted to household and related activities by the child while he was in school and after he dropped out are distinctly representative of dissimilarities in the rhythm of life, before and after drop-out. When in school, the Harijan child treated his school as a major interest and played at best a supportive role in the household affairs. But after drop-out, he had to devote the major part of his time and energy in attending to domestic assignments as well as to unsteady and strenuous outside employment which had poor remunerative prospects. (Table 8.13).

In view of this dramatic shift in their role and responsibilities, it is no surprise that most of them have passively acquiesced in the present economic status. Whatever, aspirations they might have had in their school days, the present situation was one of hard, toiling labour outside home or engagement in domestic work inside. Upon the termination of contacts with the school, their potentialities remain undeveloped, talents unexplored and their

Table 8.13
Time Devoted by Children to Household Work and Other Activities Every Day

Daily work labours	*After Drop-out* (1) %	*Before Drop-out* (2) %
1-2 hours	9 (3.1)	154 (60.1)
3-4 hours	27 (9.3)	66 (25.8)
5-6 hours	83 (28.7)	34 (13.3)
7-8 hours	94 (32.5)	1 (0.4)
8 hours or more	76 (26.4)	1 (0.4)
	289 (100.0)	256 (100.0)

energy diffused over the wide assortment of uncreative jobs. Circumstances such as these are bound to stultify the achievement motive of the individual. How else can we explain the data in Table 8.14, showing the level of aspirations of 198 drop-out cases.

Out of every 10 drop-out children, one child seemed to have no aspiration at all, about three preferred to remain as housewives (all girls' cases) or farm labourers. I wanted factory work or some skilled job, three wanted to join any unskilled job category and the remaining two wanted to start their business or take up white-collar occupations like teaching, clerical assistance etc. The fact is quite clear that due to an extremely low level of education, most of the drop-out cases have lowered their sights and desired to become what their own limited capacities or background would justify. These are reflections of unwholesome consequences brought about by their drop-out.

It was a revealing feature of the study that out of 198 children who were available for interviews, 65 have expressed their desire to rejoin their studies. In other words, three out of every 10 drop-out children were conscious even at this stage (with a comfortable gap of two to eight years) that they should educate themselves to improve their social and economic position. A question is: How many of them can successfully translate their desire into action? Whether their families would be in position to relieve them from

Table 8.14
Positions Aspired to by the Drop-out Cases: No. of Children

Aspirational Level	*Rasra Block*	*Ranipur Block*	*Total (%)*
No aspiration at all	18	5	23 (11.0)
Housewife	19	8	27 (13.6)
Farm Labourer	2	27	29 (14.6)
Factory worker	6	3	9 (4.6)
Businessman trader	12	11	23 (11.6)
Unskilled worker	39	27	66 (33.3)
Skilled worker	4	7	11 (5.6)
White-collar occupation	8	2	10 (5.1)
Total	108	90	198 (100.0)

their present engagements? Answers seem to lean more towards the negative than the positive side. Economic compulsions would not permit most of them to devote sufficient time for educational activities, even if they succeeded in re-admitting themselves.

It would be of interest to find out their present activities (till the time of this study). We learn from parents that out of 300 children, 133 are unemployed but assisting them in household work and other activities while 167 are working independently in some gainful activities. In other words, nearly 56 per cent of the drop-out cases are providing much needed economic support to their families. If we recall the earlier discussion (Table 8.12), we found that 83 children had entered into independent employment immediately after drop-out. This number of working children has doubled in a short span of 4-5 years (from 83 to 167). If we look into the present age of the drop-out cases, we find that out of 300 children, 62 per cent of them (186 cases) are below 14 years of age while remaining 38 per cent are above that age, only seven cases are above 21 years. Since the employed children constitute 56 per cent of our total sample, it is more than obvious that quite a large number of children below 14 years of age are in independent employment, a fact that underscores the economic contributions of child labour in the Harijan families. Harijan households are constrained to use child-power for livelihood.

The situation explained in this chapter throws sufficient light on the causes underlying drop-out and the consequences emanating from it. We are yet unaware of the role of child's family in his educational efforts, the extent of contribution of school system and the nature of community influences. Each of these has some part to play in the child's itinerary from home to school and back. In the chapter that follows we shall devote our attention to these aspects which, may deepen our understanding further about the educational problems of the Harijan children.

REFERENCES

1 J. Michael Mahar argues that although no untouchable girls were attending school, this was due to the need for the girls' assistance at home rather than any restrictions imposed by others.
See his essay: *Agents of Dharma* in the Untouchables in Contemporary India (Ed.), the University of Arizona Press, Tueson 1972, p. 32.

2. Mencher has noted this aspect in her study of a village in Tamil Nadu. She says Paraiyan (untouchable caste) parents were reluctant to send their children to a school dominated by Mudliar (upper caste) children whose superior status was reflected in the markedly better quality of their clothing. See her essay: *Continuity and change* in Mahar's (Ed). The Untouchables in Contemporary India, *op. cit.*, p. 54.

3. A similar observation is made by the author or Khalapur study. He writes: the major barrier to the education of untouchables was held to be economic. Untouchable parents said that government scholarships did not meet all school expenses and most families did not want to lose the income earned by their children as comherders and field hands." See Mahar's *Agents of Dharma, op. cit.*, pp. 32-33.

4. In case of urban drop-outs, Khandekar reports that nearly 72 per cent among Mothers and 60 per cent among Fathers felt sad over the dropping out of their child. Over 68 per cent of drop-outs themselves reported feelings of unhappiness over this issue. These percentages compare favourably to those obtained in our study. (See Miss Khandekar, A Study of Drop-outs, the Indian Journal of Social Work, Vol. XXXIV, No. 4, Jan. 1947, p. 383).

9

Policy Imperatives for Social Change in Dalit Society

The policy of protective discrimination as a strategy for social change is a specific expression of the liberal ideology. This ideology advocates social change in a piecemeal fashion, within the existing framework of social institutions, and prescribes non-violent, constitutional, legal and administrative solutions. The Constitution of India, which is premised upon this ideology, sets the society theoretically open and assures equality of opportunity in all realms. "The claim of the individual to welfare is sacred and irrefutable" in such a Constitution, and it "partakes of the character of a natural right" (Marshall, 1971).

This has special significance to the Scheduled Castes, who have been traditionally oppressed and are consequently underprivileged. They are in theory liberated by the Constitution, and they can now climb up the social ladder and stake their claim to higher status and the accompanying privileges. In view of the prevalence of market conditions, and their past background and present predicaments, the individuals belonging to this section of society will not be able to compete with those of the other sections. To overcome the impediments in their upward social mobility, they need some prop. The state assumes the role of a generous donor and bears the responsibility for providing the necessary help to uplift them in the form of protective discrimination.

Of course, it is conceded that not all the members belonging to these castes can be emancipated through such state generosity in the realization of individual right. Hence, the policy of protective discrimination necessarily concentrates on a few members of these castes. Also, since the process of such sponsored, non-violent and piecemeal change is by nature gradual, the emancipation of these castes is necessarily a long drawn process spread over several generations and decades.

It is, however, presumed that the initial beneficiaries the "elite" among the Scheduled Castes, would act as catalysts for social change among their less fortunate brethren. The essence of their own social mobility is expected to percolate to those who are below them, and in due course the whole community, it is hoped, will catch up with the rest of society. In brief, the philosophy of the welfare state, the ideology of social mobility and the theory of downward percolation constitutes the postulates of the policy of protective discrimination.

Of the various facets of this policy, the one to have got maximum prominence is education. Education is expected to equip the scheduled castes to overcome their caste-defined confinement to low status occupations by promoting occupational mobility among them and improving their standard of living. Educational institutions are expected to function as melting pots for caste differences and to facilitate the cultural integration of the Scheduled Castes with upper caste Hindus. Moreover, education is expected to generate a climate for change by changing their attitudes and aspirations on the lines of liberalism and humanism. In brief, education is regarded as both the foundation and the vehicle for the emancipation of the Scheduled Castes. Not surprisingly, more than fifty per cent of the funds for the welfare of the Scheduled Castes have been allocated to strengthen an elaborate programme of scholarships, hostel facilities and reservation of admission to educational instructions, to secure the educational advancement of these castes.

How far has the programme of protective discrimination been successful in realizing its objectives? Has it brought about occupational mobility among the Scheduled Castes, and if so, what is the nature of this mobility? To what extent and in what direction have the educated and the mobile among them changed their outlook and aspirations? What are the consequences, both structural and attitudinal, of the policy of protective discrimination? Based on the all-India report of the study commissioned by the Indian Council of Social Science Research on the progress and problems of education among the Scheduled Castes and gleaning relevant findings from the twenty-sixth report (1978-79) of the Commissioner for Scheduled Castes and Scheduled Tribes (1980), as also from other studies, we shall, in what follows, examine some of these questions.

Education: Prime Mover

The national study has revealed (Chitnis, 1981: 12-37 and 38-72) that the overwhelming majority of the Scheduled Caste students come from backgrounds that may be considered disadvantageous for education. That most of them happen to be first generation entrants to colleges or high schools in the family would indicate positive returns from the investment on the education of the Scheduled Castes.

Moreover, a majority of them aspire to study upto graduation and do not consider themselves bound to their traditional occupations, and they display a tendency to move out of the caste defined confinement to low status occupations. These findings seem to reflect a trend in and orientation towards upward social mobility among the Scheduled Caste students.

Of course, in the absence of data on the differential access to education between the Scheduled Castes and the non-Scheduled Castes youth from comparable socio-economic back-grounds, it is difficult to determine if the progress of the former is exclusively due to protective discrimination. Nevertheless, the mobility ideology behind the policy of protective discrimination seems to be apparently, at least, partially justified.

Turning to their social outlook and attitudes, the national study shows that the students continue to be conformist and traditional on the issue of marriage (Chitnis, 1981:73-106). They have a pronounced tendency for homophily and a different self-image. That these are found not to be rooted in their experience of ill-treatment or discrimination would point to the failure of educational institutions to function effectively as melting pots. The majority of students have a poor exposure to mass media and a low level of politicization.

The purpose of protective discrimination being the elimination of the criteria by which the Scheduled Castes are defined, the continuation of the same would be self-defeating by definition. To make use of a metaphor, "protective discrimination is a 'crutch,' and in the long run no substitute for a healthy leg" Dushkin, 1972:216-17). An important aim of education of the Scheduled

Castes is to develop in them self-reliance and an attitude of independence. But it is found that the students consistently feel that the various facilities that are provided to them are useful but inadequate (Chitnis, 1981:107-44). They invariably prefer the secure reserved jobs in government service, thereby betraying their diffidence about being selected for jobs without the assistance of reservations.

Thus, the Scheduled Caste students, instead of being fired by a zeal for change, "seem to be willing to depend on official programmes and policies' for their advancement. Given the poor level of politicization among them, there does not seem to be any prospect of organized action on their part either. The data seem to confirm the oft-repeated complaint that the policy of protective discrimination has a tendency to perpetuate itself and to breed a sense of utter and permanent dependence on the part of the Scheduled Castes, crushing and crippling their initiative.

As regards the academic life of the students a majority of them have gone through their education without suffering gaps and breaks, have no problems of comprehension, and are hard-working. Considering that most of these students are first generation educands, this is commendable indeed. But this would also mean that "in spite of the massive facilities for the education of the Scheduled Castes it is only the brighter amongst them, the good performers, who make it to high school and colleges" (Chitnis 1981:38-72).

Data reveal that though the growth in enrolment ratio in absolute terms among the Scheduled Castes is noteworthy, they are still lagging far behind other communities. While the growth in school enrolment among the Scheduled Caste children in the 6-11 age group is indeed appreciable, the growth in the 11-14 age group is not so. This indicates a lot of wastage of education among the Scheduled Castes (see Commissioner, 1980:164).

A closer analysis of enrolment in absolute terms over a period of time substantiates this fact. Of the 65.20 lakh students who had registered in standards I-V in 1968, only 12.16 lakhs (*i.e.*, 18.65 per cent) were enrolled in standards VI-VIII in 1973. this means that the rest, constituting an overwhelming majority of 31.35 per cent of the enrolees in standards I-V in 1968, have dropped out. Similarly, of the 11.19 lakh students enrolled in standards V-VIII in 1968-69, only 5.75 lakhs (*i.e.*, 51.38 per cent) enrolled in standards IX-XI in 1973.

Whatever may be the explanation for the low participation rates of these castes, there seems to be no room for complacency about their educational situation. What is the fate of those, the majority, who drop-out and discontinue their education, many even before acquiring functional literacy, is a question that the proponents of liberal ideology do not seem to be serious about. Is it that they are blinkered by the statistics on "achievements" in terms of enrolment and expenditure? Or is it that the mobility ideology individualizes failure and drops the drop-outs as irredeemable?

Social Mobility: Contrived or Spontaneous?

With reference to certain courses of study, the intended sponsored mobility fails to come off. Generally the Scheduled Caste students tend to get enrolled in a general degree course rather than in vocation-oriented diploma courses and they tend to move away from science and technology to commerce and arts courses (see Shah and Patel, 1977:Chitnis, 1981). As far as their enrolment in professional and other higher courses is concerned, the position is found to be "rather deplorable" (Commissioner, 1980:7).

The co-efficient of equality in the enrolment of Scheduled Castes which was 29.3 in 1964-65 for all professional courses increased to 39.0 in 1974-75. This is insignificant considering the fact that during the year 1974-75, out of every 100 students enrolled in professional and other higher courses, only about four belonged to these castes. For some courses like agriculture, commerce, law, nursing and physical education, the coefficient among these cases in 1974-75 was as low as 35.6, 36.3, 35.6, 32.9 and 27.4 respectively.

In several professional courses the seats reserved for the Scheduled Castes are not filled for want of suitable candidates. Even when some attempt is made to enroll the Scheduled Caste students into these courses, the result has not been encouraging. A study team of the Commissioner for Scheduled Castes and Scheduled Tribes investigated the admission pattern and academic performance of the Scheduled Caste students at the Jawaharlal Nehru Medical College in Raipur (M.P.) during September 1979 (Commissioner, 1980: 177). It was revealed that although all the candidates, including those belonging to the Scheduled Castes, are required to appear for an entrance test for admission to the College, the State

Pre-Medical Test Board had lowered the minimum percentage of qualifying marks for the Scheduled Caste candidates to 35. Since very few of the candidates belonging to these castes could secure this percentage (Achrekar, 1982) it was sometimes lowered to even 15 so that more reserved seats could be filled.

A review of the performance of the Scheduled Caste students in the College from 1964 to 1973 revealed it to be unsatisfactory. Out of forty-two students admitted during these years, four students took four and a half years to pass the final examination, six took five to six years, six took six to seven years, seven took as long as seven to eight years to pass the examination. While three were rusticated, two got migration to other colleges. Further, fourteen of them were reported to have left their study leading to a lot of wastage. All this is in spite of the special coaching given to these students during the first year of the course.

Turning to technological education, in 1973, the government stipulated that fifteen per cent of the seats in the various graduate courses in the Indian Institutes of Technology should be reserved for the candidates belonging to the Scheduled Castes. Besides the admission through the Joint Entrance Examination, till 1978, the Scheduled Caste candidates who had secured more than fifty per cent marks in the qualifying examination were also directly admitted. The cut-off value of the marks to be obtained by these candidates in the entrance examination was fixed at approximately two-thirds of that prescribed for general candidates.

In 1978, of the 41,857 candidates who appeared for the entrance examination, only 1,401 (*i.e.*, 3.34 per cent) belonged to the Scheduled Castes and Tribes. Out of the 1,919 candidates who qualified, only 11 (i.e., 0.57 per cent) belonged to these groups. However, based on direct admission, 153 Scheduled Caste/Tribe candidates were offered admission, out of which 132 joined the Institutes (Commissioner, 1980:179).

The experience of a batch of thirteen Scheduled Caste/Tribe Students admitted to the Indian Institute of Technology at Bombay in 1973 provides a good example of what promises such institutions hold for the Scheduled Castes:

> At the end of the Special (Preparatory) Course, four students left the Institute. The remaining nine students were promoted to the First Year. Of these one left at the end of the First Year.

> Two out of these, eight students fared very badly and withdrew for a semester. The remaining six registered for second year but one of them, who had not been performing well, was asked to leave later in the semester. Of the remaining five students, two were on probation *i.e.*, their performance was much below the prescribed standards. Thus, out of thirteen students admitted in 1973, only three students seemed to be giving an average performance. The rest were borderline cases (Kirpal, 1978: 168-69).

Not surprisingly, from the academic year 1979-80 the direct admission of Scheduled Caste/Tribe candidates has been stopped and they are admitted to the Institutes, as all others, only through the entrance examination. It is learnt that in 1979 only 88 Scheduled Caste candidates were selected for admission on the basis of the entrance examination against 246 reserved seats for them.

According to Kirpal (1978: 169), the future of the Scheduled Caste students absorbed through the reserved seats in the Indian Institute of Technology is bleak. It has serious socio-economic and psychological repercussions. Besides being a wastage of resources, "the feeling of not having been able to 'make it' will shatter whatever little confidence they have and render them misfits in society." Perhaps the same could be true of the Scheduled Caste students in other professional courses!

Dynamics of Social Mobility

Studies have shown that the growth of education among the Scheduled Castes has not been uniform and that the various educational facilities are unevenly distributed. The capacity to utilize the privileges has tended to vary from one sub-group to another (see Patwardhan, 1973: Commissioner, 1980). The national study found that in all the states a few castes predominate the sample to the exclusion of others which means that the educational facilities are disproportionately utilized (Chitnis, 1981: 319-26). Numerical strength coupled with such factors as urban residence, the social and occupational position of the caste in the traditional hierarchy, at radiation of occupations that provide for independent business, and the experience of organized political effort seem to explain the unique advance of some castes (see Patwardhan, 1973: Chitnis, 1981).

Protective discrimination in education seems to function effectively as a sieve for catching the most able and discarding the rest. While a small elite among the Scheduled Castes has benefited from protective discrimination, the remaining large majority has lagged behind. Consequently, the mobility that is witnessed among the *via* education is not spread over the whole community, but is confined to particular caste groups; and within these groups to particular individuals.

Not only is the spread of mobility limited and the unit of mobility the individual, but also the distance traversed in general is not very high as is to be expected. Given the trend towards increasing under-representation of the Scheduled Castes as successively higher levels of education, to cluster around liberal science degree courses and an inferior and less prestigious institutions, and to perform poorly in education, the likelihood of their equipping themselves for prestigious and highly paid jobs remains very thin.

What are the implications of the nature of mobility that is being channeled through protective discrimination in education? According to Dushkin (1972: 212), the policy of "protective discrimination as a whole seems to have fostered the growth of a "new class". That the students covered by the national study constitute only a minority and not the mass (who do not enter or stagnate or drop-out of the educational channel having entered it) points to the role of education in the formation of an 'elite' among the Scheduled Castes.

The process of elite formation and consolidation among the Scheduled Castes have simultaneously created and widened the gap between the elite and elite-information in urban areas on the one hand, and the mass of their fellowmen living in rural areas on the other hand (see Isaacs, 1965: Dushkin, 1972). Given the type of reference group behaviour entailed in the process of individual social mobility undergone by the elite among these castes, it is hardly surprising that there is an increasing alienation among them from the rest of their fellowmen. What is expected to function as a percolator becomes in reality a wedge. Moreover, with their positive reference group members unwilling to accept them as equals, the mobiles among the Scheduled Castes are rendered "marginal men' (see Isaacs, 1965: Patwardhan, 1973).

Education no doubt has the effect of weaning people away from their traditional occupations. But once weaned from their traditional occupations, what are the alternative jobs in which they will be employed? It was observed earlier that while the Scheduled Caste students tend to move away from the traditional occupations, they invariably prefer jobs in government service. Since most of them are getting education which would not qualify them for any profession or throw open avenues for self-employment, they have to depend upon the government for jobs.

The state of the Indian economy being what it is, how many jobs can the government create? There is already a heavy backlog of unemployment, and not an insignificant percentage of this backlog is constituted by the educated. The incidence of unemployment, including those of the educated, is quite high even among the Scheduled Castes.

With a steady but certain decline in the equation between education and employment, a situation of educational inflation or degree devaluation has already set in which is sure to accelerate in due course. This will definitely dilute the mobility significance of education even for the Scheduled Castes. Furthermore, the ever-restricting employment opportunities mark a physical limit on the possibility of mobility through education, so that, in course of time, even individual mobility would be difficult for the Scheduled Castes.

Even if this trickle of individual mobility were to continue, with the same conditions of operation, it would at least need a few centuries before the whole mass of the Scheduled Castes is put on the mobility channel. In the meantime, the situation of the vast majority of those who have remained outside school, either having not entered it or dropped out after having entered it, and those who would either not enter it or would drop-out if they enter it, would remain substantially unaffected.

What explains, then, the substenance of the ideology of sponsored mobility? As far as the Scheduled Castes are concerned, the policy of protective discrimination and the implied social mobility and development offer a rationalization to their predicament by way of what Tawney (1964: 105) calls "the Tadpole Philosophy." The actual possibility of social mobility for the exception, combined with the individualization of failure, becomes the primary illusion of an entire class. It legitimizes inequality, making its continued existence acceptable as a kind of safety-valve, and cooling down any stress that may be generated (see Parkin, 1972: 49). It diverts their attention from the full extent of the problem and its roots in the overall socio-economic framework.

In the light of this it is easy to understand how the palliative of protective discrimination and the illusion of social mobility created by it are adopted by the ruling class to wean away and absorb the 'ablest" elements among the Scheduled Castes, Protective discrimination is an effective instrument for the social control of groups which could otherwise prove to be potentially disruptive (Jayaram, 1981: 14).

That the policy of protective discrimination is an effective instrument for buying peace is well-known. The continued tendency to ensure this peace is seen in the uniform and uncontested extension of the policy, thrice beyond the initially stipulated period of ten years, without a comprehensive review of the implementation of the policy.

Realizing this, other "dominant' caste groups have started demanding the shelter of the policy of protective discrimination. The innumerable committees and commissions charged with the investigation of the problem of backwardness have been dismayed at the large number of petitions and deputations proclaiming backwardness in order to be listed for benefits (Dushkin, 1972: 218). Knowing full well the implications of the pressure potential of these groups, the government has extended the cover of the policy to other caste and community groups.

For instance, in Karnataka, of the 205 castes that the Backward Classes Commission appointed by the State Government could distinguish, 197, constituting about 45 per cent (excluding the Scheduled Castes and Tribes, who form another 14 per cent) of the population were declared backward. but for the concessions shown in the matter of eligibility requirements for admission to educational institutions and employment, virtually all the benefits enjoyed by the Scheduled Castes are now enjoyed by the other backward classes as well. A similar situation exists in other states also. The attentions of the special concessions and privileges to other castes and communities has virtually done away with the speciality of the Scheduled Castes. The policy has been not only perpetuated but also extended to a point where it losses its essence.

How the caste factor impinges on the educational situation of the Scheduled Castes is not clearly established. In fact, "the disadvantages suffered by Scheduled Caste students at school and college do not seem to be substantially different from those suffered by others who are economically or culturally disadvantaged", states the author of the national study. To the extent that caste is subsumed under class, she opines that as far as education is concerned, "It may be more advantageous to merge their cause with that of other disadvantaged sectors" (Chitnis, 1981: 165).

Presuming that caste is significant independently of class, the constitutional and administrative label 'Scheduled Castes" suggests too much of a homogeneity. That this is not so is confirmed by the inter-state and inter-caste variations in the educational progress and problems of the Scheduled Castes reported by the national study.

Conclusion

Elsewhere, I have analysed the class nature of the Scheduled Castes problem and have emphasized the point that the Scheduled Castes share a position of chronically inadequate material circumstances with others in the existing socio-economic framework (Jayaram, 1981). An overwhelming majority of the Scheduled Castes (about 90 per cent) live in villages, mostly a landless labourers faced with irregular employment, onerous work and low wages. But for the stigma of untouchability, they are not unlike the rural proletariat. The socio-economic conditions of a majority of urban Scheduled Castes by and large compares with the lowest social stratum in urban areas (Rajagopalan, 1978).

Poverty, illiteracy, and ill-health are not exclusive to the Scheduled Castes and are to be found in every group irrespective of caste or religion.

> The tacit assumption that a man is comfortable or depressed because he belongs to a particular caste, and that these conditions are perpetual, is wrong. In some parts of the country, Brahmins are discriminated against because they are considered solely responsible for the centuries-old discrimination against the Harijans and other castes. Is turning caste system upside down an answer to the problem? Or, is it the transformation of the class basis of the caste system, which would weaken the latter's exploitative potency, which is needed? (Jayaram, 1981: 14).

It should be emphasized here that the structurally determined "class" is more fundamental than the subjectively evaluated ephemeral notion "status ". What the Scheduled Castes need along with other exploited and oppressed sections of the society is collective emancipation from the structurally determined class position rather than the individual upward social mobility on the status *scale within the status quo.*

That such a class emancipation cannot take place *sui generis, i.e.,* from within the existing socio-economic framework and with the policy protective discrimination alone is being slowly realized. In formulating the problem from *Seminar* on reservations, Beteille (1981: 13) points out that without a corresponding change in the structure of Indian society and a corresponding change in the mental horizons of people, there can be no real or meaningful change in the conditions of Scheduled Castes and their class brethren. Intoxicating as it is with liberal ideology, is the ruling class willing to, or more appropriately, capable of, bringing about such a radical transformation is a moot question.

Ignoring this question for the time being, an important prerequisite for such a transformation is the recognition that it can come about only through a process of education whose aim is what Freire (1972: 15) calls "conscientization." Conscientization refers "to learning to perceive social, political, and economic contradictions and to take action against the oppressive elements of reality." This implies that, using education as a centre of social regeneration, a people can be awakened to their suppressed and deprived conditions and empowered with the means of changing these conditions, A small section of the people getting higher education and becoming individually mobile does not help spread conscientization. Rather it would act as a wet blanket on conscientization, keeping social awareness in swaddling-bands.

It is true that the spread of literacy and oracy through lower levels of education can play an important role in bringing about social transformation. But it is precisely at this level that the present system of schooling has failed. At the snail's pace at which the rate of literacy is growing it would take many more decades to reach a significant level. How long will it take for the oppressed sections in rural areas to reach the general level of literacy is anybody's guess.

Let alone the physical limits, the present system of education being premised upon mobility ideology and welfare state philosophy cannot be expected to undertake the historical task of social transformation. In fact, it seems to be an effective instrument for the maintenance of the *status quo.* This points to the need for a discussion on alternatives to the present system of education in the country.

While there is a lot for us to learn from the experience of Soviet Russia and Communist China as also from the educational thought of Freire, Illich and company, we have no ready solutions to be derived from them. At the same time, since a radical alternative to the present system of education would upset the apple-cart, the ruling class certainly will not take the initiative to search for it. The onus for it, therefore, falls on those who are committed to the emancipation of the oppressed as a collectively.

Notes

Achrekar, B., "Sociology of Depression and the Depressed Classes" in Murgesan, P., (ed.) *Modernisation and Conflict,* Chancellor Books, 1982.

Beteille, A., "The Problem", *Seminar,* 1981, 268, pp. 10-13.

Commissioner, *Report of the Commissioner for Scheduled Castes and Scheduled Tribes,* (2 Parts, 26th Report, 1978-79), Delhi, Controller of Publication, 1980.

Dushkin, L., "Scheduled Caste Politics', in J.M. Mahar (ed.), *The Untouchables in Contemporary India,* Tucson, Arizona, The University of Arizona Press, 1972, pp. 165-226.

Freire, P., *Pedagogy of the Oppressed,* Harmondsworth, Middlesex, Penguin Books, 1972.

Isaacs, H., *India's Ex-Untouchables,* New York, Harper and Row, 1965.

Jayaram, N., "Fresh Look at Harijan Question", *Mainstream,* 1981, 19(38), pp. 10-14.

Kirpal, V., "Higher Education for the Scheduled Castes and Scheduled Tribes," *Economic and Political Weekly,* 1978, 13 (4 & 5), pp. 165, 167-69.

Marshall, T.H., "Social Selection in the Welfare State", in E. Hopper (ed.), *Readings in the Theory of Educational Systems,* London, Hutchinson, pp. 38-55, 1971.

Parkin, F., *Class Inequality and Political Order,* Frogmore, St. Albans, Granada, 1972.

Patwardhan, S., *Change Among India's Harijans,* New Delhi, Orient Longman, 1973.

Rajagopalan, C., *Social Mobility Among the Scheduled Castes*, (Unpublished Report of a Research Project), Bangalore, Department of Sociology, Bangalore University, 1978.

Shah, V.P. and T. Patel, *Who Goes to College?* Ahmedabad, Rachna Prakashan, 1977.

Tawney, R.H., *Equality*, London, George Allen and Unwin, 1964.

APPENDIX

Historical Perspective: Final Report of the Backward Classes Committee

(Excerpt from—A State Government Report)

Preface

The question as to what steps should be taken to encourage members of the backward communities to seek employment in Government Service in adequate numbers has engaged the attention of the Mysore Government for a long time. In 1918, the Government of His Highness the Maharajas of Mysore observed that there was a large preponderance of Brahmins in the Public Service and that steps should be taken to ensure that all the other important communities in the State are also adequately represented in the services of the State. For this purpose, the Government appointed a Committee in August 1918 under the Chairmanship of Sir Leslie, C. Miller, Kt., to investigate and report on the problem. The questions referred to the Committee were the following.

(i) Changes needed in the then existing rules of Recruitment to the Public Services;

(ii) Special facilities to encourage higher and professional education among the members of backward classes;

(iii) Any other special measures which may be taken to increase the representation of backward communities in the Public Service without materially affecting the efficiency, due regard being paid also to the general good accruing to the State by a

wider diffusion of education and feeling of increased status which will thereby be produced in the backward communities.

1. The Committee submitted its report in July 1919 and after examining this report in consultation with the Heads of Departments, the Government of Mysore passed orders in G.O. No. 1827-80 — EAG 308, dated 16-5-1921 (a copy of the order will be found in Appendix I). The opinion of the Government then was that the term "backward communities" should be understood to include all communities in the State other than Brahmins. This position continued more or less till the States Reorganisation took place in November 1956.

2. At the time of States Reorganisation, there were different lists of backward communities in the five integrated areas. Yet the *status quo* was allowed to continue even after integration. This led to confusion because certain communities in the new State of Mysore were considered as forward in one area and backward in the other area, *e.g.*, Lingayats in old Mysore area were considered as backward while the Lingayats of other integrated area were treated as forward. To avoid this anomaly and to have a uniform list of Backward Classes for the entire new Mysore State, a small Committee of officers was appointed by Government in the beginning of 1959. On the recommendations of this Committee, Government issued in May 1959 a uniform list of Backward Classes in the state. The validity of this list of Backward Classes was questioned in writ petitions 567, 572, 574 and 575 of 1959 of the file of the High Court of Mysore. The High Court held that the Government Orders listing the Backward Classes in the State and grouping them for purposes of reservation of seats in technical institutions were not in accordance with Art. 15(4) of the Constitution. Therefore, the Government have set up this Committee for the purpose of determining the criteria for the classification of Backward Classes in the State.

3. The Constitution has made certain provisions for the advancement of Backward Classes. Under Article 15 of the Constitution, it is provided that the State shall not discriminate against any citizen on grounds only of religion, race, caste, sex, place of birth or any of them. But under Clause (4) of that Article, it is stated that nothing in this Article shall prevent the State from making any special provisions for the advancement of any socially and educa-

tionally Backward Classes of citizens. According to Articles 16 of the Constitution, there shall be equality of opportunity for all citizens in matters relating to employment or appointments to any office under the State and no citizen shall on the grounds only of religion, race, caste, sex, descent, place of birth, residence or any of them be ineligible, for, or discriminated against in respect of, any employment or office under the State. But, under Clause (4) of that Article, it is stated that nothing in this Article shall prevent the State from making any provision for the reservation of appointments or posts in favour of any Backward Class of citizens, which in the opinion of the State, is not adequately represented in the services of the State.

4. In pursuance of the provisions of Articles 15 (4) and 16(4) of the Constitution, the Old Mysore State as well as the neighbouring States had made some special provision for the advancement of backward classes in regard to reservation of posts in Government services and for admission to technical institutions. The principles followed for the classification of backward classes in all the States were more or less similar. The Andhra Pradesh Government have stated that they have generally accepted the principles recommended by the Backward Classes Commission while drawing up their list of Backward Classes. In Kerala they have taken the social, economic and educational backwardness of communities into consideration. In Madras also social and economic backwardness of the communities has been taken into consideration. The Government of Bombay (Now Maharashtra) have directed that the classification on caste basis should be abolished from the financial year 1959-60 and replaced by a reclassification based on income. For this purpose, they have declared that all persons whose annual income from all sources does not exceed Rs.900 per annum irrespective of religion, caste or community, are to be treated as backward. It is understood that they have since raised this income limit to Rs. 1,200 per annum.

5. So far as reservation for Backward Classes is concerned, the percentage varies from State to State. For admission to technical institutions, in Andhra Pradesh, 38 per cent of the seats are reserved for Other Backward Classes, in Kerala, 35 per cent are reserved and in Madras 25 per cent. So far as Government service is concerned, the reservation for other backward classes in Andhra Pradesh is 38 per cent, in Kerala 40 per cent and in Madras it is 25 per cent.

6. According to the orders issued by the Government of

Mysore in May, 1959, 57 per cent of posts in Government Service and 57 per cent of seats in technical institutions had been reserved for Other Backward Classes. It is this order that has been questioned in the writes referred to and quashed by the High Court on the ground that it is not in conformity with Article 15(4) of the Constitution.

Introduction

(1) Consequent on the decision of the High Court of Mysore quashing the Government Order prescribing the list of Backward Classes for the purpose of reservation of seats in technical institutions, the Government decided to appoint a Committee to advise them on the question of classifying the Backward Classes in the State. Accordingly in Government Order No. P. & D. 64 OBC, 58 dated 8-1-1960, Government constituted a Committee consisting of the following members for the purpose of determining the criteria for the classification of Backward Classes.

Chairman

1. Dr. R. Nagan Gowda, M.Sc., Ph.D., M.L.A.

Members

2. Shri M. S. Patil, B.A., LL.B., Retired District Judge.
3. Shri B. Koragappa, B.A., B.L., Retired District Judge.
4. Shri A. Bheemappa Naik, B.A., B.L., M.L.A.
5. Shri Ramachandra Rao Junde, M.L.C.
6. Shri F.D. Ghodke, Ex-M.L.C.
7. Shri K. Puttaswamy, B.A. (Hons.), LL.B., M.L.A.

Secretary

8. Shri M.B. Shetty, B.A., Visharad, Under Secretary to Government, General Administration Department.

In Government Order No. P. & D. 132SAD, 60, dated 26.9.1960, Shri Mahmood Sheriff, B.A., LL.B., M.L.A., has been appointed as an additional member of the Committee.

(2) The terms of reference to the Committee are:

1. To suggest the criteria to be adopted in determining which sections of the people in the State should be treated as socially and

educationally backward;

2. To suggest the exact manner in which the criteria thus indicated should be followed to enable the State Government to determine the persons, who should secure such preference, as may be determined by Government, in respect of admission to technical institutions and appointments to Government Services.

3. While inaugurating the Committee's work on 25.1.1960, the Chief Minister requested the Committee to submit an interim report early to enable the Government to determine quickly the classes of persons who should secure preference in respect of appointments to Government Service. In view of this request, the Committee undertook to prepare an interim report. For this purpose it met six times and after careful consideration of the problem in the light of the statistical information readily available, prepared and submitted its Interim Report to Government on 19.2.1960. The Government have accepted this Interim Report as a tentative measure with the modification that reservation for Other Backward Classes in Government Service should be only 25 per cent instead of 36 per cent recommended by the Committee (*vide* Government Order No. GAD 7 ORR 60, dated 1.3.1960 in Appendix II). The Government have also adopted this report, tentatively, as the basis for the reservation of seats for Backward Classes in technical institutions in the State (*vide* Government Order No. ED 60 TGL 60, dated 9th of June 1960 in Appendix III). In its judgment dated 16.1.1961, the High Court of Mysore has held that the enumeration made by the Committee in its Interim Report of certain communities as socially and educationally backward classes of citizens in the State is not unconstitutional.

4. After submitting the Interim Report, the Committee set to work to determine the criteria for the classification of Backward Classes in the State. For this purpose, the Committee heard representations from various organisations, associations and individuals at Bangalore. The Committee also toured all over the State and heard representations from individuals and institutions of all shades of opinion. Touring all the districts in the State and hearing representation from organisations and associations and from individuals naturally took time.

5. The Committee was very much handicapped for want of correct statistical information in regard to the population of the

several communities in the State and the percentage of literacy among them. The Committee drew up a questionnaire and obtained replies from several associations and individuals. The information collected from various organisations and also from individuals has been utilised for the purpose of preparing the final list of Other Backward Classes in the State.

6. According to the terms of reference, the Committee has to find out the criteria to be adopted for determining the Backward Classes in the State and also to suggest to Government how these criteria should be applied to determine the class of persons who should secure preference in respect of admission to technical institutions and appointments to Government Service. At every place visited by the Committee, the terms of reference to the Committee were explained to the general public in clear terms. However, there have been representations on several matters not coming within the scope of the Committee's work. Even organisations of Harijans and their leaders came forward with their grievances and suggestions for their advancement though the terms of reference to the Committee did not include Scheduled Castes and Scheduled Tribes. Still, the Committee gave a patient hearing to the representations of all castes and communities and this enabled the Committee to understand to some extent the social conditions of the communities in the State. During their visits to the districts, the Committee came to know that certain communities which are really very backward were not included in the list of Other Backward Classes contained in the Interim Report. In fact in some districts we came across certain minor communities which were so backward and uneducated that they were not in a position even to represent their case before the Committee.

7. Though several replies were received to the questionnaire circulated by the Committee, most of the replies were not very helpful. Replies and memoranda received from various organisations and individuals did not suggest any clear criteria to be adopted for classifying Backward Classes. The general demand put forward by almost every community was that it was extremely backward and that therefore it should be included in the list of backward classes.

8. The Committee could not get correct and up-to-date figures of the population of each community in the State. It was also not possible for the Committee to get the up-to-date percentage of

literacy of each community in the State. This was due to the fact that during the Census of 1941 and 1951, there has been no tabulation of the population of each community in the State and their percentage of literacy. Though the Committee could work out approximately the up-to-date population of some of the more important communities in the State, it could not get the population figures for some other communities. As regards literacy, for want of correct figures in respect of each community, the committee had to collect information from the Education Department in regard to the number of students of each community attending the High School classes in the State during 1959-60. Thus, the absence of caste-wise statistics in the Census of 1941 and 1951 was a great handicap to the Committee.

9. In the absence of up-to-date figures, the only course open to the Committee was to rely on statistics of previous Census reports. The Census Department has furnished to the Committee approximate population figures for most of the communities in the State and the percentage of literacy among them according to the 1941 Census.

Castes and Communities

1. The first question that faced the Committee was how the Backward Classes in the State should be listed, *i.e.*, whether on the basis of castes and communities or on any other basis.

2. The caste system in India is an ancient social system. It does not appear that such an institution has been found anywhere else. The caste system here is peculiar and has an institutional force with a religious background. Each caste is a social unit and the customs followed by one caste are generally different in some respects from those followed by other castes. Normally, persons of one caste do not inter-marry with members of another caste. Persons belonging to some castes do not even eat or drink with persons of other castes. Even a change of religion sometimes does not destroy caste.

3. It is not possible to trace with certainty the origin of the caste system in India. It might have been pre-Aryan institution or it might have developed after the Aryans came to India. Any how Aryans utilized the institution of castes for the adjustment of race relations. They divided the community into functional groups called *Varnas*. The first three *Varnas* are Brahmins, Kshatriyas and Vaishyas. Later on one more *Varna* was added *i.e.*, Shudras. In the beginning, the

caste system was apparently an arrangement for the peaceful co-existence of several clans, tribes or other social groups. But, with the passing of time, it developed rigidity and castes and communities multiplied themselves on the basis of occupation and other considerations.

4. Many attempts have been made by reformers in the past to abolish the caste system and to create a homogeneous well knit society. Though some progress has been made in this direction during the last 50 years, it is doubtful whether the rigidity of the caste system has weakened to any appreciable extent. Sometimes, attempts made by social and religious reformers in the past have ended not in removing caste distinctions but in creating new castes. The idea of caste has become so deeprooted in Hindu Society that it is impossible to ignore the existence of castes.

5. Though the Muslims and Christians do not recognise castes among them, the sense of 'high and low' has permeated even the Muslim and Christian Society and there are now a number of groups amongst them that are suffering from social inferiority. In short, the caste system of Hindu Society has influenced to some extent the creation of so-called high and low classes even amongst Muslims and Christians. It is with such a background that the Committee had to consider the classification of Backward Classes in the State.

6. The problem of backwardness is a direct result of the defective social order. Many representatives who met the Committee attributed the present deplorable condition of the large number of Backward Communities to economic backwardness and proposed that the only way to remove backwardness is to improve the economic condition of the Backward Classes. Some of them even suggested that the caste system should be abolished by legislation and those practising the caste system should be penalised by prosecution. It is no doubt true that economic causes have played a large part in contributing to the backwardness of a large number of communities. Denial of educational opportunities to large masses of people occupying a lower social order has also contributed to the backwardness of several communities. Poverty, ignorance and lack of educational facilities have also contributed to the backwardness of these communities.

7 The first term of reference to the Committee is to suggest the criteria to be adopted for determining which section of the

people in the State should be treated as socially and educationally backward. The words "socially and educationally backward" have been copied from Art. 15(4) of the Constitution. Thus, the primary duty of the Committee is to determine the criteria for classifying Backward Classes. As stated above, the problem of backwardness among Hindus was created by a defective social system and economic backwardness can be said to be the result and not the cause of many social evils that are present to-day. It has been pointed out to the Committee that the terms of reference do not refer to caste or community but a section or class of people who are socially and educationally backward. But in the conditions existing at the present day, it is not possible to adopt any other basis except caste and community for classifying the Backward Classes as explained above. It is also not easy to dissociate caste from social backwardness at the present juncture. Moreover, it is not easy to group people under certain occupations, as at the present day several castes have given up their traditional occupations and have taken to other occupations. A Brahmin taking to shoe-making does not become a cobbler by caste and his social status is not lowered. Social backwardness does not, therefore, go with profession. Also there are several distinct communities which are not confined to any one occupation. One of the questions contained in the questionnaire issued by the Committee was whether the Backward Classes should be listed on the basis of caste and community or on any other basis. A vast majority of the replies received are in favour of the classification of Backward Classes on the basis of castes and communities only. Taking all these factors into consideration, the Committee has decided in favour of classifying the Backward Classes in the State on the basis of castes and communities.

8. The Backward Classes Commission set up by the President in 1953 and which submitted its report in 1955, has considered in detail the causes for backwardness and measures for their removal. Though the Commission has discussed also the criteria for backwardness, it has come to the conclusion that it is very difficult to go by any standard for determining the backwardness of a community. The Commission has explained at length why it is difficult to lay down the criteria to decide backwardness. But it has not been able to recommend unanimously a uniform set of criteria to determine the backwardness of a particular caste or community. The Government of India, after examining the report issued a memorandum in

1956 explaining the action taken or proposed to be taken on the recommendations of the Commission. That Government has, however, admitted the necessity for evolving some positive and workable criteria for the specification of the socially and educationally backward classes of the people so that they may be given adequate assistance and relief in all suitable ways to make up for the leeway of the past and to acquire the normal standards of the prevalent in the country. They have suggested that an *adhoc* survey may be made to determine the numbers that would come within the category of Backward Classes. They addressed the State governments accordingly. But when the Mysore Government requested them to conduct a survey to determine the population and other conditions of every community in the State, the Government of India said that they were not prepared to meet the expenditure if such a survey is conducted by the State Government. It is also understood that the Government of India have called for one or two conferences of officers of all States for the purpose of laying down the criteria for classifying Backward Classes, but it does not appear that they have taken any decision on the subject so far. In the circumstances, the Committee had no rules or standards to go by for the classification of Backward Classes in the State.

9. Several suggestions have been made to the Committee as to how the Backward Classes can be classified. Most of them are suggestions which cannot be put into practice. One suggestion was that social backwardness was a direct outcome of economic backwardness and that all those communities which are economically backward should be listed as Backward Classes. It is, however, well nigh impossible to decide, with facts and figures, which are the communities which are economically backward and how to assess the backwardness of a community as a whole on the basis of economic standard. Another suggestion made to the Committee was that Backward Classes should be classified on the basis of profession and such of those classes of people who are following low professions like manual labour, domestic service, etc. should be classified as backward. Even this suggestion could not be accepted by the Committee for the reason that it is difficult to classify professions as high or low in the present day conditions. It is also difficult to investigate into the professions followed by each family and its number in the State. Another suggestion made to the Committee was that the economic conditions of a family only

should be taken into consideration for the purpose of classifying the family as backward, and those families (of five persons each) with an income of less than Rs. 1,200 per annum should be classified as backward. Even this suggestion did not find favour with the Committee because the acceptance of this criterion would involve a survey as to the annual income of all the families in the State. Moreover, according to the terms of reference read with Art. 15(4) of the Constitution, the Committee had to find out the educationally and socially Backward Classes and not the economically and socially backward classes. Though social backwardness might have developed as a result of economic backwardness, it is not possible to assert that all socially Backward Classes are also economically backward.

10. Another suggestion made to the Committee was that the entire Shudras caste should be considered as socially and educationally backward. The Committee could not accept this suggestion also because some of the caste and communities among Shudras have made considerable progress in recent years. A test of literacy alone cannot also be a sure guide to indicate the general educational advancement or backwardness of a community. It is common knowledge that most of the artisan classes and a major section of the traditionally trading communities are not educationally advanced though they are socially and economically forward.

11. After considering carefully the various suggestions made for the classification of Backward Classes in the State, the Committee has come to the conclusion that the following criteria should be adopted for classifying Backward Classes:-

(1) Social backwardness of a community should be judged by the status accorded to the community in society in general (apart from individuals).

(2) Its general educational backwardness should be judged on the basis of some fixed standard of education.

(3) The representation a community has in Government Service should also be taken into account.

12. With the above criteria in view, the Committee has collected material from various sources and the available data has been analysed and utilized for the purpose of its recommendations.

Educational Backwardness

1. The causes for the educational backwardness of several communities in the State are numerous. The more important causes of educational backwardness in our country, as summarised by the Backward Classes Commission, are:

(1) traditional apathy for education on account of social environmental conditions or occupational handicaps;

(2) poverty and lack of means of a large number of communities to educate their children;

(3) lack of sufficient number of educational institutions in rural areas;

(4) living in inaccessible areas and lack of proper communications;

(5) lack of adequate educational aids in the form of Freeships and Scholarships and monetary grants for the purpose of books and clothing and hostel facilities.

2. The existing social conditions are largely responsible for the traditional apathy of some of the communities towards education of their children. Certain communities engaged in occupation like agriculture, live-stock breeding, collection of forest produce, fisheries etc., either employ the children in their own occupation or for earning a subsidiary income. Extreme poverty has made them indifferent to education. There are also numerous small communities which are poor and without fixed habitation, including wandering tribes — nomadic and seminomadic tribes — who are not in a position to educate their children. The general progress of literacy in India itself has been very slow.

3. In the Interim Report submitted by the Committee it has taken the percentage of literacy of the several communities as one of the criteria for classifying the Backward Classes. But the literacy percentage do not necessarily give the general educational advancement of the people in a State. They indicate only the number of people who can read and write. Hence, to understand the educational advancement of any section of the people, the test of mere literacy is not considered to be sufficient. Several suggestions have been made to the Committee as to the educational standard to

be adopted for the purpose of classifying the backward communities. One suggestion was that the number of people in each community who have passed the stage of primary education should be taken into account while deciding whether a community is backward or forward. Another suggestion made to the Committee was that the number of students who have passed the S.S.L.C. examination in each community may be taken into consideration. Some have suggested that the pre-University class should be taken as the standard. Yet others have advocated that only the number of students studying in college classes including technical and professional colleges should be taken into consideration. The Committee could not accept any of these suggestions because it is not possible to find out the number of persons of a community who have passed a particular examination. They are not also in favour of accepting a high standard as the general standard of education in the country is not high. A large volume of opinion was to the effect that the number of students studying in the last three classes of all the High Schools in the State should be taken into account. After careful consideration, the Committee have accepted this suggestion and come to the conclusion that the number of students of each community studying in the last three High School classes during 1959-60 should be ascertained. The percentage of the total number of students in the three High School classes to the total population of the State should first be worked out. Then the percentage of students of each community in the High School classes to the total population of that community in the State should be worked out. If the percentage of students of any community in the High School classes during 1959-60 is below the percentage of the total number of students studying in the three High School classes *(i.e.,* last three classes — Forms IV, V and VI *i.e.,* High School I year, II year and III year) in the State during 1959-60 that community should be considered as educationally backward. It has also worked out the State percentage as well as the percentage for each community, to the extent population figures are available. The result has been tabulated and will be found in statement — 3. For the purpose of convenience the composition of student population of each community in the last three classes of High Schools has been calculated per thousand of population of that community.

Whereas the State average of educational standard is 693 per cent (corrected to three decimal places) the average of the Neygi

Community is 690 per cent. Thus Neygis are below the state average in educational standard.

Representation in Government Service

1. Under Article 16(4) of the Constitution, it is open to the State Government to make provision for reservation of appointments in favour of any Backward Class of citizens which, in the opinion of the State Government is not adequently represented in the services of the State. The word 'backward' here is not qualified by the words "Socially and educationally" as in Art. 15(4) and hence it is susceptible of being interpreted as backward not only socially and educationally but backward in all respects. But the Committee is satisfied that classes which are socially and educationally backward are backward generally in all respects, and therefore, for the purpose of Art. 16(4) also, the expression, 'backward' will be interpreted as "socially and educationally backward", to avoid confusion.

2. In accordance with the directions issued by Government in O.M. No. GAD(S-I) 55 SRR 59, dated 31.3.1959, the State Statistician has compiled statistics of Government appointments and employees as on 31.3.1959. From this statement, the percentages of appointment held by the various communities in the State have been worked out. The Committee's view is that if a community does not have representation in Government service, in proportion to the percentage of its population, then that community should be considered as inadequately represented in Government service, Statement 4 indicates the percentage of appointments in Government service held by the various communities in the State as on 31.3.1959. While compiling this statement all appointments under Government have been taken into account including Class IV appointments. By comparing this statement with the other statement showing the percentage of population of each community to the total population of the State, it has been possible to work out a statement indicating which of the communities in the State are inadequately represented in Government service. Column 10 of statement 4 gives this information.

3. In our Interim Report, we had excluded class IV employees while determining the adequacy or inadequacy of representation in Government Service. The Committee still feels that there is ample justification for excluding Class IV Government servants for the

purpose of calculating the adequacy or inadequacy of representation in Government Service, especially because the minimum qualification needed for Class IV service is mere literacy.

A list prepared on this basis is in statement 5.

4. It is seen from statements 4 and 5 that representation for certain communities in Government Service is grossly inadequate. In such cases Government may be pleased to take suitable steps to ensure fair representation to these communities in Government Service as a special case.

5. The figures adopted by the Committee for the purpose of calculating representation of the various communities in the State in Government Service are based on those supplied by the State Statistician. The caste as mentioned by the Government servants in these returns are very large in number. They have been grouped under the main communities as far as possible.

Note: One of the members (Shri Mahmood Sheriff) is of the opinion that the fact that the Muslims are considered to be adequately represented in Government service is due to the accidental transfer of Government servants from the integrated areas other than old Mysore State on account of States Re-organisation and that in any case there is preponderance of non-gazetted employees of this community.

But it is seen from Statement No. 4 that representation in Government service of Muslims is 15.03 per cent whereas their population is 10.02 per cent. Statement No. 5 in which Class IV employees are excluded shows the representation of Muslims in Government service as 3.54 per cent above the percentage of their population. According to the figures given in the report of the Backward Classes Commission (Vol. I) for the erstwhile Mysore State, the population of Muslims was 6.29 per cent while their representation in Gazetted rank was 7.95 per cent and in non-gazetted rank 10.52 per cent. These figures do not bear out the contention of Shri Mahmood Sheriff.

Social Backwardness

1. The term "Social Backwardness" is not defined in the Constitution. The report of the Backward Classes Commission also

does not give a correct definition of this term. Higher social status has generally been accorded on the basis of caste for centuries. The low social position of any community is, therefore, due mainly to the caste system. There are ample reasons to conclude that social backwardness is based mainly on racial, tribal, caste and denominational differences, even though economic backwardness might have contributed to social backwardness.

2. The committee is of the opinion that the term "Social backwardness" used in Art. 15(4) of the Constitution relates to social hierarchy based on the caste system. The only practical method of assessing social backwardness is with reference to the position occupied by a community in society. Therefore, for the purpose of determining the social backwardness of any community, the position of that community in the social hierarchy should be taken into account.

3. The members of the Committee have, with their knowledge of the social system in the State and with the experience and knowledge gained by them during their tours, come to the conclusion that 'Social Backwardness' of a community should be judged mainly by the status accorded to that community in society in general (apart from individuals). A contributory factor is the general economic condition of that community. Based on the above criterion the communities mentioned in statement — 2 have been classified as 'Social Backward'.

We are aware that Muslims and Christians do not recognise the caste system. Yet the fact remains that the idea of high and low has also permeated the Muslim and Christian society. In practice, the Muslims and Christians have accepted the caste as a social distinction. In the South, social distinction is still recognised between sections of Muslims and groups of Christians. Therefore, the caste system, though in a less rigorous form, is practised among Muslims and Christians also in South India. While deciding the social backwardness or forwardness of these communities, therefore, we have taken the above factors into consideration.

In this Chapter mention has to be made about the social status of Lingayats, Vokkaligas and Muslims:

(i) *Lingayats*: The Committee is of opinion that the entire Lingayat community is socially forward.

(ii) *Vokkaligas*: All sections of Vokkaligas excluding Bhunts, are socially backward. Bhunts are socially forward. The standard of education among Bhunts is above the State average, being nine per thousand according to the figures available to the Committee.

(iii) *Muslims* : A view has been expressed that Muslims cannot be considered as socially backward and that only a few sections among them like Mapilla, Pinjari, Chapparband, Laddaf, Kasab (Kasai), Katharga, Dudekula, Labbe and Pindare can be considered as socially backward. But a majority of the members of the Committee have agreed that the Muslim community as a whole should be classified as socially backward.

Criteria and their Application

1. The Committee has evolved the criteria to be adopted for classifying the Backward Classes in the State as follows:-

(i) The social position which the community or caste occupies in society.

(ii) The general educational backwardness of the community on the basis of the High School standard of education.

(iii) Representation of the community has in Government service.

2. The Committee has prepared the following statements:

(i) List of socially backward communities in the State — Statement 2.

(ii) List of communities which are educationally backward — Statement 3.

(iii) List of communities which do not have adequate representation in the services of the State including Class IV appointments — Statement 4.

(iv) List of communities which do not have adequate representation in Government Service excluding Class IV appointments — Statement 5.

3. The Committee recommends that all those communities which are socially and educationally backward should be

considered as the "Other Backward Classes" in the State for the purpose of reservation of seats in technical institutions under Article 15(4) of the Constitution. A list of such communities is in statement 6.

4. The total population of socially and educationally backward communities will be approximately 57 per cent of the population of the State. This excludes Scheduled Castes and Scheduled Tribes who are about 14 per cent of the State's population.

5. The Committee recommends that all those communities which are backward and are not adequately represented in Government Service should be considered as the "Other Backward Classes" in the State for the purpose of reservation of posts in Government Service under Article 16(4) of the Constitution. A list of such communities is in Statement 7.

6. The total population of these Backward Communities which are not adequately represented in Government Service will be approximately 45 per cent of the total population of the State excluding Scheduled Castes and Scheduled Tribes.

7. It has already been explained that the Committee could not get correct population figures of all communities in the State. There are several minor communities which are backward in all respects; but for whom population figures and figures of students studying in High School Classes are not available. The list of such communities is in Statement 8. As we know that all these communities are backward in all respects, they should be considered as Backward Classes for the purpose of Articles 15(4) and 16(4) of the Constitution.

8. The Committee is aware that among the Backward Communities some are more backward than others. Therefore, if all the Backward Communities are grouped together, the interests of the more Backward Communities will be adversely affected. The Committee after taking legal opinion has, therefore, come to the conclusion that the list of "Other Backward Classes" should be divided into two parts: Part-A: Backward Communities; and Part-B: More Backward Communities and that reservation should be made for these two groups separately with the proviso that the more Backward Communities should be eligible to compete for the quota reserved for the Other Backward Communities also. The Committee has been advised that such a course of action will not be irregular.

9. We have decided that such of the socially Backward Communities whose standard of education is less than 50 per cent of the State average should be grouped under "More Backward Classes" and those whose standard of education is above this limit and up to the State average should be grouped under "Backward Classes". Accordingly the list of socially and educationally Backward Classes has been divided into two parts: A and B for the purpose of Article 15(4) of the Constitution. A list of such Backward Classes is in Statement — 9. The same list has been adopted for the purpose of Article 16(4) of the Constitution also with the modification that communities which are adequately represented in Government Service have been eliminated. Such a list of Backward Classes is in statement — 10.

10. While considering what percentage of seats is to be reserved for Backward Classes, it is very helpful to take into consideration, the opinion of their Lordships of the Mysore High Court expressed in their judgment in Writ Petition Nos. 782 etc. of 1960—Sri S.H. Partha and others *vs.* the State of Mysore and others (*vide* Mysore Law Journal, Volume 39, page 159). They have observed that "a special provision for the advancement of Backward Classes within the meaning of Clause (4) of Article 15 is in the nature of a restraint on the Fundamental Rights and that the reasonableness of the restraint has to be tested by asking the question whether the ambit of it is wider than required by the actual necessity of imposing that restraint to achieve the object of securing advancement of Backward Classes." Besides this, we have also to remember that in accordance with the directions given by the High Court for the preparation of lists of selected candidates what is going to be reserved for Backward Classes would become the guaranteed minimum which will also be the practical maximum. Hitherto, the seats obtained by the students of Backward Classes in the merit pool were not counted against the reserved quota and, therefore, there was every chance for them to get more and more seats, year by year, over and above the reserved quota. In fact, it is seen from the figures relating to the admissions of last year that though the reservation was only 22 per cent, seats obtained by the Backward Classes in Medical Colleges was about 40 per cent and in Engineering Colleges about 35 per cent. it is, therefore, just and reasonable to reserve seats for Backward Classes in proportion to their population, *i.e.*, 57 per cent for purpose of admission to technical institutions and 45 per

cent for recruitment to Government Service. The Committee understands that in Andhra Pradesh reservation has been made for Backward Classes on the basis of their population, *i.e.*, 38 per cent. We would normally have recommended that in this State also the reservation for Backward Classes should be in proportion to their population. In our Interim Report, we had recommended a reservation of 36 per cent for Backward Classes which was in proportion the percentage of population of Backward Classes according to that report. But now we recommend that the minimum that should be reserved for Backward Classes (excluding Scheduled Castes and Scheduled Tribes): (1) for purpose of admission to technical institutions should be 50 per cent of the total number of seats available, and (2) for recruitment to Government Service 45 per cent of the posts available.

11. The Committee considers that separate reservation should be made for the two groups of Backward Classes namely: *(i)* Group—A (Backward), and *(ii)* Group—B (More Backward). It is recommended that the reservation should be as indicated below for purposes of admission to technical institutions and for recruitment to Government Service.

(a) Admission to Technical Institutions

It has already been stated that the total population of Backward Classes for purpose of Article 15(4) of the Constitution is approximately 57 per cent (excluding Scheduled Castes and Scheduled Tribes) and this is made up to 33 per cent in Group—A and 24 per cent in Group—B. The Committee has recommended that 50 per cent of the seats in technical institutions should be reserved for Backward Classes (excluding Scheduled Castes and Scheduled Tribes). The reservation of 50 per cent should be divided between Group—A and Group—B of the list as follows:

(i)	Group — A (Backward)	28 per cent
(ii)	Group — B (More Backward)	22 per cent

(b) Appointment to Government Service

Total population of Backward Classes (excluding Scheduled Castes and Scheduled Tribes) for the purpose of Article 16(4) of the Constitution is approximately 45 per cent. This is made up of 21 per cent in group — A and 24 per cent in Group — B. The Committee recommends that reservation of posts in Government Service for Backward Classes (excluding Scheduled Castes and Scheduled Tribes) should be as follows:

(i)	Group — A (Backward)	21 per cent.
(ii)	Group — B (More Backward)	24 per cent.

General Recommendations

1. As mentioned earlier, the Committee was very much handicapped in its work for want of current statistical information in regard to the population of several communities in the State and the percentage of literacy among them. Therefore, the Committee had to depend upon the estimated population figures of communities supplied by the Census Superintendent. The Committee, strongly feels that by merely omitting the names of castes and communities in the Census reports, the Caste system will not be eradicated. On the other hand, not to mention caste in the Census will work as a great hardship for the Backward Communities. Art. 15(4) of the Constitution gives power to the State Government to make special provision for the advancement of the socially and educationally Backward Classes of citizens. So long as this Article stands, as it is in the Constitution, and so long as it is not legally objectionable to classify Backward Classes by communities, it is essential that the Census Reports should contain the population figures as well as the other relevant data about every community in the State. The necessity for caste-wise statistics will be felt until all the Backward Classes in the State are able to come up or near the general level of other communities and are able to participate in terms of equality in the opportunities provided by the State. The Committee therefore, very strongly urges the State Government to move the Government of India to record in the Census report the population figures and all the other essential figures relating to literacy, economic conditions, etc., in respect of every caste and community in the State. If the Government of India are not willing to do so, the State Government will have to undertake the work.

2. The Committee desires to draw the attention of the Government to Art. 46 of the Constitution under which the State shall promote with special care, the educational and economical interests of the weaker sections of the people. The Committee notes with

satisfaction the decision taken by Government to give free education up to the S.S.L.C. to children of parents, whose annual income does not exceed Rs.1,200 per annum. The Committee recommends that this concession should be extended for education even at the College level.

3. The Committee recommends that the Government should take prompt steps to ameliorate the social, educational and economic conditions of the Backward Classes of citizens. The aim should be to bring up the general standard of those Backward Classes to the level of the forward communities, within the next 15 to 20 years. At present certain educational facilities are extended to the Backward Classes, by the State Government. But, these facilities are grossly inadequate. The Committee, therefore, recommends that Government should give free education—education at all levels—to all the poor children of Backward Classes.

4. The Committee is unanimously of opinion that the only practicable method of raising the economic and social position of the Backward communities is by educating the children of these communities in larger numbers. As the backward communities are generally poor, Government should endeavour to start hostels all over the State for students of Backward Classes. All deserving and poor students of Backward Classes should be given free hostel facilities. Where private individuals or associations come forward to start such hostels, Government should sanction boarding grants on a liberal scale.

5. Allotment of funds for the grant of Scholarships to the Backward Classes should be increased in keeping with the growing population of students of these Communities. Help should be given in accordance with the economic conditions of the families from which these students come. All the students from a family whose income is less than Rs.1,200 per year should be given free hostel facilities and free educational facilities. Others may be charged according to their economic condition.

6. To improve the economic condition of the Backward Classes they should be given special facilities by way of financial aid for industries, agriculture, etc.

7. The present day conditions are changing rapidly and the Committee hopes that some of the communities which are now classified as backward may improve their general educational and social standards in the near future. The Committee, therefore,

recommends that the list of Backward Classes should be reviewed after ten years to see whether any of the communities now included in this list may not be removed from the list. The object is to reduce the size of the population of the Backward Classes gradually so that within the next 20 years, it is reduced to the absolute minimum.

8. The Committee also recommends that Government should issue suitable instructions to all the concerned authorities to ensure that the Backward Classes are not denied their due share of the advantages earmarked for their upliftment.

Conclusion

1. We acknowledge with thanks the help and co-operation given by the Deputy Commissioners of districts during our tours in the State. We were not only furnished with the information required, but also enabled to meet people of various shades of opinion in the several places we visited. Some of the Heads of Departments and Secretaries to Government, whom we contacted for information, have been co-operative and helpful. Our thanks are due to them.

2. We are happy to record that the people of the State co-operated with us to a large extent. Many of then sent replies to the questionnaire issued by the Committee. At Bangalore and at the other places we visited, members of the public came forward in large numbers to give evidence and to explain to the Committee the social and educational conditions of the Backward Communities. Information gathered at such meetings has been very useful.

3. We wish to place on record our appreciation of the excellent work done by Shri M.B. Shetty, Secretary of the Committee. The problem before the Committee was of a difficult and complex nature and it naturally involved the collection of statistical data and factual information on several aspects of the problem. The Secretary has collected and analysed carefully all the relevant data and thus made it easy for us to arrive at practicable conclusions. Inspite of the arduous nature of his duties as Under Secretary to Government he has discharged his duties as Secretary of the Committee with promptness and thoroughness and with a high sense of responsibility.

4. The work done by the staff of the Committee has been commendable. The prompt and hard work put in by them has been

of great assistance to the Committee.

5. We are thankful to Government for giving us an opportunity to suggest the criteria for the classification of Backward Classes. Though the task entrusted to us has been of complicated nature, we have done our best to make the most reasonable and practicable recommendations, which we are sure, will be acceptable to a very large section of the people of the State. We trust that Government will bestow greater attention to the all-round progress of the Backward Classes in the State and we hope that this report will help Government in their task of improving the condition of these classes of people.

R. Nagan Gowda, *Chairman*
M.S. Patil,* *Member*
K. Puttaswamy, *Member*
A. Bheemappa Naik, *Member*
B. Koragappa, *Member*
Ramachandra Rao Judge, *Member*
F.D. Ghodke, *Member*
Mahmood Sheriff, *Member*

M.B. Shetty,
Under Secretary to Government,
General Administration Department
and Secretary,
Backward Classes Committee.

Vidhana Soudha,
Bangalore

Dated 16th May 1961

Note of Dissent given by Shri M.S. Patil

1. It has become necessary for me to record this note of dissent in order to do requisite justice to the Lingayat community. My colleagues though they had definitely concluded that the Lingayats are backward educationally and further that the Lingayats as a class excluding those that are classed as Banajigas, Jangams, Shettaru and Aradhyas are backward socially (*vide* Statement 4 under Annexure III, in the draft final report) have very recently changed their opinion by omitting the entire Lingayat community from the old lists of Backward Classes. My considered opinion, however, is that, the Lingayat community is backward both educationally and

* Subject to the note of dissent.

socially and is, therefore eligible for being included in the list of Other Backward Classes of citizens.

2. No doubt in our Interim Report the Lingayats were not listed among the Backward Classes of citizens, as our Committee then found them not backward in literacy, the only main criterion then adopted by our Committee for determining the educational status of different communities. But now for reasons given in detail in the final report the standard of higher education of students studying in the last three High School classes during 1959-60 was taken at the basis for determining the educational status of various communities. The application of this correct and proper standard to the Lingayat community as detailed below shows that the Lingayats are educationally backward. Evidently our Committee relying on this criterion had concluded that the Lingayat community is backward educationally. There is, however, now difference of opinion between me and my colleagues as regards both social and educational status of that community, and hence I am obliged to record this note of dissent.

3. The main question for consideration, therefore, is whether the Lingayats are backward both educationally and socially so as to fulfil the required conditions laid down in Article 15(4) of the Constitution of India and become eligible for being put in the list of Backward Classes of citizens.

4. At the outset the examination of the educational status of the Lingayat community is taken up for consideration. The estimated population of Lingayats in 1960 was 32,93,000 and the number of Lingayat students studying in the last three High School classes, in the entire state of Mysore, during the academic year of 1959-60 as reported by the Director of Public Instruction, in March 1960, was found to be 21,633. And this number was certified to be correct by a responsible Officer of the office of the Director of Public Instruction in the course of our discussion with him in one of our meetings. The aforesaid figures of population and of those High School students clearly indicate that the number of Lingayat students per thousand of population is 6.6 which is below the State average of 6.9 per thousand; and consequently our Committee on this very basis then concluded that the Lingayats are educationally backward. But, subsequently some of our colleagues, for reasons best known to them, moved the Director of Public Instruction to re-check the aforesaid figures pertaining to Lingayat students and secured his

report that the number was 23,369 indicating thereby that the number of Lingayat students exceeded the old figure 21,635 by 1,734. This newly reported figure shows that the number of Lingayat students per thousand of population is 7.1 which is above the State average, and our colleagues relying on this figure came to the conclusion that the Lingayats are not backward educationally. I do not however agree with this last minute decision of my colleagues for reasons given below:

First of all there is nothing on record to show that the figure supplied subsequently by the Director of Public Instruction as more accurate than that supplied previously, in March 1960, especially when no reasons are given in support of the alleged accuracy of the figures subsequently supplied by the Director of Public Instruction. Further this figure of 23,369 which pertains to the entire population of the Lingayat students studying in the last three High School Classes in the state, shall have to be reduced by not less than 1,734, insofar as according to the views of the Committee the Lingayats belonging to the sub-castes of Banajigas, Jangams, Shettaru and Aradhyas are not backward educationally and socially (*vide* statement 4 in Annexure III attached to the draft final report) and therefore the figure pertaining to students of the aforesaid sub-castes shall have to be deducted to secure the correct figure pertaining to students belonging to the remaining Lingayat community. The figure which is required to be deducted from 23,369 shall be not less than 1,734 insofar as the students belonging to these four sub-castes are highly educated and further as the entire population of those four sub-castes is round about one lakh. The approximate correctness of these figures was gathered by me in the course of our tour in the entire State. And these figures indicate that the percentage of Other Lingayat students studying in the last three High School classes is only 6.7 which is evidently below the state average of 6.9 per thousand. In these circumstances, it is evident that the figure of 23,369 of High School going boys cannot go to support the abruptly changed views of our colleagues that the Lingayats are advanced educationally. They are, in my opinion, backward educationally as found by the Committee formerly.

5. The next question for consideration is whether the Lingayats who are found to be educationally backward are also backward socially. One of the important criteria to be adopted in considering whether any section of people in the State can be treated as socially

backward is the traditional occupation of that section of people. Those who traditionally earn their livelihood by manual labour can be considered to be socially backward insofar as the upper-classes in the society treat occupational manual labour with a kind of contempt, thinking it to be a somewhat dirty occupation; and hence the communities who are engaged in manual labour for their living are treated as inferior in social life. Do Lingayats come in the aforesaid class of citizens? I answer the question in the affirmative for reasons given below:

6. It is a common knowledge that majority of Lingayats live in rural areas and that their main occupation is agriculture. The fact that they are rural inhabitants can be verified by Census figures which are available. According to the Census report of 1941 the percentage of rural population to the total population of Old Mysore State was then 81.61 per cent (*vide* Part III of Census Report of 1941) and the percentage of Lingayats living then in rural areas was 91.88 as per calculations made relying on caste-wise figures given therein, in 1941. The figures pertaining to the Old Mysore State can safely be taken as pertaining to the present Mysore State because it is well-known that the Lingayats belonging to North Karnatak and Hyderabad area are comparatively more backward than those in the Old Mysore State from several points of view. And now as seen from the statistical outline of present. Mysore State of 1959, the percentage of entire rural population is found reduced to 77 per cent; and it will not be incorrect to hold that similar reduction in rural population of Lingayats must have taken place and come down from 91.88 to 87.27 per cent only. It is thus evident that major portion of Lingayat population lives in rural areas and further it is common knowledge that the main occupation of rural population in general, is agriculture. Nearly 70 to 80 per cent of Lingayats living in rural areas are agriculturists doing necessarily manual labour in cultivating their lands to earn their livelihood. No doubt a small number of persons of that community living in rural and urban areas are petty traders, weavers, washermen and artisans. And speaking in general terms their economical condition in rural areas is poor. And they are not able to attain the proper standard of living so as to command and enjoy amenities of social life. This is the position of major section of the Lingayat community and it cannot be denied that even in rural and urban areas we can but find very few well-to-do Lingayats following occupations other than those

mentioned above. But these minor occupations can be ignored while considering the occupations and status of Lingayats as a class in general. Evidently the Lingayats as a class, speaking generally, are agriculturists, petty land holders and manual labourers, and as such they are treated as inferior in social status to some extent by upper-classes like Brahmins, who in a way consider them to be men of lower social position. This is how Lingayats occupy somewhat low position in society, especially in rural areas. They are therefore backward socially.

7. In the course of our extensive tour in the entire State of Mysore, we heard oral representations made by different communities and read written representations given by them; and these helped us in forming our impressions regarding social position and status of different communities. And I could then form my opinion that Lingayats are socially backward. This is also a relevant factor in judging the social status of Lingayats.

8. Next it may be noted that the Lingayats are not adequately represented in Government services, and they are found to be educationally backward as already explained. It cannot be denied that educational backwardness is reflected in social backwardness. All these facts, in a way, indicate the social backwardness of the Lingayat community.

9. The Lingayats who are thus found to be backward both socially and educationally are entitled to be included in the list of backward classes as per provisions of Article 15(4) of the Constitution of India.

10. Further the Backward Classes Commission of 1953 after touring the whole of India and after hearing representatives of different communities as seen from their Report of 1955, published in 1956, found the Lingayats residing in rural areas, in the Old Mysore State, to be both educationally and socially backward. And Shri T. Mariappa, one of the members of that Commission, in his minute of dissent of March 1955, has stated that the Lingayats residing in urban areas in Old Mysore State are also entitled to be classed as Other Backward Classes of citizens (*vide* page 16 in Volume III of the Report of the Backward Classes Commission). My colleagues who had definitely come to the conclusion that the Lingayats other than Jangams, Banajigas, Shettaru and Aradhyas are backward socially abruptly changed their opinion for no adequate reason.

11. Thus taking into consideration the low social position occupied by the Lingayats in the traditional hierarchy of Hindu Society, their lack of general education, their inadequate representation in Government services and the impression formed by me after hearing various representations in the course of our tour, I am inclined to believe that the Lingayats as a class are socially and educationally backward and are, therefore, entitled to be listed as Other Backward Classes of citizens. My colleagues who have been pleased to put the Vokkaligas in the list of Backward Classes of citizens should have in fairness put the Lingayats also in that list insofar as there is not much difference in the social and educational status of the two aforesaid communities. In my opinion it is just and proper to include the Lingayats in the list of Other Backward Classes of citizens.

M.S. Patil

Vidhana Soudha
Bangalore

Date: 13.5.1961.

Bibliography

Books

Ambedkar, B.R., *Castes in India, Annihilation of Caste, Communal Deadlock and a Way to Solve it, States and Minorities, Mr. Russel and the Reconstruction of Society.* (All five books were published by the Education Department, Government of Maharashtra, 1979, Bombay, Vol. 1).

Ambedkar, B.R., *Philosophy of Hinduism, Buddha or Karl Marx,* (in Dr. Babasaheb Ambedkar writings and speeches Vol. 3, Education Department, Government of Maharashtra, 1987, Bombay), *Gandhism,* Buddhist Publishing House, Private Limited, 1945, Jallandhar, *Mr. Gandhi and the Emanicipation or the Untouchables,* Bheem Patrika Publications, 1943, Jullundhar, *The Untouchables Who were they and Why they became Untouchables?* Bheem Patrika Publications, Jullundhar, *What Gandhi and Congress has Done to Untouchables,* Thakar & Co. Ltd., Publication, Bombay, 1932.

Ambedkar, B.R., *The Buddha and His Dhamma,* Siddharth College Publication, 1957.

Agarwal C.B., *The Harijans in Rebellion,* Taraporevala Sons, 1984, Bombay.

Alexander, K.C., *Neo-Christians in Kerala,* in Michael Mehar ed., The Untouchables in Contemporary India, The University of Arizona Press, 1972, Tuscon.

Aiyyappan, A., *Social Revolution in Kerala Village,* Asia Publishing House, 1944, Bombay.

Ahmed Imtiaz, *Caste Mobility Movement in North India,* The Economic and Social History Review, Vol. VIII (2), 1971.

Alter David, E., *Ideology and Discontent,* Free Press, 1964, New York.

Arora Setish K., *Political Participation Deprivation and Protest, Economic and Political Weekly,* Vol. vi, No.3, 4, 5, Jan. 1971.

Bendiy Beinhard and Lipset, S.M., eds., *Class, Status and Power*, Free Press, New York, 1967.

Benz, Ernest, *Buddhism or Communism which Holds the Future of Asia*, George Allen and Unwin Ltd., 1963, London.

Berreman, Gerald, *Social Inequality: A Cross Cultural Analysis*, Gerald Berreman (ed.), Social Inequality Comparative and Developmental Approaches, Academic Press, New York.

Beteille Andre, *Pollution and Poverty*, Michael Mahar (ed.), Contemporary India, University of Arizona Press, Tuscon, *Pattern or Stratus Groups*, Seminar, June 1965.

Balaram, N.F., *Communist Movement in Kerala*, Trivandrum, Prabhatham Printing and Publishing Company.

Boite and Anuradha Uttam, *The Dalit Sahitya Movement in Maharashtra: A Sociological Analysis*, Sociological Bulletin, Vol. 26(1), 1977.

Badrinath C. Dissant, *Protest and Reform: The Historical Context*, in S.C. Malik, ed., Dissent Protest and Reform in Indian Civilization, Simla, 1977, Indian Institute of Advanced Studies.

D'Souza Victor S., *Changing Status of Scheduled Castes*, The Economic and Political Weekly, No.14:18, 55-59.

Das, Bhagawan, *Thus Spoke Ambedkar*, Buddhist Publishing House Pvt. Ltd., Jallandhar, Vols. i-v.

Dananjay Keer, *Ambedkar: Life and Mission*, Popular Trakashan Publication 1984, New Delhi.

Fiske Adele, M., *Religion and Buddhism among Indian Buddhist*, Social Research, 1969, Vol. 36, No.1. *Scheduled Caste Buddhist Organizations*, in Michael Mahar ed., 1972.

Gokhale, Jayashree, 1979, *The Dalit Panthers and the Radicalization of Untouchables*, Journal of Common Wealth and Comparative Politics, Vol. xi, xiii, 1, No.1, March 1979.

Gur, T.R., *Why Men Rebel?* Princeton.

Gusfield, Joseph R., *Protest Reform and Revolt, Reader in Social Movements*, 1970, John Wesley and Co., New York, *Study of Social Movements*, International Encyclopaedia of Social Sciences, Vol.14, 445-450.

Irschicky, Euigne, *Politics in Social Conflicts in South India*, University of California Press, 1970, Berkeley.

Joshi, Barbara, R., *Ex. Untouchable: Problems, Progress and Policies in Indian Social Change*, Pacific Affairs, Vol. 53, No. 2, pp. 193-222, *Scheduled Castes Voters: New Data, New Questions*, Economic and Political Weekly, August 14, 1981, pp. 1357-62, *Democracy is Search of Equality: Untouchable Politics and Indian Social Change,* Humanities Press, 1987, New Jersey, *Whose Law, Whose Order, Untouchables, Social Violence and the State in India,* Asian Survey, July 1982. *Untouchable Voices of the Dalit Liberation Movement,* The Minority Group Ltd., London, 1986.

Juargeusmeyer, Mark., *Religion as Social Vision: The Movement Against Untouchability,* University of California Press, 1982, Berkeley, *What if the Untouchables, Don't Believe in Untouchability?* Bulletin of Concerned Asian Scholars, Vol. 12, No.1.

Kamble, M.D., *Poverty, Within Poverty,* Institute for Social and Economic Change, 1979.

Kuber, W.N., *Ambedkar: A Critical Study,* Popular Prakashan, 1986, New Delhi.

M. Kunhaman, *Economic Development and Social Change,* Research *Review Committee of Kerala University,* Kerala, 1990.

Lynch, Owen N., 1969, *The Politics of Untouchability,* Columbia University Press, New York.

Kothari, Rajni, *Caste in Indian Politics,* Orient Longman Ltd., 1970, Delhi.

Shastri Shankaranand, *My Memories and Experiences of Baba Saheb Ambedkar,* Bheem Sadan, Ghaziabad, U.P. 1989.

Mathew Joseph, *Ideology, Protest and Social Mobility Among Mahars of Maharashtra and Pulayas of Kerala,* Thesis submitted to J.N.U., 1982.

Oddie, G.A., *Religion in South Asia,* Manohar Book Service, 1977.

Oommen, Y.M., *Charishma, Stability and Change: An Analysis of Bhudan Gramdan Movement in India,* Thompson Press, Delhi, 1972, *Scheduled Castes: Then and Now,* in B.N. Pande, ed., The Spirit of India, Bombay, Asia Publishing House.

Oommen, T.K., *Sociological Issues in the Analysis of Social Movement in Independent India,* 1977, Sociological Bulletin, Vol. 26(1), pp. 14-37. *Scheduled Castes and Scheduled Tribes,* in S.C. Dube, ed., India Since Independence, Social Report of India, 1947-72, Vikas Publishing House, pp.153-93, 1977, New Delhi. *Mobilization of Primordial Collectivities and Social Development,* The Indian Situation Kerala Sociologists, Vol. VIII, pp. 79-118, 1980. *From Mobilization to Institutionalization, The Dynamics of Agrarian Movement in 20th Century,* Reader, Popular Prakashan, 1984, Bombay.

Patvardhan, S., *Change Among India's Harijans,* Orient Longman, 1973, Delhi.

Pratap Chandra, *Study of Ideological Discard in Ancient India,* Search for Suitable Model in S.C. Malik, ed., 1977.

Rao, M.S., *Themes in the Study of Protest Movements,* S.C. Malik, ed., *ibid.*

Rajan Babu, *Towards Dalit Education,* Dalit Open University, Deenasur.

Rajshekar, V.T., *B.R. Ambedkar's Three Commandments,* Dalit Sahitya Academy, 1990, Delhi, *Know the Hindu Mind, ibid.,* 1990, *Hinduism, Facism and Gandhism, ibid., How Marx Failed in Hindu India, Aggression on Indian Culture.*

Savaavai, S.G., *Class Struggle and Caste Conflict in Rural Areas,* Communist Party Publication, 1979.

Gore, M.S., *Non-Brahman Movement in Maharashtra,* Segment Book Distribution, 1989.

And several other press clippings, newspapers, journals and magazines.

Articles

Ailaiah, K., Lambadis: Their Identity, *Man in India,* 75(1); March 95; 97-100, (ISN-9189).

Biswas, S., Dalit Vision of Gandhi, *Mainstream,* 32(23); April 23, 94; 7-10. (ISN-2441).

Corrie, Bruce P., Impact of the Development Process on Dalit and Tribal Children in South India, *South Asia Bulletin,* 12(2); Fall 1992; 85-95. (ISN-2202).

Gosal, R.P.S., Scheduled Caste Population and Urbanisation in India: A Special Analysis, *Geographical Review of India,* 55(3); September, 93; 25-38. (ISN-5531).

Gupta, S.K., Violence Against the Scheduled Castes: Parameters and Trends, *Downtrodden India,* 1(2); May-August 94; 20-43, (ISN-8876).

Kothari, Rajni, Rise of the Dalits and the Renewed Debate on Caste, *Economic and Political Weekly,* 29(26); June 25, 94; 1589-95. (ISN-3267).

Lal, A.K., Limited Participation in an Open System: A Study of Scheduled Castes in Politics, *Mainstream,* 32(19); March 26, 94;

27-30. (ISN-1872).

Makwana, M.H., Entrepreneurship and the Scheduled Castes: A Study of Vankar Community, *Downtrodden India,* 1(2); May-August 94; 61-79. (ISN-8877).

Moose, David and Deliege, Robert, Replication and Consensus Among Indian Untouchable (Harijan) Castes, *Man,* 29(2); June 94; 457-61. (ISN-4742).

Nagda, B.L., Socio-demographic Status of Scheduled Castes in Rajasthan, *Kurukshetra,* 42(7); April 94; 31-34. (ISN-2441).

Ogawa, Kazuo, Economic Development and Time Preference Schedule: The Case of Japan and East Asian NICs, *Journal of Development Economics,* 42(1); October 93; 175-95. (ISN-332).

Sahco, Bhupati Bhusan, How Aware of the Mandal Controversy are the Marginalised?: Results of Rural Labour Survey in Haryana, *New Quest,* (108); November-December 94; 347-54. (ISN-7647).

Sharma, Rajendra, Constructing Dalit Identity, *Link,* 37(1); August 14, 94; 13-16. (ISN-5941).

Tribal Women, *Man in India,* 74(1); March 94; 1-90. (Series of Articles) (ISN-2288).

Venkateswarlu, D., Gandhi and the Scheduled Castes, *Mainstream,* 32(50); October 29, 94; 16-20. (ISN-5370).

Index